TAMING THE RAGE

INSIDE

TO

BREAK BARRIERS

Bruised Not Broken

By

Trul'ee Benevolence

The sequel to...

Changes Not Seen, Were Hidden In Plain Sight

Written By

Trul'ee Benevolence

COPY RIGHT

2008

Dedicated

To

My Boys

Thank you for being on this journey with me

R. J. D. T. J.

EVER REMINDING YOU

TO

TAKE CARE OF YOUR BUSINESS

OR

YOUR BUSINESS WILL TAKE CARE OF

YOU

TABLE OF CONTENT

Chapter 1. Grieving

Chapter 2. Raid

Chapter 3. A long way home

Chapter 4. Biding our time

Chapter 5. A cry for help

Chapter 6. No more pain

Chapter 7. Time for change

Chapter 8. Gone but not forgotten

Chapter 9. Make it make sense

Chapter 10. Mad at the world

Chapter 11. The victim

Chapter 12. Do or Die

Chapter 13. Breaking the cycle

Chapter 14. Establishing A Foundation

Chapter 15. Trouble don't last always

Chapter 16. Learning to love

Chapter 1

Grieving

……….. The morning of the funeral, the sun shined through my mamma's window brighter than it had in the past, it seemed. I woke, feeling refreshed from a good night's sleep, so I decided to walk out back where the dumpsters were, behind them is a hole in the fence where I sometimes go through, to sit and think. As I look out, I can see the amazing landscapes of flowers and trees with green vegetation placed perfectly, to make a beautiful masterpiece through out the valley below. As I sit, I thought to myself….she's gone, for real. I remembered when we were young; the time's she's threatened us with her death, saying; y'all gone miss me when I'm gone, using it as a weapon for us to do what she wanted. I finally decided to go back inside to ready myself for the day. I walk in and stood in the middle of the living room looking around wondering what to do next. I had a mental block, she was consuming my thoughts, even in her death.

All four boys looked very handsome, as they sit separately in the living room. I watched the expressions on my brothers faces, trying to see if they needed me for hugs and kisses. I was extremely sad for them, with them losing mamma so young. The knock on the door broke my train of thought. It was Joan, there on time as usual. As she walked in, I thought to myself; that we may not see her as much anymore due to mamma being gone. I surely hope that's not the case, she is good people.

We made it to the funeral home. There wasn't many people there, definitely none of our family from South Bend showed up. I thought that there could have been at least one of them here, to represent. Mrs. Shirley was there. Mrs. Sally and a couple of her children and a few others that I didn't know, it was small and intimate. Joan was the only one that mattered to me and she sat right beside me. I watched people rise to speak about my mother in ways that I have never known. However when "they" spoke of how they came by to do this or to do that, I became a bit irritated. Joan gently laid her hand on my knee, comforting me, looking at me as if to say; we know better. My sister Gail and her boyfriend Ted were there. I looked on, as she began yelling and crying out so loud and long that it became irritating, as well. I watched her fall out in the middle of the floor and cry out again. Ted rose up, to get her, to help her to her seat and still she cried to a slow whimper.

    I sat in silence watching it all but what bothered me the most was; Mrs. Sally, {the woman that suggested to my mother, that she not give me money and to basically allow me to whore my way back to South Bend, like I got here} telling me that it's OK to cry, to let it out and that it's part of the grieving process. I couldn't take it anymore. I rose to the occasion, too give them all a piece of my mind and with the look on my face, I was obviously agitated with the fiasco. I stood to my feet with no fear in my heart to raise hell in this funeral home. I opened my mouth and felt a sharp tug at the back of my dress. I looked down at Joan with a puzzled look on my face, "I wondered; why couldn't I say at least a little of what was on my mind" She gestured that I sit back down. As I slowly and reluctantly returned to my seat. I felt a sense of humility once again. She moved in close to whisper in my ear, saying; they know that they weren't there to help you with your mom Tru. They need others to believe that they were, only because it makes them look bad as your mothers closest friends if people knew the truth. I accepted what she said and sit back in silence to watched the show.

We followed the hearse in the family car to El Cajon Cemetery. It was all the way on the other side of El Cajon California. This is where we laid my mother to rest. I thought to myself; it seemed like a long ride, however, I looked over at the boys, concerned of their well being and ask if they were alright, we OK, Alfred said. My children looked bewildered, not knowing what was going on. So, I smiled and offered my hugs, to any one of them that wanted it. It was a sad moment for our small family, those that were there looked on as we mourned the loss of our mother. Joan put her arms around me to comfort me and whispered; it's going to be alright. With my head held low, I thought; I will not give them {my audience} the satisfaction of seeing me cry. The ride home was anything but quiet. My brothers talked about everyone that stood up and made remarks about mamma. They were laughing and joking especially about the ones that lied and said that they were there, or they did this or that. I allowed it because I felt that this was their way of coping with her death. The laughter was a healthy outlet for us all.

When we made it home, there were two ladies in the apartment that were from Joan's church that brought food for our family to eat. When I saw this, I looked over in Joan's direction with the same look that I remember my mother giving her, not weeks earlier. {I had this deep sense of love for her that I couldn't express only because I felt that she only had compassion for us and that it was in her nature to do good and show love}. She would soon prove to be a valuable lesson learned. I wanted to be alone, to lye down and reboot for a while but there was a knock at the door and when I opened it, there were people wanting to come in that I had never seen before, that I assumed wanted to give their condolences, so I stepped aside to allow them in, with a smile. Here, were the group of folks that we laughed about on our way home, as well. The memory of the conversation, made me smile as they passed by me, to go into the apartment. They were a group of people that appeared to be church folk, by the way they dressed.

As they filed in, I could hear the phone ring in the distance. I heard one of the boys yell, that it was my sister Denise. As I sit trying to catch my breath, I watched the phone being passed around the room. When it finally made it to me, I spoke to her and told her that I loved her and explained that I was exhausted, and I'll speak to her when things calm down, she agreed and I passed the phone to my brother. As the day moved on, I noticed the room began to empty. My oldest brother Bernard and his uncle Chance, stormed into the apartment in good spirits, laughing loud and goofing around. Chance looked like a Cowboy with the hat and boots to match. I didn't know a lot about him but I overheard my mom telling someone that he was a nice guy. He was a short man, with a stocky built, with a nice bearded face that had a smile on it the whole time that he was there. His raspy voice carried through out the apartment and his energy was positive and much needed. He and his family live in a place called Pomona California, they moved there from South Bend, as well.

One hour after they arrived, he announced that it was time for him to go. He was a riot and I had never seen my brothers love on and enjoy anyone as much as they did their uncle Chance {as they called him} and I wasn't sure that I was ready for him to leave, however, I said nothing. He walked over to me, looked into my eyes and quietly ask; if you need me too take the four boys with me, I can? Before I could answer; I know you could use some time alone? I felt moisture in my eyes. I nodded, Yes, before I knew it. He said; now go on and get'em ready. As soon as the words left his lips, I didn't waist anytime getting their things together. Bernard, told me that he was going too, that pleased me. I could hear the kids having fun with Chance in the living room. I'm smiling at some of the jokes they were sharing with him, I hear the phone rang, it was their father Alfred Sr. Trell, call out to Little Alfred; daddy wants you! I paused for a moment to see if I could make out what was being said. Minutes later, little Alfred called out my name. Memories came rushing in, it was as if I'm in the room watching what he is doing to my little body again. I could almost feel him touching me, I can smell the alcohol on his breath and in his skin. My brother stood in front of me; what's wrong with you, Tru? I just took the phone from him; Hello. He spoke slowly, how y'all holding up? We're OK under the circumstance; I replied. I'm sorry that I couldn't be there for y'all but if you need my help with the boys and if your coming back this way? I'll be here for you. I stood in silence, {I couldn't believe that this man who never helped when she was alive would step up for his kids when his wife has died}. Will you help if we stayed here? I ask. I could try, he said. I'll call back another time and talk about that. He suggested that we take care and hung up. I couldn't believe him. My brother Trell walked up to me as I held the phone in my hand and ask; are you still on the phone? I looked down at him and shook my head, no. He walked away as he always had in the past when his father ignored him. I had heard my mom's friends arguing / talking about my brother not being Alfred's, and that he was his brother Trell's child, years ago. This was the reason for the distance between Alfred and my brother. So.. I continued getting the boys things together to leave.

Chapter 2

The Raid

When everyone was gone, I noticed a silence that was unbearable. I needed some noise so I walked over to the radio and turned it on and sit on the floor right in front of it. Involuntarily my thoughts took me back through the events of the day. I see all of the faces and all the fake smiles on them. The lies that made me want to step outside myself earlier, along with all of the empty promises. The pain that was bellowing up inside was too much. All that I could think of, was how she spent my whole life punishing me for being me and died without a word of apology. I could feel the warm salty tears running down my face but what snapped me out of my thoughts, were kids running in the apartment down below again and then the door slammed shut so hard that it shook the building. I rose from where I sat and looked at myself in the mirror that hung over the radio and cried out loud because I realized, that I was as ugly as my parents said... I snatched the mirror off the wall and threw it at the wall in the dinning room. I went on a rant, slamming and throwing any and everything that I put my hands on.

How dare you not tell me who my real dad is! I yelled. How dare you take that to your grave! I shouted. I sat back on the floor feeling the pain in waves. I hurt so bad inside. Feeling winded, I managed to pull myself together a little. I could feel a slight pain on my forehead, blood trickling down the front of my face. I looked into a broken piece of glass and saw that I had cut myself. I managed to cleaned myself up and went next door to Mad Dog's apartment to pay them a visit. I noticed that there were quite a few people flowing outside from his apartment to the guy who stayed a couple of door away. His name was Rick, I've been to his place to cop a time or two but the atmosphere was different, he put me in mind of a person who believed in dark spirits, so I never went back.

Mad dog opened the door and greeted me with a smile, how are you holding up? He ask. Better than I thought I would, I replied. I made my way past him with a half smile on my face. It didn't take long for the pain associated with the death of my mother to subside. I was in a bad space in my head but the drug helped manage it. I could hear their front door being opened and closed the whole time that I sat in my hideaway in their walk in closet. A place of refuge from the world, in their world. I sat on top of a crate with a blanket on it, for comfort to smoke in peace. I needed more dope, so I got up and put the glass pipe underneath the makeshift cushion to go into the living room to retrieve more to keep my numbing process going. I slid the door open further to step out and heard what sounded like, loud thunder that shook the whole building along with the shredding of wood. I had no idea as too what was going on out side this temporary safe haven that I made for myself. So I turned, to go back in to hide from what I thought may be a robbery about to go bad. Everything seemed to move in slow motion for me after that. I can hear shouting but I can't make out what's being said. I huddle down behind the clothes and remained quiet. I could feel all of the commotion from the vibrations of the floor. I made up my mind, that I would remain here until this all blew over.

Suddenly, the door flew open and made a loud thud that caused me to jump. Two minutes later, I felt a hard object poking me and the clothes surrounding the area where I crouched. Come out of there, Now! I heard the voice yell. I crawled out slowly on my hands and knees. I was told to lie down on the floor and put my hands behind my head and interlock my fingers. Cross your ankle over one another and lay still! He shouted. He repeated the command louder; cross your ankles over one another and lay still! I must have been moving too slow, he yelled; Move! Now! I then, rushed to do as he ask. While I lay on the floor I could see bodies laying on the floor through out the apartment. I noticed, big guns in their hands that were drawn on us and the officers had on full riot gear. This seemed unreal to me, it's as if I'm in a bad movie or a horribly written skit. Everyone who spoke, was shouting. I could hear the shouting echoing outside in the court yard, as well. The officers began to check the pockets of people laying in the living room. I could feel the anxiety rising inside me and I could also feel myself sobering up, I thought to myself, they done blew my damn high.

I tried to remember if I had anything in my pocket that would be a cause for me to go to jail. I don't even believe that I own anything that's illegal. The process was long, gruesome and quite terrifying. It was my turn and I was afraid. I heard a female voice behind me speaking in normal tones, saying; are there any weapons or sharp items on your person? No; I said. What's your name and date of birth? I answered her however it was obvious that I was scared shitless because, my voice was trembling. She continued; just relax, I'm going to go through your front pockets first and make my way to your back pockets, OK? I nodded, yes. I was ask to turn to the right and then to the left for easy access to my front pockets.

When she was satisfied, she said; uncross your ankles and I will help you to sit up. I looked up to see a pretty Latino or Mexican woman with dark hair, that was pulled up into a bun. Her eyes were kind and her tone was welcoming. She instructed that I sit there and wait, she winked and walked towards the other officers telling them; this one is clean. I watched, as others began to sit up throughout the apartment as well. A male officer returned to where I sat and instructed that I stand. He grabbed my arm forcefully and walked me towards the door, leading outside.

As I approached the threshold, I knew then where the echos were coming from that I heard earlier. There were two other raids being conducted at the very same time. There were police everywhere, going from this apartment to Rick's place and downstairs to a white couple's place, which, was truly surprising because I never knew of any activity going on there. They were very quiet and kept to themselves. As we walk out further, I observed two big Ambulance that were parked out front of the building that were being loaded up with people in hand cuffs, which made me shiver. I could see that there was a large fire truck pulled up close on the side of the building where there were just windows. The officer and I walked to the start of the stairway, he turned to looked at me and said; your free to go. I couldn't believe my ears, my face felt warm and it seemed hard to breath. You sure? I ask; yes, she said; your clean. Feeling relieved, I quickly walked down and around to the other set of stairs and then ran down and disappeared out of the side doorway leading out into the streets. Shaken up by what just happened, I stopped in between the apartment buildings and just cried. I pulled myself together, ran into the apartment, stood on the inside of the door and thanked God for sparing me from going to jail today. For four days after my narrow escape of incarceration, like the addict that I am, I wondered around aimlessly in the night looking to cop some dope from one place or another, in hope of medicating this pain inside. I was meeting all sorts of characters and seeing things that should have scared me straight, but didn't. I was told about a house by another addict on the streets, that had what I needed. When I found the address, I knocked on the door and waited. I was surprised to see my friend Debbie standing there. We hugged briefly, it was obvious that we were happy to see each other. I entered the huge house that looked as if it were a beautiful piece of property at one time. The front door itself, was huge. As I stepped into the entryway, I realized how massive it really was. I ask her; where is the dealer? {I just wanted to cop and go home}. She turned and led me through this maze of clutter, that lead all the way back to doors leading to the pool area, which I could see through the large glass doors that possibly hadn't been cleaned in some time. She slid the glass doors open where there were pool toys for kids and adults and all sorts of games just left as they were, with an enormous in ground pool that had all the furnishings surrounding it, however you could see the neglect. I continued to follow her through, to a small house on the other side of the pool. She stopped at the door, smiled at me, and knocked softly. There was a big black guy that answered, he signaled for me to follow him. As we walked through, I could smell weed as we approached. When he opened the door, I saw a large area that had three tall candles sitting on cast iron holders that had the St. Mary printed on the front and they were lit. There was a small light over the bed that seemed to make things a bit creepy.

   I wanted my shit to go, however when I looked closely, I saw this old woman, {that I later learned was 70 years old} laying in her bed under this light with a small mound of what appeared to be freshly cooked up crack cocaine on a tray, with a glass pipe/stem in her hand. I was stumped. Her name was Miss Ella. She motioned for me to come closer. What's your name sweetie? she ask. Tru; I replied. What you need, Tru? She replied. I want a half; I said. She scooped up a heap of rocks on a card and put it on a small scale beside her. She removed what she had weighed up and put it into a bag and handed it to me and I paid her. I thanked her and turned to leave. I heard her small voice call out; come smoke with me, tell me your story and I'll tell you mine; she said. I told her that I had to get home. I think you should sit, she replied. I felt a bit threatened by her response, so I sat in a chair beside the bed but she insist that I sit on the bed. As I crawled up onto the double wide king size bed, she began to tell me her story as to how she got here in life and I sit to listen. From what I gathered, from her broken English, her family came from Trinidad and had a couple of successful businesses in this area. She and her sons decided to dabble in the drug business as well, and years later here they are. The big guy who let me in, was one of her boys and he gets high as well. I'm 70 years old and I can't quit; she admitted. I felt sad for her and wondered, was this my fate as well. It was time for me to go, I thanked her for sharing her story and promised that I'd be back and said my goodbyes and was allowed to leave.

Chapter 3

A long way home

Sunday, Chance brought all of the boys home. I was happy to see them all, as they were to see me. When Chance and I finished talking in private. I thanked him, for this time alone. It's my pleasure baby, I knew that there was no one else that would give you this, he then turned and said his goodbyes and left. The boys were eager to tell me what they had experienced. They were all talking at the same time, my head going in all directions to attempt to show them all, that I'm paying attention to them. Finally, I had to insist that they go one at a time so that I could listen to them all. My brother Alfred was the most exited, so he went first. The fishing was the best part, Tru. They all joined in to agree. After they all had their say, I reflected for a moment. I was Grateful that Chance had taken the time to help my brothers in their grieving process as well.

This was the start of a new school year and the boys were going to school without their mom. I wanted to believe that there was a change in store for us all. I went out the week before to buy new school clothes for them, so that they were ready to go. Monday morning, the boys were ready, Jamie and Roland were so exited that they were play fighting with each other. I walked out with all four boys to wait on their buses. We were greeted with the sun shining high with not a cloud in the sky. Once the last child was gone, I didn't quite know what to do with myself so I cleaned and played a couple hands of solitaire until I got board and went to lie down. I lay in silence and thought about my mamma until it hurt. I then pushed her out of my mind to think of something else but my thoughts were interrupted by a faint knock at the door.

I eased off the bed and quietly walked to the window and peeked out to see if it was someone that I wanted to deal with but what I saw was my baby boy Jamie standing there alone. I hurried around the chair that was sitting in front of the window to open the door. I looked both ways to see if anyone was with him and there wasn't. What are you doing here Jamie? I ask. I came home; he answered. What do you mean you came home? Before he could answered, I told him to go in the house, I closed the door and ran out to the streets to see if someone was pulling off...nothing. I quickly made my way back to him to further my questioning. {I could not believe that my baby walked all this way from school alone. It seemed like I'd just put him on the bus an hour ago}. I told him to sit at the dinning room table, I gave him a snack and went into the bedroom to get ready. When I returned, he was on the floor playing with a toy. I sit down on the floor beside him and ask that he show me the path he took to come home. OK mamma, he said proudly, and off we went. He went up the hill, explaining the whole way, I smiled, thinking; look at him. As we continued walking around the winding street, he remained focused and on task. Past the church, he pointed and went through the whole in the fence which was a shortcut that I had taken a few times in the past. We made it to Canyon Drive, which is a big street for a little guy to cross, my heart is pounding even more because we are now approaching Mission Avenue, which is the main artery of the city. This street, runs from the beach up through the city and down through too the valley that connects to a four way intersection that leads to other avenues to continue on through to Camp Pendleton Marine Corps Base.

Although I had walked this route a few times with my children in the past, I just didn't think that they, themselves would ever attempt to walk it alone. The distance from the school to our home may have been four to five miles. Finally we made it to Mission Ave, it was busy as usual. I bent down to look him in his eyes and ask him to show me what he did to cross over, he nodded with a smile. I watched as he walked over to the pole, pushed the button, As we wait for the light to change, I looked up at the large overpass that he has totally ignored. I continue to follow behind him, looking into the eyes of people in their cars who were watching and smiling at this little genius guide us to our destination, {if only they had known what brought us to this point}making it to the other side, he turned to wait for me{as if to say; so now what, mom}with a smile on his face. When we made it across, I ask; why didn't you use the overpass, son? He said; its easy to walk here, looking in the direction from where we came. Walking from school is dangerous for a little boy your age; I added. He looked at me and said nothing. I grabbed his hand and we walked into the school together. I could feel the tension building inside of me. I needed someone who knew what I was feeling about this shit. As I walked into the main office, there wasn't anyone in there but two small children sitting side by side against the wall. I mumbled; is this is how y'all lost my boy.

Excuse me, I said; in a stern tone. A tall heavy set caucasian woman with unusually thick ankles, appeared from one of the four rooms, may I help you? she ask. Yes you may; I replied. My name is Trul'ee and this is my son, Jamie. He reported to school this morning via bus and an hour later, he showed up at our home, alone. I want to know how this could have happened under your watch? I didn't know who this woman was but because she answered I assumed that she was the person that I needed to speak too. She looked down at my son with a puzzled look on her face and ask; can you hold on just a minute ma'am while I look up his teachers name. I stood watching her scramble around to find the information. I impatiently waited for the response. His teacher's name is Miss Beard, I'll call her to the office; she said.

We sat in silence and waited. When she came into the office, by the look on her face, she had no idea as to why she was called but when she was told, her eyes widened. I watched the two of them pass the blame from the bus driver to the class helper and finally to my child and that's where I drew the line. Excuse me! I said. He is five years old walking around in a big city alone, how could you place blame on him, someone here dropped the ball; I said. Someone didn't check their list to see where he was, and when that happened he did what he thought he should, he came home to his mother; I preached. The two of them were full of apologies and wanted to give him snacks and take him to his classroom to meet the other children. No! I said; he's going with me. Pay attention to the children, Please. I looked down at my son, I then turned towards the door and we left the building. We walked hand in hand across the street to the indoor swap meet and brought him a toy and went home to play.

Two days had passed since the incident at the school. Debbie paid me a visit. She let me know that she was tired and needed somewhere to relax and possibly crash for a few days, I said; yes. I immediately told her; I haven't used drugs in a week and that I didn't have a taste for it. I understand; she admitted. I sometimes don't want it either, she said as she lit up. I calmly, left the room. I came back in with a plate of chips and dips that I ate alone with a glass of cool-aid. When I finished, I laid across the bed with her reminiscing and laughed about the house where I saw here on that evening. The old lady, among everything else that has went on in our lives. We talked for hours, finally it was quiet. I could feel sleep come on. I lay back, with my eyes closed and arms crossed in the back of my head. I felt something strange. I thought that Debbie was shaking the bed but when I looked her way, she seemed to be sleep already. I lay still for a minute and felt it again. I was determined to know the source, so I held my breath and waited. There it was again, a movement in my pelvic area, I knew then, that it was a baby. I began to cry in silence. I knew that this was a bad time to be pregnant. I felt lost and alone and didn't know what to do. I still didn't believe it, so I laid there and waited with my hand on my stomach to see if it happened again…it did. Shocked, I called out to Debbie, she turned towards me…I'm pregnant; I said. With her face contorted she announced; I am too. I looked her in her eyes to see if she was shitting me, we both busted out laughing. We are pitiful and we know it; I shouted out through the laughter. We consoled each other while crying. I have to do something different because I don't want to have a baby in the state of California, they'll takes it like they did Trisha. I have to leave here; I added.

The day light broke through my mom's window as it had in the past reminding me of her. It made me sad to think that she and I hadn't resolved our issues before she died. I could feel the warmth of the sun on my face and somehow it made me feel better. I sat on the edge of the bed contemplating my next move. I dread the thought that was going through my mind, however something had to be done. With my head held low, I picked up the phone and dialed Jamie's mom's number. My throat was dry and my mind was consumed with negative things that I imagined, that he would say to me. Larnice answered the phone, my words would not come out the right away. Hello; she repeated. Hi Larnice, this is Tru, how are you? I'm alright, how are the kids doing? She ask. They are doing fine; I answered. After the small talk, I ask to speak to him. Jamie! She called out. I heard him answer in the distance. While I wait, I practiced in my mind several different ways that I would start the conversation. Hello! His voice startled me. Hey Jamie, it's me; I said. How you holding up girl? He ask. I'm OK for the most part; I said. We went back and forth about me and the kids. I need you! I admitted. I feel that I have no one else to call on that will help me with these kids but you; I said. I spoke to their father after the funeral and he didn't sound as if he would be of any help, I paused, waited patiently for a response. Finally, he ask, what do you want me to do? I don't have no money, I don't have a house, so how am I to help you? I have a proposition for you; I said. He laughed out loud. I need a house, somewhere to bring four kids and a baby. A baby? Yes, I'm pregnant. Who's is it? He ask. Yours, I said. I knew something was wrong with you because I was feeling nauseous for a while; he admitted.

 I can send you money for the deposit and first months rent and then send more later for utilities to be turned on. How much are you looking to pay? He ask. $300.00 a month, I guess. I believe, $800.00 should do it for now and I'll take care of the rest when I get there. He agreed and we ended the conversation. After placing the phone down, I sit for a while in deep thought. I worried about Trell and Alfred Jr. relocating. It just seemed like a bad Idea at the time because they have been in California for quite some time and the thought of them getting to know a place that they left as small boys, made me wonder if I was doing what was best for them as well. I spoke to their father once more to assure myself as to what I thought I heard him say. If I brought the boys there, are you going to help with them? Yes! He said; surprised that I would ask again. I had no choice but to take him at his word. So, I sat down with the family and Joan to discuss our strategy. It was hell trying to persuade two young boys into believing that leaving their home was better for them. I saw the fear in their faces, that made me feel bad. Joan had already put in two years of her life taking care of my mom, I wouldn't dare ask her for anything else in reference to us. She was the angel from heaven.

In the weeks to come, my brothers were showing signs of anxiety. Trell would have questions constantly about the move but Alfred?… let his opinion be known daily,{he did not want to go}. I feared that he would make a run for it eventually. I inconspicuously kept a close eye on him. Monday afternoon, Alfred was late coming home from school, I panicked, I ran into the apartment to prepare the other kids as to what to do while I go out to look for him. I locked the door behind me and went out to the streets ready to descend down the hill. As I walked a few steps and turned the curve, there he was coming in my direction, I couldn't be mad at him for what was going through my mind. I gave him a hug and turned to finish the walk up the hill with him. I let him know that he was a sight for soar eyes and to, not do this to me again.

All seemed well with me and the kids. I loved watching them play together in the apartment, while they played I began packing things that I thought would be essential for my brothers quality of life there. Their favorite toys or clothes and video game seemed to be those things. I ask the two of them to go into our mom's room and choose something of hers that would help them to remember her by, this was hard for them and it made me cry because my mom didn't have anything that they would want. Watching them search hurt even more, finally I pulled it together and went in to help them. I chose a handkerchief for the both of them and sprayed some of her cologne onto them.

Wednesday, put us a day closer to our departure date. I was a bit anxious to get this move over with. I walked out and waited in front of the building for all the boys to come in from school as usual. All but Alfred made it off the bus. I was furious because my intuition told me that this boy had ran. I looked down the hill to see if I could catch a glimpse of him coming up, I run up the hill to see, nothing. I rushed the boys in the house and called Joan to explain the situation, she said; I will be right over. I grabbed snacks for the others, sat Trell down and drilled him, asking him, where his brother may have gone. With a confused look on his face he shrugged his shoulders. I knew this was to detour me but I wasn't falling for it. By the time Joan showed up, I had gotten three places out of my brother. We found him at the 3rd place on our list. The lady of the house had no idea what was going on but when I explained what he was doing, she hurried him out of her house, admitting that she wasn't a kidnapper. When I got a hold of him, I held on to him by his shirt as he swung his arms, kicked and cussed at me until I grabbed him by the neck and squeezed enough to let him know that I meant business. I held him in place telling him; I will choke the shit out of you, if you don't get your ass in that car and sit down, that he did.

The next day all of the kids were made to stay home from school because of his antics. I just couldn't take a chance on that happening again with either one of my brothers especially, since our bus was leaving out tomorrow afternoon. I promised that if they behaved that I will buy them what ever pair of tennis shoes{within my price range} that they wanted for their first day of school. As uncomfortable as it may have been, I held onto Alfred as we loaded onto the greyhound bus. I continued to say positive and encouraging things to keep him calm hoping that something would sink in. However, he shouted; I don't care what you promise to do for me, I'm still not going to be happy there. I smiled at his remark and continued to guide them to the back of the bus to be near the bathroom and for comfort due to the three seats in the last row. I had to step off once more to say my goodbyes to Joan. I cried while holding on to her. I reminded her as to how much she meant to our family. I turned away to wipe my eyes, my heart hurt having to leave her. I reached down and grabbed a large duffel bag full of snacks and a large box of Kentucky fried chicken, blew her a kiss and boarded the bus. The ride home was uneventful thank God, they all ate slept and played the games that I brought.

Chapter 4

Biding our time

South Bend Indiana! The bus driver call out. I awake out of my sleep and immediately started getting the boys ready to disembark. As I got the little ones together, I carefully watched my brothers response to what they were seeing outside. I ask; what are you feeling right now guys? I waited for the response from either one and finally I see them both shrug their shoulders as if they didn't know what to say. I looked to see that Jamie was there to pick us up. As the bus driver pulled our boxes and bags from beneath the bus, I felt a deep sense of regret however, I know that it was much too late for that now. It was a challenge getting all of our belongings into the car along with the kids. I had to get out and rearrange the boxes and the kids. I had them sitting on top of each other and each of them were holding something on their lap. I prayed that we didn't get stopped by the police as Jamie had complained about several times. I sat quietly and watched out as we made the slow ride through the city to our destination. When we came over the tracks and made a right turn to come up Linden street, I knew that we were going on the Lake. He pulled up to a house on the corner of Wellington and Linden and I dropped my head. I knew from the look of this house that it was not large enough to hold all of us. It was a tiny single family home with one level, the front door was on Wellington street and the back door sit on the side of the home on Linden. There was no garage nor a car port. I could tell right away that there were no windows that indicated that there was a functional basement. I instantly regret my decision to come here but then I had to remember the main reason of my decision and that was to save my baby.

I instructed the boys to remove what they could carry. We had fun with it, laughing at each other for not being able to handle what we chose too haul into the house. When we stepped inside, my fears were true. The living room was the size of a mid sized bedroom, too the right was a small kitchen that had a red and white steel fold down table with four chairs that was from the 1960's. I could see three doors from where we stood that were towards the back of the house. I walked in that direction and noticed that the floor moved under my feet every step that I took. Alfred ran on before me, he stopped at the room to the left and looked in and said; are we all supposed to fit in here? I turned my attention to see what he was referring too. This room was much smaller than the room they all shared in California. I tried to make light of the situation by telling him that this was only temporary and that I'll find a bigger place for us but in the mean time I will buy you all bunk beds to sleep in. I could tell by the look on his face that he didn't care. I turned to look into the other bedroom, which was small as well, I said a prayer and walked back towards the front door to instruct the boys on where to put things. We attempted to settle in for the night but it was a challenge for them because it wasn't home.

The next morning, I woke up in good spirits. I just laid in bed feeling my baby bulge that felt truly amazing. I hadn't put my feet on the floor yet when I heard Jamie yelling, I knew that I had to investigate quickly. I walked in to see my brother Alfred standing by the sink with fear in his eyes however his stance told a different story, he was ready for what ever. With my hands in the air, showing that I come from a place of peace, I stepped in. It's OK, I will buy more cereal Jamie. You taking his side, ain't you? No, I'm not, I just want them to eat if their hungry; I admitted. He marched out of the kitchen, angry as usual and stormed out the front door. Alfred mumbled under his breath; I hate him. I pulled him in for a hug to explain that hate is such a dark and ugly word, are you sure this is the word that your feeling right now? To my surprise he said; no. I wondered why Jamie was so upset about the cereal, he doesn't even eat it. Everything that my brothers did, bothered him. I was sort of relieved that the pressure wasn't on Roland, I felt that because my brothers were older they could handle him.

The first of the month was here already and the check was in the mailbox. He took me to cash it. I payed the bills, got groceries and brought the kids a video game for their Nintendo 64 which to me, seemed like a great idea. Jamie did not, we argued in front of them until I went into the room. I layed across the bed for a bit, not realizing that I had fallen asleep. When I woke up, it was morning. When I got up off the bed. I walked through the house to talk to my babies that were awake as well. I loved this time of the morning, my boys are usually in good spirits after a good nights sleep, of course. I love their big smiles, it was what I needed. Where is Alfred and Trell? I ask. In the room playing that game, Little Jamie replied, with a slight attitude. What, they weren't letting y'all play? I ask jokingly. He just shook his head, no. I walked in the direction of their room, stopped and knocked on the door and stepped in, immediately noticing, Alfred isn't here, where is he, I ask Trell. I thought he was in there with the kids; he said.

I ran back through the living room and out the front door looking both ways in hopes that he was outside. Unfortunately, he wasn't anywhere to be found, so I walked back into the house and went back to the bedroom, sit down on the bed and put my head in my hands. When I finished sulking, I reluctantly, got up to get ready to go out and search for him. I decided to call his dad first, too see if he had heard anything from him, he said; no. So, I opened my drawer to get some socks and my chain purse, I remembered I needed to get more milk. I moved my hand around inside but when I felt nothing I searched with both hands to cover more space. I couldn't seem to feel my chain purse, so I emptied the content of the drawer and moved to the drawer beneath it, in hopes that it had fallen through. Dissatisfied, I cleared all of the drawers to search in the bottom of the dresser with no success. I couldn't believe where my thoughts had lead me{he took the rent money}. I slowly rose to my feet in utter defeat and stood there thinking; what would I do if he did take it and spent it all? I bent to my knees to say a prayer, afterwards I looked under the bed and underneath the table and realized that I was wasting my time. My mind wandering the whole time where could he be, finally I knew where he was and off we went. We pulled up in front of the bus station and I stalled. I just didn't want to believe that he would do me like this however here we were. Can you tell me if a young man, light skinned with a small frame built, came in to buy a ticket to Oceanside California, please? Yes, he said. My heart felt as if it had shifted in my chest. I couldn't get my questions out fast enough, he told me that he sold my brother a ticket and that the bus leaves out at 3:15 this afternoon. It felt as if I had been punched in the stomach. Betrayed, I couldn't believe that this guy sold a ticket to a minor; I thought. I argued my concerns. I decided to wait for him to come back being careful to stay out of sight in case he walked in early.

After two hours of waiting finally he walked in. I was so nervous that my belly churned. I walked slowly, coming up behind him finally close enough that I grabbed his shirt from behind. He violently turned to see that it was me and snatched away and took off running. The two security guards that were there waiting with us were in tow. Jamie and I weren't far behind. Alfred ran as if his life were in danger, he flew down a long hallway through a door that buzzed when he opened it which lead to the outside. We found ourselves heading towards the airstrip, I watched as he ran underneath small planes that were parked. I could see that the security guards were gaining on him, however I had doubts that they would catch him because he was bobbing and weaving to knock them off course, as for me I was done. The cramps in my belly let me know this was too much for my baby.

I stood watching all three of them chase this little guy around and around in circles, it was sheer comedy. I could see that Jamie had stopped running as well, my brother had turned in the direction in which the planes were preparing for take off. I looked on in fear, finally there was an officer that sprinted from another part of the building and finally caught up with Alfred and tackled him to the ground. I watched as they stood to their feet, I could see from a distance that my brother was still resisting however I could tell that the officers had quite the grip on him. As they moved closer, I could see that my brother was very angry from the expression on his face. As they passed by, I'd hoped to see some remorse in his eyes when he looked in my direction, there was none. They walked him to a small office where I was ask to attend. The officers handcuffed my brother to the chair that he sat in. Paperwork ensued, I immediately ask; are you going to file charges against him? Yes ma'am; he replied, we have to make a report as to the incident that happened today. I would like to take him home because he's a minor. There was a pause, when we are finished, you will be free to take him home. I thought about the entire chase that my brother had taken them on, I couldn't help but smile and shake my head, in disbelief. I also remembered the ticket that was brought with the rent money and ask if I could get a refund? Of course Miss Tru. As soon as we are done with this process we will go to the window and get your money returned to you.

There was a sum of $225.00 recovered from my brothers antics which left me $125.00 dollars short of my rent money. I looked in his direction with sheer discuss. When we were released to go, I was afraid to say anything to him for fear that he would talk crazy. In that instant I would have tried to tear his head off. I said nothing while we rode home in silence. When we made it to the house he had this attitude that indicated to me that he would run again if given the chance. I spoke to him in a calming voice asking; will you give me a chance to make things better for us? Finally, with remorse in his eyes; he agreed. I involved the boys in as many different activities as my money could afford, taking full advantage of all things that were free of course. The Charles Black center was available and free to all the young and underprivileged kids in the neighborhood however my brothers didn't seem to be as interested in what was going on there, so I did what I could with my boys when this occurred. As far as my brothers were concerned, I did what I could to keep them busy in hopes that they wouldn't want to leave any longer, it wasn't easy with Jamie being mean to them every chance he could.

As the baby grew inside me, the larger and more incredibly uncomfortable I became. My nose grew to a size that was awkward on my face and my arms were huge, I gained thirty pounds in such a small amount of time. When I walked, it was obvious that I was miserable. There were times that my feet were swollen to the point that it was hard to even sit. I felt ugly, my depression had hit an all time high, I felt worse than I had ever felt in the past and I didn't know what to do about it. I would lay in bed in the dark during the night and during the day I laid in the room with the curtains drawn. I was large, unattractive, uninvolved and unloved in my mind, however I knew that I had to keep it together for the kids, which was quite a struggle. It got cold early in Indiana, which made us all want to hibernate sooner due to us not being familiar of the cold weather here yet. I made sure that I got the boys coats way back in October from Christ child society. They gave them brand new clothes as well, I was also instructed to go to St. Vincent Depaul to apply for a Christmas basket, which helped out tremendously. I learned the system, I found what was needed and I retrieved it for the boys. There were things that they wanted that I couldn't afford but I could try to provide the things that they needed.

Chapter 5

A cry for help

December 9, 1989. I awake in excruciating pain. They were sharp, hard and unbearable, no matter which way I turned, there was no relief. I knew that it was time to go. I couldn't wait any longer, I yelled out in pain with every contraction. This child did not want to settle down at all and that scared me, it felt different than the other kids did. We finally made it to the hospital but as I passed the threshold I felt a need to push. Nurses were frantically saying; not now. I was rushed to the maternity ward and prepped for delivery. Things seemed to move fast. I was checked to see how much I had dilated, I felt the need to push again, not now, I heard. I was there alone in the delivery room and my emotions were all over the place. As an impulse, I pushed and again I was asked not too. I wanted this child out of me right now, it was hurting me, finally I was told that I could push and that I did. Fifteen minutes later the baby came out with no complications, he had all of his fingers and all of his toes. He was put on my chest blaring out, letting everyone in the room know that he was here. I watched as the nurses moved him away to clean him and check his vitals. He was a beautiful dark skinned baby with long fingers and toes, his name was already chosen by his big sister Yasmin, Darion Demonte Brazen. Congratulations were given by the staff however, I didn't feel as if I could celebrate as of yet, I was still having what felt like labor pains and they were even stronger than they were while I was in labor.

On a scale of 1-10 how severe are your pains? A ten; I replied. I moaned in pain, the doctor turned and instructed the nurse that I be given an epidural for the pain. I was ask to sit up and hold my breath, once it was administered it wasn't long that I could breath without pain. The afterbirth was removed and I was able to rest. I watched as they took the baby away, as soon as I turned over to close my eyes in walked Jamie asking; where is the baby? There was a part of me that was happy to see him, actually anyone because I felt alone. But he was the only person that I had in my life that cared even if it was his weird way of caring. I explained to Jamie that the baby was taken to the maturity ward. Why isn't he here with you? he ask. I'm exhausted, I needed some rest. He made a short snarl and turned to walk out of the room. Little did he know, my mind was in turmoil, my heart felt a storm coming on. When he left the room I felt as if I wanted to cry but I was much to exhausted, so I turned over to get comfortable and suddenly felt as if my mind was drifting into a dark place. I remembered that I decided early in this pregnancy that I wanted no more children, I signed papers to have a tubal ligation. I looked down at the paperwork again and turned to the nurse that was on duty at the time with tears in my eyes. I thought that I had this procedure years ago when the baby was taken from my tubes? She looked at me with concern in her eyes and replied; it sounds like you had an ectopic pregnancy Miss Trul'ee, however I will check your medical history to find out and I'll return with the answer as soon as I can.

I watched as she walked out, feeling dumbfounded trying to remember what I signed and what procedure was done on me way back when. Finally she walked back into the room with a paper that stated that I had an ectopic pregnancy and I had a Laparoscopic Procedure done. I immediately started to cry, I felt uneducated and just plain stupid. The nurse attempted to comfort me by telling me that it was a long time ago and not to worry however it didn't matter to me, I still felt what I felt. Two days later we were home, my boys were exited to see their new baby brother. Trell and Alfred were equally exited and from the looks on every ones faces they seemed happy but I was wrong because when Jamie left the house the boys gave me an earful of grief about things that he did. I couldn't believe that Jamie would treat my brothers so differently and be so mean to them. My brothers threatened to leave if things didn't get better. I understood their frustration so I promised that if they would give me a little time to heal from having my baby that I would find us a place of our own.

As days prolong, I found it harder to interact with the family. I was tired, weak and had no apatite. I just didn't want to get out of bed. I would instruct the boys on what to do from my bed. I called them in sometimes to help with the babies bottle. Finally, not able to cope I spoke with Jamie, explaining that I don't know whats wrong with me, I don't have the energy to do anything. Can you help with the baby at least? To my surprise he said; yes. He kicked in right away. He had Darion, morning, noon and night after that. I couldn't believe it. I had never seen Jamie as attentive with any of the other kids as I had with Darion. But as days passed I could outwardly hear a storm brewing within Jamie, he kept complaining about a guy that kept knocking on the front door, we all herd it as well but were told to not answer. He made several remarks that if the guy didn't stop, that he would beat his ass. I had to ask; who is this guy? Don't worry about it; he said. I did as I was told and left it alone. I was emotionally, spiritually and physically empty, I really didn't care about what was going on out in the living room or anywhere else for that matter. I felt as if I were sinking farther into that black whole and it scared me. I heard loud knocking in the front part of the house that vibrated all the way through, to the back of the house. It was 7:30 in the morning, I knew that this must have been the guy that Jamie spoke of, he wanted something and he made that apparent. He knocked for a while and when no one answered he stopped. The kids were waking up, my babies came in to lie down with me, it seemed as if they could sense that something was wrong with me but didn't know how to communicate it. I just held them both in my arms. I ask were Jamie and the baby were? Roland said; their in there on the couch and he won't let us fix no cereal. I shook my head, lord, here we go about this cereal again. I let out a snarl and tried to lift myself out of bed but it seemed to be harder than I thought. Give me a minute; I said. I pointed towards the door with my finger to let them know, to leave out, I'll be right there;I said. When they left out I cried into the pillow, it broke my heart that I couldn't get up to get my children what they needed but what was worse is that I didn't want to get up. With all of the strength that I had I began to ease out of the bed. I pulled myself up, holding on to the walls and furniture. I began to make my way past Jamie and Darion as they lay on the couch sleep. Boom! Boom! Boom! I crouched down to the floor, my heart beating hard as hell. I stayed down for a moment because it scared me that bad, but as I stood to my feet I looked down in the direction of my pelvic and realized that I had peed on myself a little. I continued into the kitchen with what strength I had left to fix the boys their cereal. Minutes later, Jamie flew past the kitchen cussing and fussing at whoever was at the door. I heard the door open and then him yelling at someone about knocking on his door like they are the police or something. I could also hear the guy trying to speak but he couldn't get a word in. Trell and Alfred had heard the commotion from their room and ran through the house to get outside to see what was going on. I looked out of the window and saw Jamie swing and slap the guy across his face, Damn! I said. The slap was so loud that I clinched my teeth imagining the pain that it must have caused. I couldn't believe{I've never seen him hit anyone but me and my son}what I had just seen. They were rolling on the ground in the dirt like kids, my brothers thought that all of this was funny but all I saw the danger in it. By the time I made it to the door the guy was on top of Jamie attempting to restrain him but Jamie was throwing blows, some connecting and some not, I smiled, he was flailing around like a fish.

STOP! STOP! I yelled. I see Alfred out of my peripheral running towards the commotion, before I could say anything, he jumped up in the air and dived on top of the guy attempting to put a choke hold on him. I couldn't believe this! {he don't even like Jamie, why is he helping him} I wondered. After what seemed like an hour, I snapped out of trance that I was in and began yelling loudly; STOP!! STOP!! THE POLICE IS COMING! I repeated it several times until finally they eased up and everyone began to relax. The guy stood back near the end of the sidewalk, still on guard. I didn't blame him at all. Because, he was still being surrounded by the same people that attacked him. Jamie and my brothers were busy looking around to see which way the police were coming from,when they both realized that I had lied, Jamie gave me a look of discuss, he then turned his attention towards the man as if he had, had the upper hand or something. Breathing hard and talking loud was not the answer, I thought. However, Jamie felt the need to scold the man further, about knocking on his door. The guy finally spoke in a professional tone, Mr. Brazen, I was ask by the company to come collect money or confiscate the product. Jamie intervened; you ain't getting shit out of here! he shouted.

I smiled before stepping closer, in hopes to make him feel comfortable, what is your name sir? Milton he replied. I apologize about all that has happened her but if I may, what product are referring too? The television ma'am; he replied. I looked over at Jamie and then back at Milton, how much is the payment? He said; One hundred and 10 dollars ma'am, I'll make the payment; I said. I just need you to follow me to the bank OK, he agreed. I looked in Jamie's direction with no eye contact, turned to walked in the house to get ready. When I made it to the bank my thoughts would not allow me to fully focus on what I came to do but after a couple of attempts, I was able to withdraw what I needed for the payment. My heart was heavy,

I just couldn't believe that all this happened over a television. I knew at that moment, that I had to try to make it through this thing that I was going through to make a change in our lives. After taking care of the bill, I made it back to the house, my plan was to avoid all contact with him and get back in the bed but he wanted to justify his actions. I really didn't want to hear it but I stood there to keep an argument at bay.

I was finally allowed to move without conversation, I ask if he could bring the baby in for a visit and then turned to ease my way into the bedroom where I sit in silence. My mind was all over the place again, I felt confused, emotionally drained and unstable. I was scared to even hold my baby. I sit holding him tight while rocking back and forth thinking about my mom and the choices that I've made in my life, which made me very sad and ashamed. I called Jamie in to get the baby so that I could return to the dark place in my mind, alone. Five days had past before I knew it. I just didn't have the strength to get up and do anything. Jamie called me lazy to my face. He came in the room as if looking for something. He stopped, turned and gave me an awful look. Are you going to ever get out of that bed? I couldn't answer because I didn't have an answer. He yelled; you do remember you have a baby to care for? I heard him but it just didn't register. I knew that I needed a doctor. I called our family doctor the next morning when it became apparent that my physical, mental and psychological state of being, was at risk. I was told to come in the next morning for an evaluation and that I did. The long and short of it, was that, I was suffering from a severe case of postpartum depression. I was given Prozac and a therapist to talk too. Telling the real reasons that I needed these sessions was not an easy task for me, especially if I didn't know why I was feeling the way that I was. I entered the doors of Madison center twice a month for six months. I was feeling much better and confident about the direction in which my life was heading. However the devil was still knocking at my door.

Although, Alfred came to Jamie's rescue that morning. The animosity between them was still apparent. They seemed to grunt and growl at each other every chance they had, the near mentioned of the names in front of the other, would change the temperature in the room. My brother would mumble words about him under his breath even when Jamie wasn't talking to him. He turned to me, looked me into my eyes, Tru, you promised to get us away from him when you felt better. While nodding my head, I replied; I am Alfred, give me a little more time, OK. He gave me the side eye and slowly walked into his room, I smiled, knowing that he was right. The very next morning I woke up in good spirits. I went to the boys room to ask if they wanted to ride with me to get a newspaper but Alfred was gone. All that I could do was shake my head and turn to walk across the small hallway to my room to get ready to go out and search for him. I looked for him all day, until finally feeling defeated, I turned to head back to the house. When I made it home, I sit besides the boys hoping to absorb some of their wonderful energy. I slowly picked up the phone and called the police to report my brother as a runaway. I gave the police all of the information that I could possibly remember about him with the exception of what he had on this morning. It saddened me, that he felt as if he just couldn't deal with this situation that I put them in, any longer. If something happens to him; it would kill me inside.

The next day, I decided to take the kids for a walk, it was a lovely day for a stroll. It felt good getting away from the house and taking in some fresh air. The boys loved it, they played, ran and jump around while Darion attempted to get out of the stroller to be with his brothers, it put a big smile on my face. Trell and I walked and talked about future plans in our own home, things that we dream of doing once we acquired one. My mind still wandering…. thinking of where my little brother could be. I stopped in my tracks and gently grabbed Trell's arm and ask; is there any place that you hadn't thought of, that Alfred could be? Naw, I stood for a moment studying his eyes, hoping to find truth in them. When I was satisfied, we both continued on with our walk. I see people doing yard work, sitting on their porch people watching, kids playing ball in the streets and old guys just shoot'in the shit with one another. When we finally made it inside the store, all three of my kids faces lit up. The saying; [like a kid in a candy store] couldn't be more real. I didn't need to shop, although the little store sold a lot of household items you may need if you couldn't or didn't want to go to the groceries store. I came for one thing and one thing only and that was a news paper. I brought four suckers and that newspaper and we proceed to walk back home, choosing to take a different route for a different scenery.

When we made it back to the house, I decided to sit on the two step concrete porch that was barely attached to the house. I wasn't quite ready to go in yet. I sat down and gave God thanks for the beautiful day and the mindset to move on in life. I watched the boys run around until their candy high wore off and one by one they went in. I decided to go in as well, as I passed through, Jamie was in the kitchen cooking something that smelled awfully good for dinner, one things for sure he knew how to get down in the kitchen. As I walked by, he ask; where were you'all this afternoon? At the store; I replied. To my surprise he had no rebuttal. Now-a-days he was more verbal than physical towards me, my brother and the boys. I really didn't know if it was because he was growing out of it or if it was my brothers presence in the house. At any rate I never got cocky or took a chance on it. I continued on through to the bedroom, I got the baby cleaned up and ready for his bottle. The boys and my brother Trell came in playing around, you could hear Jamie's voice from the front yelling; stop all that noise!

The next day I sat secretly looked through the newspaper to find a house for me and the kids. I was nervous as hell, every noise that I heard in the house I would stop, put it away and make sure it wasn't him coming in to catch me. {My plan was to find the house, then, sit down and talk to him about it because in my mind I thought that I needed somewhere to go right away in case he snapped}. I would search and call each number that I thought suited our little family, to no avail.

The next week, I rode to the gas station to get a Sunday paper because I knew that it had a greater selection in it, than any other day of the week. I found an apartment on western avenue. It was a three bedroom apartment that was upstairs. I could see it as early as tomorrow if I wanted. I arranged to meet with the guy, while my older boys were in school, Darion could hang out with me. I was exited and leery at the same time because I didn't think that any of these apartments on western avenue would be kid friendly because of the traffic that flowed through, however I met the guy anyways. He told me to drive around and park in the back. When I made it through the narrow alley, I started to keep on driving but I stopped to survey the land and my intuition told me that this was not a good place for a woman with children at night or during the day for that matter. I noticed a brown older model car coming through the alley and I assumed that it must be him. As he parked, I turned my attention toward the stairs that lead up to the apartment. He walked up to me and introduced himself as Harold. We exchanged pleasantries, and proceed to walk up the stairs. When we made it to the top, I turned to look down as he fumbled for the keys. I mumbled; this would be a long way down if one of my kids would happen to fall, still I chose to continue on with the showing of the apartment. When he finally opened the door, I looked past him to see what looked like a very nice place back in it's day. The ceilings were high and everywhere you looked, the molding was beautifully positioned around each doorway and window. Walking through the kitchen, I noticed that there were plenty of cabinet space with a large area for dinning. I walked further in, and I couldn't help but notice how beautiful the molding over the archway was. The artwork was still in tact after all this time. The windows surrounded the entire front of the apartment which let in an abundance of natural lighting. Two of the bedrooms were adjacent the living room and the third was off the kitchen. I finished the tour feeling satisfied, although the apartment hadn't been kept up by it's landlord. I turned to Harold and thanked him. I admitted that because of my small children this wouldn't work for us and said my goodbyes.

I made it back to the house feeling somewhat liberated about making a first step towards getting my own place. Jamie walked in, and my mood changed instantly. He started talking to me about issues involving his daughter. I guess he felt as if I wasn't paying attention to him so he yelled my name. I'm talking to you. I looked up to speak to him and in walked my brother Trell from school. Jamie paused for a while waiting on my brother to pass through, to go to his room as he always did. Instead he had something to tell me about something that his teacher said. He was excited and didn't know that he had walked in on a conversation. Jamie shouted; boy! Are you restarted or something? Don't call him that; I said. Can't you see that we talking? He added. When my brother attempted to answer, Jamie said; get yo ass out of here and go to your room! I looked into Trell's eyes to see the tears that began to form along with an angry glare. I reached for his hand to comfort him but he snatched it away and did what he was told to do. I watched Trell walk away, I felt bad because this is my fault. Don't baby that boy...Jamie continued on with his conversation as if nothing happened. I sit quiet pretending to listen with an occasional lift of my eyes toward his direction but my mind was elsewhere.

The next morning, after the kids were off to school and Jamie went Job hunting. Darion and I went to a place not far from where we were living called, La'salle Park Homes to apply for housing. These apartments were subsidize housing for low income families. Once we found the office. I said a quick prayer and went inside. There was no-one present but one woman by the name of Miss Barbara. She was a light skinned nice looking lady with small freckles on her cheeks. When she spoke, here voice reminded me of Joan, back in Oceanside. May I help you? she ask. The tone in her voice made me feel as if everything was going to be alright. I told her that I would like an application for housing. How many are there, of you; she ask? Myself and four children, I answered. Are they all boys? Girls? She ask. Boys, I said. You will need a three bedroom but the waiting list is at least three months long. Ma'am, I moved here from Oceanside California after my mother died, with my two little brothers, my two children and a baby on the way, {as I pointed down at Darion} in hopes that their father or my family would help me with the boys. I'm living a few streets away from here with a man who is at the moment very verbally abusive to both me, my brother and the boys. If you can, help us with any size apartment, please. She turned and rustled through a drawer that appeared to have files of some sort in it and handed me three pieces of paper and ask me to fill them out. My heart was pounding, while tears began to well up in my eyes. As I pushed the tears aside, I filled the papers out. I could hear her rustling through another drawer looking for something. She pulled out an envelope sat it on the desk and turned to me and ask; do you have your social security card and birth certificate? Yes ma'am. I handed the paperwork back to her and she copied everything that was given to her. I watched as she got it all together. She looked into my eyes while handing me the small manila envelope that she found and said; God put it on my heart to do this for you, good luck Miss Trul'ee Benevolence, and congratulation on your new home. I was so happy that I heard myself giggling and then I cried profusely.

Chapter 6

No more pain

I couldn't seem to compose myself all day. I fixed dinner, got the boys ready for the evening with a smile on my face while humming, sweet love, by Anita Baker. It was a type of euphoria and I loved it. However when Jamie noticed my new found state of being, he wasn't in agreement with it. It was fine with me because, God had shown favor and for that I was truly grateful. Why are you trippin? he ask. I'm just happy Jamie; I replied. I will explain later when I get the boys in the bed. I sat on the couch and ask that he sit with me, while pointing to the chair across from me. My nerves were on end. I didn't quite know how I was going to bring this too him but I knew I couldn't just leave him without saying anything regardless as to how mean he has been in the past, he has always opened his doors for us. I sit searching my mind for the right words to say. Come on girl; he snarled! I took air into my lungs and then exhaled. The words that fumbled out, were sounding unlike my own. While feeling awkward, I found an apartment for me and the kids... Jamie, I said quickly. I figured you didn't want us here anymore. I remembered you saying on numerous occasions that you were tired of us, complaining about one thing or another, so..I found somewhere to take them. I waited for his response for what seemed like for ever and saw a look in his eyes that I had never seen before. One of remorse, sadness, one that made me feel a bit of regret. However, it was one that was short lived. "I didn't say it like that" you go ahead and do what you gotta do, girl. I'll be alright, he hissed. I watched with a careful eye, waiting for what was to come....That never came. He walked out of the front door to the car where he sat smoking his cigarette, finally driving away.

 I packed up what little we had, while moving very quietly in his presence. He returned to sit on the couch with his arms folded and legs crossed on the coffee table watching television and didn't say a word. That to me, indicated that I should not bother him. If I needed to get something that was near him, I chose to leave it sitting right there. I had to borrow his car to move. All I had were garbage bags full of clothes and boxes of toys. The things that I had gotten from St. Vincent, I thought that I would leave here for him, it was only right; I thought. When the kids and I turned the key for the first time to our new apartment, their excitement made me smile. As they ran through the apartment testing the echo's through out, I walked through inspecting things to see what I was working with. I was excited as well but a wave of sadness came over me when I thought about my little brother Alfred... I could now here the kids upstairs picking out their bedrooms. I decided to run on up to join them and watch their anticipation. When all four bedrooms where assigned to each child, I alerted the boys that it's time to go, we had to finish moving. When we walked into the house, I could feel the tension in the air. I wanted to ask him if he wanted to come and see the apartment but I decided that now wasn't the time, so my brother and I went to the bedroom and proceed to break down the bunk beds, careful not to misplace any of the small pieces, because I did not want to come back here to look for them.

Finally, getting the beds torn down enough to be transported was a task, but we did it. I put a blanket on top of the car first and carefully put the large pieces of the bed frames on top and the smaller pieces inside the car where I could find room. I had gotten all of the extension cords that I could find in the house and tied them together to use as a rope to tie down the frames. Once he and I got all of the frames moved into the apartment, although tired, we headed back out to get the mattresses. We made it back to the house to find that Jamie had moved the mattresses to the living room and propped them against the wall. I smiled inside and out because of his kind gesture. My brother and I prepared ourselves to carry them out but Jamie intervened. He and I carried the box springs and mattresses out and put them on top of the car and tied them down together. Thank you; I said. He nodded and went back in the house where he sat back on the couch in the same corner in which he was in the beginning. So my brother and I continued on with the move. My boys looked at me as if they wanted to go this time but I explained that we will be right back and I will buy pizza for dinner. Cheering erupted in the house as I closed the door behind me.{ Funny how being a parent, you seem to know what your kids are thinking when your in tune with them}.

We were done and because I was so tired I ask; Jamie, would give us all a ride to the apartment. He agreed. I watched the look on his face to get a reaction, there was none. I told him that I will call him. Me and the kids got out and went into our new home. The pizza came to the apartment just as we made it there, the guy and I walked to the door where I could free up my hands to give him the money. I noticed that there weren't any curtains or blinds up to the windows, so I looked through the bags and found blankets and candles so that we could go upstairs to have a picnic in one of the bedrooms. I spread all of the blankets out on the floor and laid down and told them a crazy bedtime story and off to sleep they went one by one.

The next day was a busy one. I had to transfer the kids from the schools they were going too and enroll my boys into Harrison elementary and my brother into Navarre middle. I needed to go groceries shopping for the apartment as well. I also went to St. Vincent in hopes of getting things for the new place. Learning the bus system wasn't the most difficult thing that I had done today but having Darion made it a bit more challenging for me with me having to get on and off like I did. After being out all day, finally we were able to return to the apartment. We were approaching our stop, as I reached for the cord someone had already pulled it, so I got my baby, the stroller and his diaper bag and readied my self to get off. I walked in the direction of our apartment and heard some commotion coming from that direction that put my maternal instincts into overload. I turned to go in through the other opening to avoid whatever was going on. I turned slightly to notice someone coming up beside me. She must have noticed that I was out of sorts and ask if I needed any help. Before I could answer, she took the diaper bag and the bag of food that I was juggling from my hand.

She walked quietly beside me all the way to my apartment and when we made it to the door, I opened it and she sit the bags on the inside and said; my name is Willie Mae Bullock. She had such a stern voice, one that commanded my attention, just like Ainnie's. She was a dark skinned, older, average looking lady with a kind smile, and a mole beside her nose, that gave me the thought of a beauty mark. She may have been 50 years old or so, with a southern accent… I live ova yonder; she added. I smiled, "nice to meet you" I'm Trul'ee. As I watched her walk away, I noticed that her apartment was located right across for ours. I felt at that moment, that God had sent yet another one of his angels to watch over us.

I had awaken to get the boys ready to begin their day. I knew that I had a busy one ahead of me and I wanted to get started early. We all noticed that there were more people outside, being that it was a Saturday. My boys were anxious to get out side and play. After brushing their newly cut hair, they were allowed to go. I sit on the porch and watched them play for a while and decided that they would be safe while I got a little work done around the apartment.

Fast forward….One month had passed, and Jamie came by to let me know that he needed somewhere to stay for a little while. He added, that he didn't want to go back to his moms place to live. Of course, I said yes. He knew that I would open the door for him because he had always opened his for me so many times in the past. I didn't expect change nor did I demand it. I understood, those things not said. Unfortunately things between us were the same. He began moving the very next day. He brought almost everything that I had left there for him. The couch and love seat was much needed, now the kids had furniture to sit on but when I looked at that television set, I remembered all of the ruckus that was caused on that day, because of it. It wasn't long after he moved in, he began getting on my brothers case about everything that he did or didn't do. I would intervene sometimes to reduce the pressure that was building between them however, Trell was fed up and would walk by on occasion, looking at me, shaking his head. I knew that I had messed up but, I didn't want to see it in my kids faces, so..I would try to do things to make it right but he wasn't falling for it. I guess, I came up with an idea...I thought that if I told Jamie to invite his buddies over, maybe he could let off some steam by playing cards and having a good time in hopes that it would get him off my brother Trell's back for a minute.

Saturday night was perfect, the weather was nice and people were sitting out in front of their door enjoying the nice breeze. It was close to 7pm, when we heard a knock at the door and in came a guy that everyone around town called Bro-man. He was a big man, that had a look about him that he could hurt somebody real bad but he was a nice guy in my opinion. He and Jamie had been friends for years, they say. Behind him was a gentleman that I had never seen before. I went behind them and locked the screen door and offered them a seat. Jamie lead them to the dinning room table and offered them a beer. I proceed to get the boys up so that they could go upstairs and play{I'm a firm believer that kids should not be around grown folks}with their toys. After all the kids were upstairs, I made my way back to the table to see if the guys needed anything. I turned to politely introduced myself to the new guy. Hello, my name is Trul'ee, I'm with Jamie; I said. My name is Darcy; nice to meet you. He was an average looking man, light skinned, thin built with a bit of facial hair on his chin. I excused myself and went to the kitchen to finish the chicken wings that were cooking for the boys to eat. The music was sounding good and everybody was having a nice time. I was in the kitchen grooving as well. "Tru" bring us some beers! I hear in the distance. I grabbed the beers from the fridge and took them to the table. Bro-man was talking as I walked up, they all burst out laughing. I smiled at them and sit the beers down and turned to leave out just as Darcy began to speak. I noticed that there was something different about the tone in his voice, it seemed rehearsed. I made it back to the kitchen, my mind was baffled. I stirred the cheese sauce for the chips. I still couldn't contain my thoughts. I fixed a nice platter that consist of chips, celery, carrots, chicken wings and two different sauces for dipping. I grabbed the paper towels, I was moving so fast that I almost forgot the hot sauce. When I made it to the table, I purposefully ask questions that would generate a conversation while placing everything on the table.

I made a funny, that cracked them up and then... he spoke. Without thinking I looked over into his eyes to verify what my ears just heard. "IT WAS A GIRL! A WOMAN!" I screamed in my head. She had my attention...not in a lustful way but,in a curious one. I had never seen a person like her, I was intrigued by her presence. I moved away from the table quickly because I felt myself staring. I went back in the kitchen to process what I had just heard. I told myself to let it go, stop overthinking, however as moments passed I just couldn't let it go. I wondered; how does a person become this way? What made her want to be a boy? I had to let this go because it was consuming too much of my thoughts at that moment. I called my son down to get the platter of food for them to take back upstairs, threatning them not to make a mess and it was business as usual……or so I thought? Days came and went and nothing changed between Jamie and I. He was the King of the Castle and he ruled with an Iron fist. My brother had reached his limit and when my sister Denise moved back to South Bend, he moved in with her. It hurt me to tears. He was only 14 years old and had to make such a grown up decisions because of my choices. I couldn't understand why I couldn't break free from this man. He had a hold on me and I couldn't explain it to anybody, if I tried.

…….He jumped up to reach for my neck, I somehow dodged him and moved to the right of the couch, standing there to see what his next move would be. "Ain't nobody gone want you with four kids bitch, watch and see" I don't even know why I come back; he shouted. I watched him turn and walk out and slam the door behind him. Although I've heard those words before, they still cut like a knife. I sit on the stairs to think about what I was going to do next and it occurred to me that I had the opportunity to make changes in my life, now.

An hour later Jamie, his cousin Al and his mom pulled into the parking lot with a flatbed. Larnice sit in the car while Jamie and Al came in to get his things. I remained outside where I thought it would be safe. I walked over to say hello and noticed a look of discuss on her face that I truly understood. She had a few choice words to say about the situation and when she was finished, I walked over to stand on a patch of grass close to my apartment. When I saw him bring the furniture out, it bothered me. I had been paying on it all this time more so than he was but because it was in his name…. I stood in silence until they were finished, when the last item was loaded, Jamie turned his attention towards me. I heard his mom, "come on boy, I ain't got all day." He gave me a stare that meant something fierce.

When they left, I thought that maybe I would be able to relax a little, get my mind right. But remembering that stare that he gave me, put me on edge. As days passed I felt better but it stayed on my mind. I began to concentrate on more positive things. I wanted more for my little family and I had to do something to make that happen. Willie Mae was becoming a true friend, she was very resourceful and informative about things that me and the kids needed. Although my brother chose to remain with my sister. I continued to care for him. I began to feel that all was good with us and with that came a desire to get my education now. So…I walked over to Willie Mae's house and ask if she could watch the boys a few evenings during the week for two hours. She said; yes. I was on my way to bigger and brighter things, I thought. The program was called General Educational Development for adults, they had classes at the old Central High school, down town.

I was too ashamed to tell her where I was going, as far as I was concerned this was my little secret and I intended on keeping it from her and everyone else. There was an embedded fear of mine also, that someone who knew me would come walking through those doors or too be taught by someone who graduated when I should have. Still I continued on with my journey in hopes that neither fear became a reality.

Four weeks had passed, things were real good. I learned more this week in class than I had the last week. Every wonderful thing with my boys were better than ever. We had a nice cozy home to live in finally, with a couch and love seat, a nice coffee table with end tables to match that, I owned. God was truly Blessing. It was Friday and two of my boys laid on the floor playing their video game while Darion played with his action figures. I sit on the couch doing homework while watching the boys be in their element. The phone rang, snapping me out of my pleasant thoughts. Hello; I sang into the receiver. Hello; Tru, this is Joan; she said. I was frozen with happiness. Are you there? She ask. Yes, I'm here. How are you guys holding up? she ask. We are doing good, we recently moved into another place, it's not a mansion but it's home. Well, I want to come there to visit you guys; she said. I stood in silence, with my mouth held wide open in awe. Tru? Are you there dear? She ask; again. That would be wonderful! I shouted.

We finished our conversation, with her telling me that she will let me know in a couple of days when she will arrive. We all were very excited that she was coming to check on us. I really couldn't believe that we meant that much to her that she would travel all this way to see us. Wow! She called the next day to make me aware that I had a week and a half to prepare for her arrival, that was quick; I thought. I began working on the spare room, pouring all the Love that I could muster up, in to it. In the days leading up to her arrival, there was a positive vibe correlating through out the house that I had never felt in my entire life, it was euphoric. My children seemed overly loving towards me and themselves, it was amazing that just the mere mention of Joan's presence would bring on such an amazing amount of positive energy. This, to me showed that we all loved her in our own unspoken way.

The day was finally here and she was due to arrive at our home at 10:30am, my nerves were frazzled. I wanted everything to be perfect. The goal was to impress her with how clean and organized things were in my place as apposed to my mom's. I paced the floors, checking and re-checking to make sure that everything was in it's place. And then……

The knock at the door startled me, my heart stopped beating while taking my breath away momentarily. It was her! I thought out loud. My feet would not cooperate with what my brain was telling it to do. Finally the sound of Trell's voice snapped me out of it, we all moved towards the door to greet her {I wished at that moment that my brother Alfred was here as well} with smiles and anticipation. It was truly wonderful seeing her, she looked absolutely amazing as usual. Hair was perfect as always. She was wearing a burgundy two piece pant suit with a gray silk blouse that tied into a bow positioned at the side of her neck, with a pair of gray opened toed shoes that match the blouse with a quarter inch heel that showed off her perfectly manicured toes. I couldn't help but stand in awe, she was the epitome of what a beautiful Black woman should look like. She reached for me, to hug me and I didn't hesitate to responded. I invited her and her daughter Jenny, in to sit so that we could all catch her up on how each one of us were adjusting to life here in South Bend. I chose to leave out all of the bad things on purpose because it just felt like the right thing to do at the moment however, I did fill her in about Alfred. I know that he's alive, I just can't catch up with him. Trell, chimed in with his version as well.

Denise was there as well, she made Joan aware that she was glad to finally meet the lady who cared for her mom. I sit back and watched in silence how she and my family laugh and talk until dinner. What did you cook Tru? Smothered pork chops with mashed potatoes, gravy, seasoned green beans, yams and biscuits; I replied. After dinner, she told me that I put my foot in that food. She also made me aware that she was exhausted from the flight and wanted to rest. I told the boys to say goodnight as I lead the way upstairs. I placed her bag in the room that I prepared for them. I looked up to see the expression on Joan's face that showed, that she was pleased."She didn't realize all that I had went through just to see that look on her face but it was priceless." After pointing to the new towel sets that sat on both their beds, I ask if I could get them anything else. No, thank you dear; Joan replied. I smiled and closed the door behind me. This was a very good day.

The next day we all took a drive around town to show them the small city that we live in. There wasn't much here to see within these four corners. We were surrounded by a bunch corn fields and vast farm land. Notre Dame University was the attraction as far as I was concerned. There was the mall and a couple parks in the area but nothing exciting. We drove along the river and through town and around north side boulevard. She said that it was nice, but I think that she was being modest. I smiled, as I thought; there is nothing here to compare to anything in California but still I was pleased to hear those words. We finally made it back to the house where she finally met my only friend in the world, Willie Mae. They exchanged pleasantries and Willie Mae expressed that something was on the stove and that she had to go, nice meeting you; she said and closed the door behind her. When my friend left there was a calm in the air that set a series of events in motion. I rose up off the couch to put on some jazz. Joan turned to meet my eyes with a loving gaze to tell me; we're leaving early in the morning. I instantly became saddened only because I wanted more time with her. She ask that I send the boys upstairs for a little while, because she has some important business she needed to share with me. I brought the boys into the kitchen, handed out snacks and instructed them to go upstairs. I then walked over to the stereo to turn down the volume. She spoke slowly….."I have stage four lung cancer" she said with a sweet and even tone. I could feel the warmth rising inside of my body. My feelings and emotions had not yet caught up with what I had just heard. Finally, it felt as if a light had came on inside my head, "she's dying" I screamed inside! I may have repeated it three or four times before responding. I felt so very bad for her and her family for what they were about to go through but somehow without realizing, I made this about me. How could God take yet another person away from me. Why would you bring such a wonderful human being into our lives just to snatch her away; I thought. I looked into her eyes and began to cry so incredibly hard that I felt my jaws began to hurt. She is such a beautiful person both inside and out. As looked up at her, I saw a reflection of my sadness in her face. The more that I cried, she cried. I tried to pull myself together but the more I selfishly thought about her being taken away from me, the more it hurt and the more I cried. I felt a calm come over me, as if I had left the room involuntarily and someone else came in my place. It didn't hurt anymore, the empathy was there but all other emotions were somehow turned off without my permission. I'm so sorry for what you have been through and are about to go through; I said. I truly wish that I could be there to help you as you had helped my mom, that is the least that I could do for you. She turned to look in my direction with a bewildered look on her face; I promise to call as much as I can to keep you guys updated on this disease, God's got me; she admitted. However, it's been my belief from past experience, that when it's been diagnosed, it's a death sentence. I sit in silence attempting to keep my face together…for her. I looked up as if to actually see the kids and called them downstairs, we stood to our feet and gave each other a long hug to end our conversation. She and I woke early the next morning to say our goodbyes, we hugged, this time seemed different, I walked them out to the car and watched them drive away, not knowing if I will ever see her alive again….

Our lives continued on without one day going by that I didn't think about her. She and I spoke on the phone once a week to catch me up on the progression of the cancer. I noticed that the small cough that she had in the past had became more aggressive. I was very patient while talking to her by waited for her to breath again to say her next word. There were days towards the end when she didn't feel up to talking and her husband would call for her, to fill me in at her request. He was a very kind man, a gentle giant I would sometimes say but the more I spoke to her, I realized that it had been the most compassionate and endearing moments that I had ever felt talking too any human being. Saturday Evening at 4pm. I got the call that she had died at home surrounded by her family. Her body was still there when he called me. I could actually picture them all standing around her in my head, and it hurt so bad. Telling the boys, took me a few hours to do, I had to get myself together first. Trell was the one that took it the hardest because of the ties that Joan had to our mother. I understood. For the next few days we all spent time comforting each other over the loss of her. I decided to cook a special meal on her behalf, we sit having dinner reminiscing about the past until it was time for bed.

Chapter 7

Time for a change

The days following Joan's funeral were uneventful but my thoughts were many. I would sit with Willie Mae for a bit and then take the kids home to cook dinner for them. Sit and think again about those who had also died in my life. I missed different qualities in them all. My mom, because of the title that she carried. Aunt Darlene because of her knowledge that she spewed onto me. Joan, for showing love when she didn't have too. Last, but most loved, was Ainnie. Who taught me how to take care of myself and made sure that I knew that I was pretty, even when others thought that I wasn't. I believe, that in some ways, I still wanted and needed them alive. I spoke to them all, telling them how much I needed them. As for my my, I hadn't realized that I was still angry with her, after all of this time. A knock at the door brought me out of my thought. Yes; I shouted. I wiped the tears that had formed and ran down my face as I slowly looked out to see, her/ him. I opened the door hoping that I locked the screen door and with a smile, said; Hello, how are you? Jamie isn't here. I didn't come to see him, I'm here to see you; she said. What could she possibly want with me? It was getting dark out and I didn't want anyone to see inside my home, living in the projects and all. So, what is this about? I ask. And if it's not important can you come back in the daylight hours? Yes, I can; she replied. Later, I lie awake most of the night wondering, what could she want with me. I have never seen her, nor anyone who looks like her in my life. My thoughts circled until I was finally able to relax my mind enough to fall asleep.

The next day went just like the day before, business as usual. When I got my boys off to school and the baby to my friends house I went to class. When I made it home that evening, I picked up the boys and began to prepare the chicken wings that I had left out thawing. There was a knock at the door. I instinctively looked up at the clock on the wall that said "5:30pm" I peeked out and it was her again. I opened the door noticing that I had locked the screen door this time, Hello; I said, with that same smile on my face that I had yesterday which made me chuckle, I knew this because it felt the same. How are you? I ask. I'm fine; she said. I came back hoping that you were home and that we could talk for a while and get to know one another, I have wine and a joint if you smoke; she added. "I was curious as to what she really wanted with me" I reached down to unlocked the screen door and told her to come on in, in spite of what my intuition told me. I offered her a seat as I closed and locked the doors, not taking my eye away from the area where she sit, I instructed the boys to take a snack and a juice and go upstairs to play, they all passed with curious looks on their faces, surely wondering who this guy was. When the last child made it upstairs, I turned towards her/him and offered a glass of ice for the wine. {She} happily accepted, get a glass for yourself; she added. So... how are you and the boys doing since Jamie left. For some reason it stung a little when I heard her say that. How did you know? I ask. I think everybody around here knows by now, news travels quick around here. We are doing well, just handling our day to day; I replied.

So... what do I owe this surprise visit from you? I ask. I just thought that you were cool people when I met you before and that you could use a good friend; she said. I watched as she opened the bag to bring out a bottle of MD 2020 and a 40ounce of Old English. I wanted to reply in a timely fashion but I couldn't quite think of the words to say behind that. Can I put one of them in the fridge for you? She handed me the bottle of beer and ask; you can use a friend, right? I smiled; yes I can, I guess. She poured us a drink and she lifted her glass, cheers. I had no idea what she meant and by the puzzled look on my face, she knew that as well. She explained that it was something that people said before they drank, like a toast. Well I didn't know what a toast meant either but I decided to leave it alone. She told me a little about her past and I shared just a little about mine. But the more I drank the warmer it became inside the apartment and inside me. Why are you the way you are and what made you want to be this way? I blurted out. "I couldn't believe that I allowed that shit to roll off my tongue like that" but I had to know. She paused for a long moment and...sounding just like a grown man, she laughed out loud for a while, as if mocking me in some sort of way, I wasn't sure if I had pissed her off or humored her. Finally the laughter stopped, she began to speak, dragging each word as if contemplating her next. She took in a breath, I've been this way for as long as I can remember; she said. I've never thought of myself as a girl, although I knew from a very early age, that my body was different from my brother's, however I never let it stand in the way of anything that I wanted to do. I played baseball, basketball and football with the boys and was pretty good at it, I interrupted, I didn't mean any harm, I was just curious.

This way of living is similar to breathing for me, I'm this way without trying; she explained. I have another question? I admitted. Is having sex with a woman different from having sex with a man? I have never had sex with a man; so I wouldn't know; she claimed. I told her to give me a minute. I ran into the kitchen and grabbed more snacks. I called the boys down, gave them what I had in my hands and instructed them to get ready for bed, and off they went. I'll be up to check on you shortly, I shouted. There were two over sized pillows that lay in the corner of my living room that I brought out and laid on the floor with snacks for us and more wine and beer. We layed on the floor and continued our conversation well into the night. We were having such a good time, I thought we might wake the kids. It was fun, it was 1:30am and I had to say goodnight, I could tell by the smile on her face that she enjoyed the evening as well.

Back to business for me and the kids. With class, their school and coming home to sit with my only friend, sorta filled our day but this routine of mine was getting a bit monotonous. I found myself sitting out on the porch a few times during the week at night watching the stars and dreaming about far away places that I wish that I could see. It was Friday night and I sat out late watching people going wherever it was that they were going. I noticed someone coming in my direction.

As I looked closely, I noticed that it was Darcy. I could feel a smile began to form on my lips. When she was close enough, I ask; what brings you this way? I'm coming to see you silly. Feeling a bit giddy I ask; what's in the bag? Without saying a word, she slowly pulled out two bottles of wild Irish rose, I smiled remembering how the last wine she brought, made me feel. Are you ready? she questioned. Let's do it; I replied. I got up off the porch, ran in the house and got two glasses. We sit outside for a while, having a good time laughing and talking shit. Somewhere around 11:00 o'clock it began to get a bit chilly out so, we gathered everything and move it on the inside. I fixed some chips and dips for us and continued laughing and having fun.

She ask to use the restroom, I guided her up and showed her where it was, I turned on the light and headed back downstairs to wait for her. In the meantime, I took the opportunity to call my sister to check on my boys. Seconds later, I could hear her footsteps coming up the hallway, did you find everything alright? I ask. Yes I did, she replied while running down the stairs and stopping directly in front of me, looking deep into my eyes as if to read my mind. She gently held the side of my face and slowly kissed my lips. I kept my eyes open to see what was actually happening to me. She moved back slightly, still focusing on my lips. Softly apologizing for being too forward, yet grabbing my hand, bringing me closer to her as she took her other hand and placed it to the nape of my neck and kissed my lips forcefully. She seductively began licking around my lips while slightly nibbling on them. I closed my eyes this time, taking in this new feeling that made my clitoris hard while feeling the warmth of something moist in my panties. I stood before her in shear amazement. "I couldn't believe that a woman could make me feel this way" I pulled away and excused myself. I'll be back in just a bit; I said. I changed the music and ran up to find something more comfortable to slip into. While taking a quick shower, the excitement and anticipation made me nervous but I wanted more.

I finished showering and crept down the stairs, I thought I saw a flicker of light and to my surprise, I walked into a dark candle lit room with the pillows thrown to the floor, with our drinks poured and placed on place mats beside them. I was impressed with what I saw. I had no Idea what was about to happen to me but I was excited to find out. She held out her hand for me and I slowly took hold of it, allowing her to lead me to the floor of pillows. She kissed me in such a way that I felt it resonate throughout my entire body. I felt her hand move behind me and go underneath my shirt. I could feel my bra loosen, as she used one hand. She slowly pulled my shirt up and over my head, resting her tongue on top of my nipple, suckling and blowing causing it to erect. I looked down at her, still in disbelief as to what was happening to me. I watched as she took my entire breast into her mouth, massaging it with her jaws and her tongue, it felt amazing. I wanted to scream but I moaned instead. She moved back and forth between my nipples. I felt her slowly move her hand beneath me, gently pulling my jogging pants down. I felt myself lift up to help her maneuver them past my hips. The warmth that I felt inside made me ready to receive whatever she wanted to give me.

She moved close to my ear and whispered... your in good hands baby. I had no doubt, she continued to passionately kiss her way to my belly button, sticking her tongue in and moving it in a circular motion. I could feel her warm breath moving downward to my inner thigh, I yelled out in pleasure. It was too much but I wanted more. I could feel her moving slowly towards it. I could feel it began to throb and pulsate. I began to squirm uncontrollably until I couldn't take any more, stop! I said; forcefully. Breathing erratically. What's the matter baby; she ask. I'm sorry, it's just that I've never been touched like this. It makes me react in a way that I.... it's overwhelming. As I spoke, I could feel my body calming down, I watched her crawl up from her current position and kissed me on my forehead. No need to apologize; she said. She lay beside me, slid her arm underneath my head and held me in her arms reassuring me that it was, OK. As we lay in silence I could hear her breathing, her heartbeat was at a steady rhythm. As minutes passed, I couldn't believe that she was still holding me in her arms, "this was a first for me yet again again." I broke the silence; let's go upstairs to my room. We began to gather everything up off the floor, replaced the pillows and went up, hand in hand. I went to the bathroom to freshen up again and when I returned the bed had been turned down and then she left out, came back and stripped down to her T-shirt and underwear. There, we slept through the night.

The alarm went off, I turned to look behind me to see if last night was real and there she was. I crept out closing the door behind me hoping not to wake her, I went to the boys rooms to wake them for school and remembered that they weren't there. I chose to remain at home today so that I could experience more of her. I returned to the room where she lay in waiting. I climbed back into bed after freshening up and we picked up where we left off last night. Her lips tasted as wonderful as they did, then. Every move that she made was slow and calculated, my body seemed to mold into her every touch. I covered my eyes feeling the intensity as if on a roller coaster with all the highs and lows. I could feel her breath on my hip and then her wet tongue that caused me to squirm to the point that I wanted to come unglued. She moved towards it, I braced myself while holding on to the pillows above my head….she slowly but surely found her way through to my silky soul. I took in as much air as my body would allow and exhaled. It was as if I were free to feel her every move. Although I didn't know what to expect, I knew that her tongue felt magical. There wasn't a place that she didn't explore, she used it as if it were a serpent, it slithered into places that I wasn't aware that existed, until she found my abyss. She went in with a circular motion that was made while going as deep as she………..OH! MY! GOD! I yelled out.

She slowed her rotation to a sweet massage moving my bottom to coincide with what she was doing and OH! MY! GOD! It happened again! You are truly a master at your craft; I thought. The massage came to a slow ease, allowing my body and all my census to calm down, as she kissed my body, making her way up, with the sweet scent of my pussy glazed on her face. All that I could say was; WOW! Her smile was modest but sure. She held me in silence for a while and then ask; can I use your shower? Absolutely; I responded. In her absence, I laid there in a dream state, thinking that I have never had anyone to care for my body in that way. When she returned, I excused myself to go shower, she reached for my hand and kissed me passionately and then allowed me to pass. I smiled all the way down the hall but when I realized that I was this happy. I felt guilty for some reason. I thought that maybe I didn't deserve to be happy as "he" has said in the past. This thought was short lived because when I opened the door of the bathroom, I could smell bacon and again I smiled. She and I stayed together making love and playing house for four days and on the fifth night she was gone back to her life.

Not a day had gone by that I hadn't thought about her. Those days that we spent together were the most unforgettably moments that I've ever spent with another human being. Everything that she did to me had never been done to me before. I questioned; am I like her now? Cleaning the house, I happened to look up and out of the living room window to see Darcy walking in the direction of my back porch, when I heard the knock at the door I stopped in front of a heart shaped mirror hanging on the wall to check my hair to make sure that I looked presentable. When I opened the door she had such a big smile on her face, again there was a bag in each hand, what is this? I ask; in a playful tone. It's a peace offering for staying away from you so long; she explained. Smiling, I stepped aside to allow her in. I took the items from her to put in the refrigerator, assuming that they were alcohol. I have to cook dinner for the boys; I admitted. I'll help you. It was really nice that she and I playfully prepared dinner together, this was another first for me.

I heard rustling at the door. I immediately knew that it was my boys home from my sisters house. I opened it to see them playing happily, which was what they did every day. I let them in with instructions to go upstairs and change clothes and wash up. When they all came down dressed and ready to eat, I decided that now would be a good time to introduce her to my children and that I did. None of them showed special interest in her, they were cordial and anxious to be let outside. One hour guys and in you come to eat, I announced. Out the door they went, handsome boys you have there; she said. Thank you, I said, as I walked into the kitchen to finish dinner. I called the boys in to wash up and eat, I watched as she offered to help them, I was truly surprised to see how the kids took to her, especially lil Jamie, he never took to people, well. When they were all done she ask; do you have any board games? No, I don't. I will bring some when I come over next time; she replied. Dinner was even better with her present. She had conversation with the boys at the dinner table that had them using their minds, they were all smiling and laughing and that made me smile. She helped me clean and I put the boys down for bed and returned to her. The night was amazing as every other night had been. She and I were together quite a bit. She kept a smile on my face, while tapping on my heart strings however, I was afraid to reveal this to her. The closer we became, the more curious I was. I wanted to know who she was and where she's from, those relationship questions, I guess. She seemed OK with answering them all however, the question of where she lived seemed to be a problem for her to release. Finally she answered; I live with a friend. I couldn't understand why that was so hard for her to answer. So, I chose to not ask anymore questions, this was a red flag for me.

It was a beautiful Saturday afternoon and people were out early setting up for their day. Doors and windows were opening and music was blaring. The boys and I were cleaning our apartment with a little bit of Anita Baker playing in the background. They were upstairs getting their rooms together and I had the downstairs. I stepped out on the back porch to shake a couple of rugs and noticed there were people outside that had turned their attention towards the corner of my apartment building, I then noticed it as well. I could hear tires screeching and smell rubber burning. I could hear yelling but I couldn't understand what was being said.

I watched as mother's scrambled around to get their children in to safety. Curiosity was getting the best of me, I wanted to see what had their attention around there, so I crept towards the end of my building and peeked around hoping to catch a glimpse of what was going on. It took my eyes a minute to adjust however when things came into focus, I could make out a car chasing a person through the courtyard. Without breaking my stare, I looked closer to see that it was Jamie's car. I immediately turned to the person running and saw that it was Darcy. I watched as she ducked and dodged the car and finally ran up onto one of the neighbors porch. Something in my inside, told me too laugh….. and that's what I did, not a smile or a giggle but an all out laugh. Although I knew deep down, that this shit wasn't funny, I did it anyways…again. But, due the dangers of what I was witnessing, my mind would not process it as danger. I honestly had trouble processing what was going on between these two and just when I thought the fiasco was over, he revved the motor again and drove straight through the courtyard leaving tread marks in the dirt while shouting; dike ass bitch! to her. I watched as she walked into that same back door of where she was standing which was directly cater cornered of my place. I looked around to see if Jamie was coming back through and when I was satisfied that the coast was clear, I sit out back and watched that back door for what seemed like an hour. As I sit, I wandered what transpired between them that brought all this on? I felt in my heart that it couldn't have been about she and I because I was very careful, making sure that no one knew.

As the days go by, every time that I passed by the window in my living room, unconsciously I would look out at that back door across the way, looking to see if anyone was going in or out. The phone rang, I picked it up and heard Jamie's voice, my heart jumped. In a solemn tone; Hello; I said. What's going on over there? Are you a Dike now! He shouted into the phone. I felt my body began to tremble a bit, I didn't know if I should admit my dealings with her or play it off {LIE}. I chose to lie. I don't know what your talking about; I said. Yea you do…..Bitch don't have that gay shit around my kids, you hear me! And he hung up. I sat there caught up in my feelings, I was instantly embarrassed that someone knew or thought they knew about what I was doing. I searched my mind trying to guess who could have told him about this. All of the happiness that I felt while being with her was gone after talking to him, I felt dirty and ashamed, the light that burned bright in my heart was turned off instantly. It showed in the sudden shift in my behavior when she came over that night and noticed it written all over my face. What's wrong baby? She ask. You two out there cutting up, that's what's wrong; I said. Now, was all that about us? Her face turned beet red, I need the truth; I stated. OK, I ran into him last night, he needed something and I knew somebody that had what he wanted; she said. My heart jumped and my mouth fell open; are you talking about drugs? Yea; she replied. Do you do drugs? I ask. No, not like that; she stated, I dibble and dab a bit. I could feel my heart begin to harden after that response. I knew this was the beginning of the end for us.

Things between us changed after that night, I was more protective of my privacy, I even decided to be transparent with her about my drug problem in hopes that she would understand the severity of my addiction. I demanded that she not bring drugs or anyone affiliated with them around me or my boys and that no-one is to know about what goes on in this house pertaining to she and I, as well. Also, under no circumstance was she to use the front door to enter or exit this home. This was the only way we were to continue seeing other. She looked at me for a while, are you serious? She ask. When I finished with all of my demands, although not happy, she reluctantly agreed too to them all.

The next time that I saw her, there was a change, she wasn't doing or saying all of those wonderful things that she had in the past. I understood, however the lovin was good and this was the reason that I continued to see her. As time passed we began to have disagreements about minor issues. She had become verbally aggressive, more so, when she drank. I also noticed that she stopped abiding by my rule about the front door. She began to make demands on who can and can't come to my home. I could feel that things were spiraling out of control, the arguments and controlling behavior led me to feel as if I had lost myself. I told her that I couldn't do this anymore and that I'm done! She looked at me as if, looking through me, turned abruptly and stormed out of the door slamming it behind her. I breathed a sigh of relief after locking the door, I felt that I had just missed a storm.

The next day, I walked around the house taking inventory, looking for shards of glass while thinking; I should be farther along than I was in spite of my drug addiction, this caused me too loathe the life's choices that I had made for myself and my children, even more. Although I was determined to keep my head above water, asking myself, what else had I done so far? Nothing. I decided that I would go back to class and work hard at my diploma and not allow any more distractions but as weeks passed, I couldn't help thinking about her from time to time. Friday nights were the worst. There was a knock on the back door, I opened and it and there she was. I was afraid to entertain the feelings that I was experiencing. Hey, what's up? I ask. You; she said. Can I come in to apologize? You don't have to come in for that, I said. Playing hard to get, was hard. I stepped aside to let her pass and smelled alcohol on her breath. I immediately regretted my decision. My lips were pierced together as my thought whispered....tell her, that she has to go. She turned towards me, looking me in my eyes as if she wanted to say something kind.

YOU WANT TO FIRE ME!? She said, with conviction. An off white substance fell from her pocket as she turned. It hit the table which made a thump. I looked down and knew what it was immediately. My mouth fell open but before I could truly focus and respond, she attempted to retrieved it from the table but it rolled off and fell to the floor. Once she picked the rock up from the floor, she proceed to smashed the end table with something that was in the other hand. Before she was able to lift her hand up for a second time, I was on top of her, whooping on her ass. We fought for what seemed like an hour. I could feel her strength and I know that she felt mine as well. We fought all the way through to the kitchen where we stopped. Both of us winded, trying to talk shit to one another. All that I've done for you; she said. Sex? I ask. Thank you but now you gotta go before I call the police, I warned. She pulled out a medium sized switch blade that curved over, she stood there as if ready to cut me. I quickly opened the drawer next to me and pulled out two butcher knives. My stance indicated that I was ready, however I kept talking to her, hoping to defuse the situation. I believed at that moment, that the devil was busy because nothing I said worked. That girl rushed me and the knife went in. I could see the fear in her eyes, it was as if she knew that she had made a big mistake. I watched her as she backed away from me with her face contorted, a tear that I noticed hanging there, finally ran down her cheek. The immense amount of shock that I felt when I watched her grab and hold her side. My mouth involuntarily fell open. I cautiously reached out towards her to help but she stepped away, mumbling; you stabbed me.... over and over again. With the knife still in her hand, I attempted to help again. I noticed that she was trying to come for me and stopped. I ran next door to call the ambulance and my kids dad because I knew, that I was going to jail.

Things became even more chaotic. I ran back to my apartment to find her sitting on the stairs. Give me the knife, the police are coming along with the paramedics; I announced. She then threw the knife across the floor. I grabbed the towel to pick it up, careful not to put my fingerprints on it, just in case I needed it for myself, as evidence. I could here the sirens in the distance. I hustled upstairs to get my boys ready to go with their dad. My heart pounding and my thoughts were all over the place but it didn't detour me from my main objective, I had to get my boys to a safe place before the police came, it felt like deja'vu. I knew that my children knew something was wrong by the looks on their faces, they had to have heard the commotion downstairs. Roland looked up at me and ask; are you OK mamma? I looked down to answer him but our attention was drawn to all of the emergency lights bouncing off the walls, that made me instantly nervous. I continued to get my boys downstairs pass Darcy and all of the ruckus. When we made it to the front door I see Jamie standing to the side waiting and observing all of the madness. You gone be OK, girl; he ask. I nodded; yes and whispered; thank you, kissed my boys as I waved goodbye and walked towards the officer. I turned to go back into the apartment but hesitated for a second, thinking about how I made it to this point. I was afraid of what was to come, I didn't want to go to jail, ever. The officer were waiting for me inside the door. I reluctantly walked over in his direction, although I couldn't see her physically, I could here her moaning. God please don't let her die, I prayed. What happened here? The officer ask. I began to fumble over my words, he quickly intervened; just tell me your name first. As I began to give him the answers that he needed, my attention was drifting towards her. The door swung open and startled me. I watched as they brought the gurney in. It just got real to me. I stopped the interview, to ask if he would please go over to see if she's going to be OK. He dropped his note pad to his side and walked to speak to one of the paramedics, when he returned, I tried to read his face, but I got nothing. She's in good hands; he replied. Not truly satisfied with his answer, my focus remained on her. He finished his line of questioning and told me that I was free to go, for now. What did that mean; I thought to myself. I was too afraid to ask, so I just kept still watching the events unfold right before me. I stood in the same spot watching as they lifted her body up and rolled her passed me. My heart sunk when I saw that she had an oxygen mask on her face. I tried calling out to her but she wouldn't open her eyes, I felt even worse.

As the last of the emergency workers left my apartment. I began to feel as if I could breath freely. I slowly closed the door, trying not to draw attention to myself. Heavy in thought, struggling with believing that I was a free woman after what I've done, of course I thanked God for sparing me from having to go through that unwanted experience again, however I couldn't help but worry about Darcy because she too is now going through an unwanted experience. I racked my brain thinking of different things that I could have done to deescalate the situation and have prevented this from happening to us. I sit on those same stairs as she did, thinking, what a mess I've created for my family once again. Two hours had passed, I had worked myself into a big ball of nerves by then. There was no one that I could contact in reference to her, so that made matters worse. A knock at the door brought me out of my thoughts. I opened the door to find that the same officer that was here earlier, standing there with his pad and pen. May I come in? He ask. I stepped aside, I could feel myself begin to shake from fear. May I help you, officer? I muttered.

I need your entire name and a show of Identification, please. I nodded and went right away to retrieve it for him. Who lives here with you? He shouted up at me. I yelled; myself and my three boys. I ran back downstairs to face him and noticed how incredibly handsome this young man was. At that moment I secretly knew that I wasn't ready to write men off, as of yet. He began to write down my information and handed my card back, not yet letting go. If she dies, you will go to prison for a long time; he said, with a stern look on his face. She has a punctured lung and is in intensive care fighting for her life. I couldn't hold back the tears at that point, he opened the door to leave and turned to say; let's just hope that I won't have to return. I bowed my head to indicate that I understood. Before the door closed, I ask; what hospital is she in? Memorial; he said. I stood in the door and watched as he walked out into the night.

The next day I decided that I would call the hospital to see how she was doing. I had no Idea what I would say to her, had she answered the phone. Hello, who is this? {I could tell that this wasn't a nurse} Hello; my name is Trul'ee, I am Darcy's friend. I would like to know how she's doing. Well, this is her sister Passion, I will tell her that you called when she wakes up, OK. How is she doing? I ask. Well, they had to operate on her, so that she could breath better, although she's still on oxygen, she's stable. I thanked her and hung up, realizing that Darcy must not have told her that I did this too her. I was determined to get up there to do some damage control soon. The boys were brought home the next morning happier than ever to see their mom. Although he didn't show it, I believed that Jamie was somewhat relieved that I was home as well.

Three days had passed and in my mind, it was long enough, I had to make an appearance. I went next door to Willie Mae's apartment but she wasn't available to keep the boys. So I packed snacks and told them that we were going to hang out today. A bus ride later, we were finally at the hospital. They allowed the boys and I into the intensive care unit however I didn't know how things between her and I would turn out so...excuse me ma'am, will it be alright if I allow my boy to sit here in these chairs while I step in to say, hello? I assure you that they will be no trouble{giving them the eye}....She agreed. I gave them snacks and instructions and turned to knock and quietly stepped into the room. To my surprise she was wide awake. I was surprised to see that the oxygen was still on her after these few days. I must have hurt her badly; I thought. I sit in a chair that was near the bed and ask; do you still want to kill me? Put one finger up for yes and two for no. I could see a slight smile across her lips. Sounding winded, with a raspy voice; I'm sorry, I didn't mean for any of that to happen, I wasn't myself that night; she admitted.

I could see how much energy it took for her to speak, so I ask that she not. We sit in silence for ten minutes, the boys are right outside the door and we have to get back before dark; I said. She whispered, can I see them? I didn't see a problem with that, so I brought them in. Jamie Jr. was the first to walk in, I noticed his eyes looking at all of the equipment that was hooked up too her. Roland gave her a half smile and said hi but didn't seem to care about anything else. Dorian, held his arms up for me to pick him up, all he did was look down at her. My older boys began to ask questions however, I thought that it was best that I shut it down for now. It was time to go. I told the boys to say goodbye, Jamie walked over and gave her a hug without being told, that was sweet. Roland stood back, smile on his face and waved goodbye to her. As we walked towards the exit, I felt confident that all would be well between us and the fact that she was going to live, meant that I wouldn't have to go to jail, that was an added bonus.

She called me every day after that, discussing her progress, I could hear in her voice that she was getting stronger. Five days later, she called to tell me that she had been released. I was happy for her but just a bit worried for me. I didn't quite know what was really on her mind, I guess my guard was up due too past experience. I waited, counting the days until she would surfaced again, wondering if she would be of sound mind when she did. For days, since that night, I kept finding small pieces of glass as I cleaned under the couch, the chair and in the rug, no matter how much I vacuumed. I became obsessed with cleaning, wanting to spare my children the anguish of more pain. When I was satisfied, I put the broom and dustpan away. I heard a knock at the door. I peeked out to see her. I stood, being very still, contemplating weather I should or shouldn't open the door. I also took into consideration that she came to the back door as well but still I pondered over it. I decided that I would hear what she had to say, {be it that I almost killed her}which was the least that I could do. So….. I went out of the front door locking it behind me, went around the corner to the back door. I did this because I wanted to spare my children from any further drama. I stood a safe distance from her, carefully watching for signs of violence, which I could tell that she noticed by the shaking of her head and the smirk on her face. I'm not going to hurt you Tru; she mumbled. I came here to let you know how truly sorry I am for what I've done to you and the boys. I remember smoking something that tasted and smelled a little different, everything after that was a bit hazy. I would never intentionally come her to harm you baby; she added. Before answering, I searched her face looking for sincerity and found humility. I can't have this type of behavior around my children, they have already been through enough; I said, sternly. She and I sit on the porch for a couple of hours. I listened to sweet nothings and dire promises. I had never had a person speak as if I meant this much to be kept by them. I tried to put on a persona as if I wasn't taken in by her words but I was.

Chapter 8

Gone but not forgotten

It seemed as if I couldn't focus on anything. My mind and heart were in total disarray, to the point, that when I reached for something from the cabinet, I couldn't remember what that something was. My legs felt bound, hard to manipulate. I felt unbelievably flushed, as I began to shiver and shake within every part of my body, as I felt the tips of her fingers slowly moving up my inner thigh. Creeping so closely and now touching my silky soul. I began to shiver even more with anticipation as she caressed and massaged it with care. My breathing became erratic, as I felt the gentle touch of the other hand fondling my breast, causing a slight erection of my nipples. While, seductively twisting and turning firmly while causing an unusual elongated appearance. My body became warm as she slowly slid inside of me, maneuvering each finger as if playing a 1997 Gibson. I could feel every cord being stroked. She breath on the nape of my neck, I felt her soft moist tongue all while caressing my breast that caused a moist sensation down below, which had me holding on to the oven door. She stopped abruptly and dropped to her knees and placed her lips over my silky soul and blew on it…..Oh! My! God! I yelled. As she teased and tasted my essence, I couldn't help but hold on tighter to the stove because I was…. Oh My God! I yelled out in pleasure again. As she slowly moved her tongue from the back to the front, seemingly allowing me time to collect myself. She slowly rose up, while wiping the glaze from her face. I could see a smile of satisfaction, I smiled too. I hugged her to balance myself and followed with a passionate kiss. I couldn't stop smiling, words weren't necessary at this moment so I excused myself to freshen up before the boys came home from school. Things weren't perfect between us but they were good. Our pillow talk on most nights consist of dreams and ambitions that we both had for ourselves. I shared my desire of traveling to see places that I had only seen on television or in magazines. She wanted to become an artist, I could definitely see this happening for her because she was very good at it. Among other things she and I also discussed having a child, we both agreed that this would be down the road of course but it was tossed in to the basket of dreams, as well. She was at my home often but on the days that I attended classes, she wasn't allowed to stay because I didn't trust her. She ask on a few occasions where I was going but I never told. This was something that I wanted to do on my own, no interference from no one or nothing.

 As days turn to night, the cravings were becoming more unbearable. I could smell it, taste it. I've actually envisioned the pipe in my mouth and felt the high that followed. My children has been my reason to stay clean all of this time however the desire to have it is overriding all logic. I've kept myself busy to suppress the urge to get just one. So I sit still sometimes and concentrate on something else or someone else. She's not working anymore actually, {she} is actually a trigger for me. In the back of my mind, I know that she knows where it is, and….one day, I know that I will send her on a run. Willie Mae knows about my addiction however, she can only empathize with me and not truly be able to understand how overwhelming this drug can be. She talks to me, telling me her version of how sweet life is without the use of drugs. Now, I'm empathizing with her. I see things much differently than she does. We live in the projects, borrowing from one another to maintain. The seed had been planted in my head and now I must nurture it.

Shopping for the tools that I use to smoke this drug is a humiliating thing, but necessary. I could see the look on the face of the guy selling me these things. I imagine what he could be thinking about me but I buy them anyways. One glass pipe, chore boy and a lighter, I then turn to leave. The moon is bright but it's still dark out. My thoughts consume me, all that I've worked so hard to accomplish so far is at stake but all I need is just one to knock the edge off, I tell myself.

The sun is shining bright and more importantly my children are at school and the babysitters. There are boys as young as 15 years old standing out early this morning selling that drug. I choose one by the name of Jimmie, who I've known since he was younger, through his family. He was quite surprised to know that I wasn't just speaking to him but that I needed to cop. When I made it home, I sit at the table noticing that there was a bit of hesitation in my hands. I knew that I was making a very big mistake. Yet again, remembering my past actions. The level of anxiety that I was feeling about what I was about to do, was overwhelming, however my addiction wouldn't allow me to stop. I began by getting the chore boy burned, opened the package, there was an unbearable wave of fear but I took in a deep breath. Looked at the clock on the wall to check as to how much time I had. Put the bolder on, fired it up and listened to the sizzle as I took in the smoke. It didn't feel as satisfying as I thought it would but I felt it.

By the time the boys made it home I was done. Although the affects of the drug hadn't worn off yet. I mimicked, everything that I would have done had I not done the drug, it just took more effort to appear normal to my children. As time passed I began to come down, back into mommy mode. I tossed the paraphernalia into the garbage outside. I told myself that I was done, forever. In the weeks to follow the cravings continued. But I was able push it aside. With talks about the baby again, made me very happy. I've always known who I wanted, to be the sperm donor. He is a relative of mine, I wanted the child to have my blood running through it's veins. Since we have no money, and had to do it this way the prayers were going up. He was on board all the way but, I had stipulations. Number 1.That he not want any ties to this child Number 2.That this be a secret between us three. Number 3. No visitations, under any circumstance. He agreed, so I continued making arrangements for the conception of the child.

It was a beautiful night in June. The skies allowed the moon to shine bright, yet again. I came indoors to check the room one more time to make sure that all was well. The bed was made with a royal blue comforter, with a splashes of pink in it. Candles were strategically placed through out the room to emulate a relaxing yet, romantic setting. There was a knock at the door, I skipped down the stairs to find him standing in the doorway. I greeted him with a hug, as I always have and told him that she was ready. I handed him a washcloth and ask that he freshen up first. When he was finished, I lead him to the room where she lay, waiting. I could tell by the look on her face that she was uncomfortable, so I reached over to hold her hand through out.

I cringed when he mounted her. There was no four play, no kissing, no touching, just straight fuckin and when the act was done. I looked into her eyes and mouthed, thanked you. I thanked him as well and ask that he let himself out. Once he was gone, I grabbed the bucket of soapy water that I had placed beside the bed and began to gently wipe her down in that area. When you feel better, feel free to shower OK; I whispered. I have to go and get the boys from Denise's; I said. As I got up to pour the water out, I noticed that my emotions were all over the place. We are about to have a baby,{speaking it, into existence}. However, when I turned to look at her, there was a look of uncertainty on her face. So, I laid back down beside her and held her in my arms as I know, she would have done for me. When I wake an hour later, I announced that I had to go, I kissed her and left out.

When the boys and I returned to the house, she was gone. I looked on the dresser to see if she had left a note...nothing. Three days later, she surfaced. Why did you leave like that? I ask. I at least thought that by now, you knew to leave a note, I would have done the same for you; I said. To be honest; I knew that you would have tried to stop me Tru; so I left before you made it back; she admitted. I had to go out and do my thang, one more time because I know things are going to change while this baby is inside of me,{I couldn't get mad because I understood what she meant} you understand? She ask. Yes, I do; I answered.

Fast forward….. We are four months pregnant now and I'm in total bliss. I love the part when it's quiet and we are laying in the bed together and she allows me to talk, sing and rub on her belly to interact with the baby. Shopping for the baby was my new norm, although I didn't know the sex of the baby. There were pampers, wipes, bottles and unisex clothing that I felt I had to buy. I noticed that she is still small for four months. You can't tell that she's pregnant at all, I smirked; I thought about how I wish that I was small like that when I was pregnant. I remember, getting pretty big in my back and my belly not to mention my breast and nose. I was able to feel this child moving around which put me in a peaceful state of mind.

It's getting dark out, I can tell that she's antsy and a bit agitated. I believe that I know what's going on with her but I say nothing. Are you hungry? I ask. I'll fix you and the baby a special dinner if you like. Nah, I'm good, I'm going out to take a walk and get some air. Well, are you sure you don't want to eat, first? I ask. I'll be right back; she says. She kissed me on the cheek as she passed me to go out the door. I didn't see her for five days. I worried more for the baby than I did, her. At that moment, leaving her crossed my mind for a brief second but this was our baby, I thought. I couldn't do that, to a child of mine. One of us had to be strong and stay clean. No matter how hard it was. I called Madison Center in hopes that someone could point me in the right direction as to where I can get help with my addiction problem. There were several places suggested however, they were all AA. There happened to be one there at the center. I was also informed that if I had Medicaid, transportation would be provided for free. So I chose Monday and Thursday in the evenings and on occasion, there were times that if I had to bring my boys, I could.

The first few times I just listened and found that their problems as an alcoholic wasn't much different than mine as an addict. So, I thought that I would stay a little longer to see how they made it through. She came to the back door but her presence brought on a very tense argument that I felt the need to defuse quickly because of the baby.

What do you want for you and your baby, Darcy? She sat down, put her face in her hands. I want to put this drug down once and for all. I want stability in my life, with a Job, car and a house; she added. You can have that while being here with us, if this is somewhere you would want to be? She rose up from her seat and hugged me; Yes, I would love that, we can work on things together, she added.

As the weeks turned to months, things seemed to fall into place around the house. Darcy was drawing again. She loved showing the boys her technique. As the baby grew inside of her, plans for the future became a priority for us. On 3-17-1993 we had a beautiful baby girl with big beautiful eyes. She was light skinned, like her mother, with a head full of hair. She was named Carmen. Passion, was the one chosen to go into the birthing room with her, which was quite alright with me because I knew that she was coming home to me. Two days later, I received the phone call that they were being released that afternoon and were coming home, to us. The boys and I were very excited as we made things ready for them. Upon arrival, the scent of baby flowed through my nostrils. I couldn't wait to get her into my arms so that I could ingest more of her scent. Once I had her, I turned to reach for Darcy, so that I could help her up the stairs to the bed, the covers were already turned down. Once she was in bed, my attention was solely on this beautiful little girl before me, counting fingers and toes and kissing the bottom of her feet, I had fond memories of doing these very thing to my boys when they were babies. I took a glance around the room, taking a mental note of all of the things that we had accumulated just for her. The six foot Bunny that sat in the corner was an added bonus, a gift from people who cared. She is home, where she belong. It was a delight to get up and fix bottles, change pampers and just sit up with her, watching all of her different facial expressions and movements. I couldn't help but wish that I would have been allowed to experience this joy with my own children without interference from their father, I missed having the choice to breast feed, which made me sad all over again but I was in love with her, already.

Two weeks had passed since her arrival and we all were still enjoying the many changes she seemed be going through. I found that I had to be careful to include my youngest because I could see a little Jealousy going on with him, which was understandable because he has been the baby for a while now. The next day, after checking the cabinet and the diaper bag, I realized that there was no milk for the baby. We were down to our last can and the wic appointment wasn't for another week. Instead of asking "them" for a can or two until the appointment, I decided to buy them because the store was much closer than the wic office was. Darcy volunteered to go but I told her that I will go instead so that she could continue to rest. She insisted, adding that she feels fine. "I really didn't trust that she would return but this was for the baby" so, I agreed. I gave her the money and ask that she bring some ice cream back as well. She left me and the baby with a kiss. Four hours later and she still hadn't made it home. I made up my mind, that I would get all of the kids ready to walk them to the store to get the milk myself. Once we all were ready, I opened the door to find a bag with what looked like cans in it, I bent down to pick it up and sure enough it was. I looked around to see if I would catch a glimpse of her but… I grabbed the bag and told the boys that they can play outside for a bit.

She was gone for four days with no word. Of course, the baby was fine here with me but I couldn't help but worry about Darcy. She had just given birth not two weeks prior. Passion had gotten into a habit of calling every day to ask about the baby and it was always Darcy there to filled her in. However, the next day, Passion was getting agitated because she wasn't available. She pressed me as to where she was, with no satisfaction she resulted to other means. She insisted that the baby be turned over to her, her true family. One hour had passed with no further phone calls from her. A knock at the door broke me from my cleaning process. I went to the front bedroom window, looked down to see her with two police officers. Immediately my heart began to thump around in my chest. I bundled the baby up and slowly walked downstairs. I opened the door and was greeted by two large white gentleman. Good evening ma'am, my name is officer Wade and this is my partner officer Drake. May we come in? He ask. What is this about officer? Mrs. Passion here, pointing in her direction, has a concern about a newborn that's here in your care, looking down at the baby. I assure you that the baby lives here sir and is not being held here against her will. I stepped aside to allow them in. No need to worry ma'am, this is a routine check. I watched as Passion attempted to step in with them they ask that she remain outside. I had a slight grin on my face after hearing that. I closed the door, Officer Wade blurted out; Miss Passion believes that; in her sister's absence the baby should be in her care, surrounded with her family. I care to differ sir, mom and baby lives here with me and I am the other mother of the baby. Well ma'am, I need to see some evidence of this. Holding my daughter tight in my arms, I turn to head up the stairs to take them to my bedroom. He, went in first, followed by Officer Drake. They both seemed to have a surprised look on their faces when they saw the babies clothes folded neatly on her little dresser. Her bassinet with pink lace surrounding it, was nicely made up and ready for her.

There were two four drawer dressers with everything that she could possibly need in them. On top, was baby lotions, powders and other things for her upkeep. There were receiving blankets, burp towels and a small pillow in another drawer that I opened to prove my point that she's home. Definitely not excluding the six foot rabbit that sit in the corner smiling at us. Officer Wade announced; I've seen enough, as far as I'm concerned, the baby belongs here. As we turned to walk out of the room, I breath a sigh of relief. When the officers were let out, I closed the door behind me and went back up to the baby. I decided make a slight detour to look out of the front bedroom window first, to witness Passion pointing and flailing her arms. I assumed that whatever they were telling her, she was not in agreement with it. Two days later, Darcy came home with the long face again. I chose not to argue about the when or where because I already knew the answers. I so remember the look of bewilderment and feelings of fatigue and the humiliation. Go up and take a shower Darcy and we will talk later OK; I said.

When she returned, she laid across the bed and began showing the baby love. It was beautiful watching her play with her child. In a soft tone, I ask; what makes you want to use this drug? Because, whatever your reason, I want us to try to get it out of our lives. We can't thrive this way; I added. She laid there as if thinking of an answer. I don't have triggers,{as they called them in the meetings} I have cravings and they are strong however, I have to fight them off on a daily bases and it isn't easy. I do this for my kids, although I've learned that this has to be for me in order for it to work; I said. Now, what do you want for yours, as I pointed to the baby. I guess I just don't have the strength that you do when it comes to this stuff. I know that I want better for both me and her but I'm not quite sure how to go about it; she said. Maybe you can come to meetings with me? I think this may be the thing that we need. I suggested. I don't have insurance; she admitted. You don't need it, they say all you need is the desire to stop using; I added. I waited for a response but there was none, she laid there and fell asleep. She and I stayed busy, playing games with the boys, putting puzzles together, anything positive to keep our minds occupied and our thoughts free from the use of drugs. I was finally properly introduced to her sister and the family. I found that Passion was a very nice person, she invited me back to visit as often as I liked.

Carmen is two years old, now. She has grown into her own personality with a sassy temperament to boot. I loved it, I loved everything to do with this little girl. I kept her hair done when she was there, there was always something clean there for her to wear whenever she came. But by this time things between Darcy and I were a bit sketchy. She used the baby as a pawn with me and for the most part, it worked. There were times that she would take the baby to Passion's home where she would remain for days. I wasn't feeling much like her mother these days. We, were in a disagreement about one thing or another. The major issue for me, was that a women was attempting to control me. I couldn't allow this, not from a woman, and I would speak on this often. The arguments were so severe sometimes, that it would get physical. I would tell myself; as I patched her up afterwards, that it wasn't my fault, I was only defending myself. In the mix of all the madness, I began getting high again, that took a terrible turn on my self esteem and self worth. There was a method too my madness, in an attempt to separate the drug activity from my children. I felt that if, they were physically away from the act that they would have any idea that it was going on. While they were in their rooms or I in mine. I believed that I was blocking out the fact that they couldn't actually hear me and those whispered conversations in an attempt to keep my boys from being exposed, I had a front row seat to my own shit show. Things had gotten so bad that I didn't trust myself with my own money. I paid the bills, brought groceries and took what I would hope to see in the morning, to my friend Willie Mae to put up for safe keeping. Sometimes, it worked and some times it didn't. On occasions, my boys needed school clothes cleaned and I didn't have the money for it, however I'd grabbed the dish soap from the kitchen, put the clothes in the bath tub, washed them by hand and hung them up to dry in the bathroom. As days passed, I felt worse than the day before, no matter what I tried to do to make myself feel better, nothing worked. With the arguing, fussing and fighting and added pressure of attempting to keep all of this madness from the kids, was too much to bare.

Good Evening, welcome back to the land of the living; Darcy mumbled. As I lay there trying to get my eyes to focus, I noticed that I couldn't move as I once had. My limbs felt as if they were weighed down with led. As my eyes began to fully focus, I could see others in the room, sitting on my bed as a matter a fact. I immediately looked down at myself to see if I were decent in front of these people whom I didn't know. I attempted to sit up but the room started to swirl around so I thought against it. As I lay back down, I looked to see that they were passing a pipe, getting high. I turned to speak to Darcy but nothing came out, my mouth and my throat were so dry that it hurt when I tried to speak. I signaled to her that I needed water, she rose off the bed and darted down the hallway to the bathroom to return with a cup of water. I slowly drank, waiting for the moment that I felt confident to speak.

Where are the kids? I ask. They are in the bed sleep; she replied. Why aren't we? I ask. Without words, she got up off the bed and signaled to her company to come with her. As they moved down the stairs, I could hear small chatter and then the door opening and then closing. When she returned I could see the glaze over her eyes. I know that bewildered look, oh, too well. How many hours was I asleep? I ask. "I knew, that it had too have been a while because my body was so very stiff." Two hours shy of five days; she said. No, no way; I replied. How did my boys respond to not having me present for them? I ask. They were OK; of course they were concerned but I cooked for them and got them off to school. The babysitter? I told her that you were ill; she added. Tru, you were really out of it, you never moved. Not even to go to the bathroom for all of those days. It's as if your body shut down on you. There were several time that I checked your breathing by putting my ear to your lips and your chest, I tried shaking you to wake you but you wouldn't respond; she said. Why didn't you call 911? I ask. I didn't really think you wanted me too, she replied. I believed that they would have taken your kids away. I sit in silence, thinking; that was part of the plan. I took the lithium in hopes that I would pass on to give my children a better life than what I've offered them.

Two hours later the boys came in to see me sitting up in the living room chair, by the looks on their faces there was love in their hearts and with all of the kisses and hugs I could tell that they missed me immensely. I could feel their love but it brought on sadness from a place that was indescribable. Instead of being able to embrace the love and reciprocate, I fell even deeper into depression because of it. I kissed them and announced that I wasn't feeling very well and that I was going back to bed. Moments later, I heard a knock at the front door. I then heard footsteps coming up the stairs and then a light tap on my bedroom door. When the door opened slightly, I could see the face of my only friend in the world. Gurl, {exercising her southern drawl} I had to come see if you made it out of the woods yet. I could feel the tears trying to escape my eyes, there was so much that I wanted to tell her, but I couldn't. How are you feeling, Tru? She ask. She told me that you were really sick, I came back the day before yesterday and brought soup, crackers and 7up and you were sleeping, so I thought that I would try again today; she admitted. You are the best, thank you; I said. We shared a hug and she excused herself and left. My tears were allowed to flow freely. From that day forth my emotions were all over the place. I couldn't seem to get them in order and the more I thought about things the worse I felt, it was as if I were falling apart.

My patience were short with everyone, little things would trigger me into a small fit of rage. I found myself apologizing quite a bit. When is the baby coming home? I ask. She looked over at me with a smile that I didn't quite understand, she's on vacation with my family and won't be back for another four days. Well, how long has she been with them? I ask. The whole time that you were out and two days before; she admitted. Her family and I were used as pawns as far as the baby was concerned but what were we to do, we loved her. The next day I received word that my brother Alfred was found and put into a juvenile facility out near Roseland Indiana. I was happy to know that he was alright but sad that it took incarceration to find him. It was also told to me, that because I am his guardian, that I must come and sign papers and make arrangements for his release although, he was sentenced to be there for a year or less with good behavior.

When I was finally allowed to see him, I noticed that he couldn't look me in my eyes, I understood. "I chalked that up to remorse for the way he acted towards me the latter part of last year. I just couldn't believe that he's been gone this long. What have you been doing to survive out there and where have you been staying? I ask. He slowly looked up at me; I get it where I can, sis. I'm out here makin it work for me. I thought to myself; who are you and what have you done with my little brother? I just couldn't stay with you and Jamie no more, that dude was crazy. He and I don't live together any more so you can relax; I admitted. When you get out you are assigned to come home with me and I'll get you back in school and back on the right track; I said. I came to visit him often, I brought the boys and my brother Trell as well, in hopes to use this as a, scared straight tactic for them.

With all of the crazy that's going on in my life. It seemed more constant and no matter what was said or done, it never let up. I knew that she and I were at our end. I hardly saw the baby, this went on until the day I no longer saw her again. My drug use became intolerable, I could no longer keep my thoughts together nor could I focus on anything positive. I thought about different ways that I could release the pressure that was building inside, however it was all negative, so I prayed more. I prayed for my children and myself, that we make it through this thing, unscathed. I called Jamie and ask if I could drop the boys off at his home for a while. There were always hoops to jump through when dealing him but he finally; said yes. Upon returning home, I walked around the apartment to see what I could possibly accomplish while the kids were gone but I decided to take a bath instead. As the water ran, I gathered everything that I needed, came back and placed them all on the lid of the toilet.

 I sit in the water and all I could manage to think about was how I continuously screw things up for me and my boys. I keep choosing toxic people to co-exist with and the fact that I can't stop using this horrible drug that's slowly killing me. I needed to just relax and take a moment to breath...or not. I reached under the towel and pulled out the razor too admire it. I checked to see if it were sharp enough and place it just above my right wrist, I closed my eyes, lowered it and began to move the razor from left to right, feeling only pressure while it cut through. I looked down and was not satisfied with the results so I sliced through again, only to see a small amount of blood, so I sliced through yet again and noticed white cartilage that looked like the gristle on a chicken bone. I cut through once again, this time feeling a bit of pain and decided that this was enough, maybe I wasn't doing it right; I thought. When I surveyed what I had done to myself, it was the size of a bow dollar or bigger. I reached over and grabbed some tissue to slow the flow of blood that was now present. I rolled it up and used it as a bandage until I got to the linen closet and found a white face towel, in which I wet and applied to the wound. I walked outside to the parking lot and saw someone that I knew and ask him for a ride to the hospital; he agreed, without questions. It was a quiet ride and gave me time to think about what am I going to do next, can't live right and obviously can't die right.

I walked into the ER prepared to give them a fictitious story in hopes that I wouldn't get locked down in the psych ward. I explained, that I cut myself, they didn't seem to care. I watched as they sewed me up, I struggled to hold back the tears, from the pain inside, not out. I couldn't help but think of all of the sadness and uncertainty in my life. I could remember wanting and begging for my mother's love and then recognizing the lack of, that I never quite recovered from. Also, her leaving me and moving to California without my knowledge, I was filled with all of those feelings and emotions all over again. This landed me in a possessive, obsessive and controlling entanglement that lead to him mentally, physically and emotionally abusing me. Thinking of all that I've endured was a bit much but I couldn't stop. You seem very sad…the voice chimed in next to me. If your wound makes you this sad, we have people that you can talk too, if you like? This voice was very calming. This brought on more tears. I bowed my head in embarrassment and remained silent. Finally, he finished, the young man stood in silence, as if waiting for me to answer the question that he had ask. Thank you; I said, I'm fine. I watched as he slowly left the room.

One week had past, my brother Alfred was released from the juvenile facility into my custody, as they said he would. I wanted to believe that he would think that things were better than they were with us in the past but I was wrong, he ran away again, taking my kids video game after being home for only one week. Fueled by anger, everyday from that day forth was spent, taking care of my business. Because, for far too long, my business has been taking care of me. I went over a had a long conversation with my only friend, money exchanged hands and she gave her blessings. I spoke to my brother Trell and then to my sister Denise, wishing them well.

Chapter 9

Make it make sense

I purchased three plane tickets to San Diego California with all of the money that I had left. Where my sister Gail and her boyfriend Ted would be waiting for our arrival. As we flew over, I couldn't help thinking about the people that I blessed with furniture, odds and ends for their homes, when I left. It kinda made me feel a bit better about everything. Ted was there alone, to pick us up in this small white car, that barely fit me and the kids with two boxes. It was an all day travel, getting from South Bend to San Diego and over to Vista California, where my sister and her then boyfriend lived. When we were settled in for the ride to Vista, I ask; where is Gail? She had to do something; he said. It was actually a good thing that she didn't come because it allowed us time to better get acquainted. He was an even nicer guy than I remembered, he seamed concerned about our welfare and kept the conversation light as though making sure not to make me feel uncomfortable. It was obvious that he was truly in love with my sister by the way he spoke about her. I was actually happy that she found what my sister Denise and I didn't, in a mate. He spoke with intelligence and once again, I listened and learned to every syllable that he uttered. I hadn't heard any one speak in this way in a long time. Finally making it to their apartment, I looked around and noticed, it was nice. While unloading the car, I also noticed my son eyeballing this park. Which was there just for the apartment building, it was nice as well.

The kids and I followed him up the stairs. Darion, complained the whole time, he didn't understand why he couldn't go to the park but I informed him that I would bring him down later if he's a good boy, of course he agreed. When Ted opened the door, I was actually impressed with what I saw. It was a very spacious apartment, that was separated by a large kitchen with an opened concept. There was a bedroom on either side of the kitchen with a bathroom in the master and one outside of the other bedroom with a large living room and dinning room that flowed through to a large out door patio. I was instantly proud of my sister for the life that she made for herself. I loved what I saw and voiced this to Ted and thanked him for loving and caring for her all of these years. By the way; where is she? I ask. She should be here soon; he said, as he walked pointing to a room. This is where you and the boys are for as long as you need it. Although, I had no reason to disbelieve him, I struggled with what he said due to past traumas in my life. Instantly, my thoughts went back to when I was a kid led to believe that the things that I went through were normal. It definitely wasn't about any lie that he told you, Tru; It's your past, that has you messed up; I said to myself.

I thanked him and walked in the room to see that I had to make room for us. It was apparent that they loved their daughter by showering her with many toys and things to ride. Without sounding overbearing, I ask Ted if I could put a few of her toys on the patio to make a little room for my boys to play while we were in there? Sure; he said. When I was finished cleaning and organizing the room, the first thing I had to do was take my baby downstairs to the little park that he saw earlier. I sit and watched my children play, they played as if they hadn't done this in such a long time. It brought me peace and allowed me time to think about my next move. Although my thoughts were all over the place, I knew that I wanted my time here in California this time, to be better than the last. As selfish as it was when I thought of it, it was even more selfish when I said it out loud. I wished that Joan was still alive, maybe she could shine some light on my situation because I had no clue as to what and how I was going to do this.

A car coming into the driveway caught my attention because of the music. A song called Regulators by Warren G was on the radio, that was the jam. I noticed that it was a woman but when she drove up to park, I see that it is my pretty sister, I smiled. However, I noticed that she didn't smile back. Maybe she didn't know that it was me over here; I thought to myself. So I figured that I would walk up to her so that she could see my face better. So I gathered the boys and proceed to walk in her direction. When I made it to the car; ma'am may I help you with something? She turned to look into my eyes showing no emotion what so ever. I hugged her but felt no positive energy flowing from her. I hoped that her allowing me to come here, was something that she wanted to do and not something she felt obligated to do, thinking that she owed me for caring for mamma? I had to redirect my thoughts about this because, I didn't want to feel as if she didn't want me here, I just made it here and I needed her. As I helped her with her things, she seemed very quiet going up the stairs. I wanted to believe that she had a bad day and this not brought on because of the distance and time that we spent apart. But when we made it into the apartment, I tried to bring up funny things that happened when we were young that I knew she would remember, it didn't seem to phase her, she was cold as ice. I could see how aggravated she was with Ted as well. He hadn't done anything that I was aware of, so I politely excused myself, took the boys and went to the bedroom.

When the boys and I awake from a long nap. I got the them up to wash their faces and brush their teeth and realized that we had no towels, so I walked through the apartment noticing that there was no dinner cooking nor was there anyone sitting around. So, I continued towards their room and knocked on the door. I waited for a response and then slowly turned the doorknob. I peeked my head in to find only her and baby Q. When I saw that my sister and niece were alone, I thought that

I would use this time to talk baby talk with my niece as she lie in the bed beside her mom but as I looked up, I find that my sister's face had not relaxed since earlier in the day, so I chose to stop. What's wrong with you Gail…. For real? I ask. I'm just tired; she said. I'll tell you what? You just relax and I'll fix dinner for the family, OK. She nodded and I went to work in the kitchen cleaning and looking for the things that I needed to prepare a meal. There were a lot of items in the freezer but not much to work with. She seemed to sense that I was having trouble finding something among the frozen french fries, Ice cream bars, TV dinners, pop cycles and hot dogs. We don't cook much around here, we usually go out to eat; she said proudly. Who was I to judge, if I had the money, we would probably eat out as well; I thought. I decided to prepare the kids hot dogs and french fries and called it a night.

The next day, I woke the boys up to get ready. While they brushed their teeth and washed their faces, I went to tap on the door to ask if it were OK to feed my kids. He said; yes! as if surprised that I asked them. I'm only being polite; I said, with a laugh. Also, me and the boys are going to the welfare department this morning, OK. Would you like me to give you a ride? Ted ask. No thanks, we're going to catch the bus and see the sights but, thanks anyways. There were many things going through my mind as we made our way through the city. One of them being, I needed to get money to properly feed my boys and get housing for us, as well. As I watched the boys play around at the bus stop, I couldn't help thinking of the people that I left behind. I actually wondered how they were doing and hoped that they wondered about me too, silly me. After riding the bus for forty five minutes through the beautiful city of vista, we finally arrived at our destination in Oceanside to see that the place was packed. There were people sitting outside waiting for their number to be called as well as indoors. I took a number and sat down. I placed the kids in front of me on the floor with the small toys that they brought with them because there was no seats available for them to sit. As I looked around, I noticed all of the different nationalities and ethnic backgrounds here needing the same thing as I. I watched as one after another were called back. I began to get a bit anxious as I saw people that were standing in line before me be called back and finally my number was called. I quickly grabbed the boys up, gathering toys and snack and ran up to the desk, to be ask my date of birth and told that I had just a little longer to wait. By this time, I had been there for over an hour already. Forty five minutes later my name was called.

I answered all of the questions, crossed all of the T's and dotted all I's and was told that I would receive emergency food stamps today and I am to come back tomorrow to get the money part of it. I was grateful as I sit and waited for my name to be called again to receive the certificate. Once I received the physical check in my hand, it made me nervous a little as I realized it was a check to be cashed at a bank to receive actual money from. I shook the feeling and gratefully said; thank you. My children and I went to the bank with the three hundred dollars. When I stepped into the bank, I was in my feelings because this was the bank that mamma used when she was alive. Couldn't no one tear her away from her money but God, finger hut and me. When we were finished, I looked down at the boys telling them; we're going to eat now, giving each of them five dollars as we walked to the bus stop. We stopped at the store that was near their apartment to pick up groceries, we managed to get just enough for us to carry. When I made it in, I washed the boys up and went into the kitchen and got busy preparing dinner.

I put together some smothered pork chops with onions, mashed potatoes, green beans and hot water cornbread that Willie May taught me how to make. I was pretty proud of the meal that I prepared. Smiling the whole time while watching my sister devour what was on her plate. Sucking on her fingers, was an added bonus but when I saw that she seemed more relaxed and approachable, it took me back to something I had read years ago, the way to a persons heart is through their stomach, it just seemed to be true with her, at least. After dinner, I gave all four of the kids chocolate ice cream bars for desert and watched the different shapes and designs that appeared on their faces from the chocolate. My sister was laughing out loud like the old days and that made me feel good that I had did something that brought this on. I'd hoped that we had overcome this wedge between us. Thinking back, I was the best sister ever, according to her before they moved out here. She was my favorite as well, I took her everywhere with me, brought her clothes and shoes as if she really were my child.

It was bedtime for my boys, when bathed and teeth were brushed, we prayed....Now I lay me down to sleep, I pray the lord my soul to keep, if I should die before I wake, I pray the lord my soul to take. God bless everyone. This was the prayer that I taught my children because death always seemed just around the corner for me. When the kids were settled in bed. I came back into the dinning room to find Gail and Ted still sitting, talking. I excused myself and butted in. I'm going back to the welfare office in the morning; I said, as I handed them a $100.00 dollar bill. The boys and I will be leaving out pretty early in the morning. I'm letting you know so that you guys can lock your door behind me. Why don't you leave the boys here with us; Ted said, better yet, you should take the car, so that you can save on your travel time; he added. I immediately turned to see the reaction on my sisters face. She sat motionless with a look of uncertainty. As I turned my attention back to Ted. I thought I noticed a twinge on her face, that maybe I could have imagined, are you sure, guy? I ask. We would be perfectly fine riding the bus, I added. I'm OK, but thanks anyways. I turned to my sister, at a loss for words. I heard Ted, forcefully tell me to take the car. Without looking at him, OK. I will.

The next morning I felt reluctant to take their car for several reasons. One of them being the hesitancy and uncertainty that I saw in her eyes. The fact that I was feeling unsure of myself and my ability to control my urges where truly a factor. So I shook my head violently; get a grip Tru! I grabbed the keys off the table and whispered through their door, I'm gone. I pulled into the parking lot and saw that there were a lot of people there, same as it was yesterday. I walked in and took a number and sit down. As time passed, I realized that I had been sitting there for almost an hour and a half, again. I felt a little nervous about the time only because I didn't want to upset my sister, thinking back when we were young. I was the one who always kept her laughing, she was so pretty and sweet, she made it easy to love her.

I could hear my number being called in between the thoughts of my deeply rooted memories. Number 59; a voice called out over the PA system. I rose up to make my way through the sea of people waiting to be helped, in this large space you could hear the rumble of people talking that would quiet down when the PA clicked on. Finally making it to the front desk, my anxiety was real. I had to pay special attention to my hands, I kept wanting to put in my mouth to bite a nail. I received the check in my hand, I looked down to see that it was for another three hundred dollars. I thanked her and made my way through those that were still waiting and went to the bank that my mom used, once again. As I maneuvered my way through the city, it felt good to know that I could be of help to my sister and her family, me and mine. I made a right turn going down Canyon drive to go to Ralph's supermarket. As I drove down the winding road, I realized that my subconscious thinking was hard at work. I began battling with what's right and wrong in my head and before I knew it, I was on the dark side of town {as some would call it}. It felt as if my heart was going to pound out of my chest as I pulled to the curb, attempting to talk myself out of what I was about to do. I could feel the acceleration of the car beneath my feet. Before long, I was parked up the street, exiting the car, locking the door, to walk back to a known dope house. No amount of words that I could have said to myself at this point, that could have turned me around because the urge was much too strong. I could smell, taste and hear the sizzle in my mind.

The next morning was tough, walking out into the daylight with the sun beaming so bright that my eyes actually hurt, it felt as if I was having a deja vu. I felt out of sorts, out of my elements, it took me a while to get my bearings as the sun continued to beam down on me. As

I continued, slowly walking to the car the reality of things begin to hit me..…. I FUCKED up. I continued walking towards the car having irrational thoughts as to how I can get out of this predicament but rationally thinking? I knew that it would be obvious to all involved that I had smoked up all of the money last night. Once I made it to the car, I sit there for a minute to think but as I looked up, I saw two unmarked police cars parked in different places, watching the house that I just walked out of. Thinking, that I could be tweaking, I looked again, started the car up and slowly pulled away from the curb, praying that they let me go. I turned a few corners and had to pull over to get myself together to somewhat get my nerves built up. I sat there for a while playing different scenarios out in my head. Finally deciding, that I will NOT do this to myself. I started the car and pulled away from the curb driving in the direction of their apartment. I pulled into their parking lot to realize that I was a little afraid, not much because I knew in my heart that she loved me.

With the sun still beaming down on my head, it felt as if all of the life was being drained out of me. I dreaded going up those stairs. I looked in the mirror to check for imperfections or anything that could show on me from the night before. Here we go; I said to myself. I lightly tapped on the door, while looking down to realizing that I have the key but out of respect I continued to knock. Ted opened the door with a big smile on his face, while stepping aside to allow me in. As I walked in; I'm glad your OK Tru. Thank you Ted; I'm sorry about last night, I hope the kids weren't any trouble; I admitted. They were good boy's; he said. Note to self; his smile and concerns seemed genuine. I could hear all three of my boys running towards me before I could even see them. It was nice to hear them calling out my name in excitement. I sit on the small love seat and began to show the boys love, my niece walked in and stood in front of us as if she wanted the attention too. Come here Miss Q, come to auntie; I said. Before I could speak another word my sisters voice was loud and clear, so loud that all of the kids were startled. I hurried and rushed my boys into the room that we shared in hope that they wouldn't hear most of it, at least.

She took advantage of our car by acting as if it were hers, she has no respect for us! She shouted. She repeated this over and over again getting louder and louder each time she spoke. I knew that people outside could hear every word that she spoke but when I saw that my niece was starting to cry, this made my emotions stir. Although, I couldn't cry due to the drug, it made me sad, still. Ted surveyed the room and then turned his attention towards my sister; Enough Gail! He shouted. I think she got the point; he added. That made her even angrier. You don't care about my feelings, your siding with her? She yelled. OUT! She shouted in my direction. Get her out! She shouted again. She continued saying; I knew that we couldn't trust her! She said, with force. It hurt to hear my little sister speak about me like this, although I deserved this. I turned away as did Ted, he walked over to my sister to whisper something in her ear and they both went into their room and closed the door. Behind closed doors seemed to be a place where you were able to speak in private however every word that she spoke was loud and spoken clearly. I went into the room to shield the boys from her angry rant that could be heard by all.

Almost and hour later, I hear a slight knock on the door, come in; I said. When he opened the door, I saw it in his face. The storm had passed. Tru, we have to find somewhere for you and the kids to go. He looked at me as if to read my face, I had no words. I'm sure I displayed no readable expressions because, I believe I was in shock. Don't worry, I'm sure we'll find something; he added. Fighting back tears, how much time do we have? I ask. Today; he replied. Tears began to run down my face involuntarily but I quickly wiped them away. I had no way of knowing that what I did would put our lives in this predicament. The two oldest boys were looking in my face to get some kind of a response. I got up and went to the rest room and cried hard but quiet, only because I didn't know what else to do. I walked out giving the impression that I was ready to move forward with this but I knew in my heart I definitely wasn't. With no family but her and no friends but him, I felt all alone. Ted and I walked over and sit on the couch. We looked through the phone book for homeless centers for hours, being turned down for one reason or another. I still couldn't believe that I was having to go through all of this for one night of sin however I remained focused and continued to to finger though the pages. After three and a half hours, we called two places that might be an option for us. One was a place for recovering addicts and their children, the other was a battered women's shelter. The entire time that Ted and I stressed over finding somewhere for us to go, my sister remained in her room stirring around as if waiting for the results of our find. It was eerie. After getting the OK, I reluctantly got up off the couch and attempted to pull myself together. I walked into the bedroom and gathered the plastic bags that had our belongings in, and twisted them up into a knot. Sadly, I got the boys together and without saying goodbye to my sister, we followed Ted to the car. Once in the car, I sit quietly feeling destitute. He moved through traffic so swiftly that coming off the freeway was a breeze, it felt as if we made it there in no time. We followed the instructions that were given to us; that he pull close to the curb, up the street from the facility. I said my goodbyes, thanking him for his help and rounded up my boys to start our way towards the Battered women's shelter. I had no idea what was to come of us but I know that this felt bad.

Before I touched the gate, it began to open and once we were safely inside she pulled a lever that secured the gate, locking it. I immediately noticed that the fence was well over my head, there was no way to see in from the outside nor could you see out from the inside. She introduced herself and the name of the facility. As she walked us through, she pointed out the many attributes and safety features that were put in place to keep all who come here, safe. There was a beautiful pond in the middle of the grounds, with small palm trees planted strategically through out. The were two cats laying around as if they had been here for a long time. It looked like the perfect place to heal from a horrible situation. As we moved closer to the house, the kids and I noticed a tree swing and a place for them to play. She continued, pointing out the laundry room and the fact that there were nine rooms for nine mothers and their children. As we walked through, it appeared that we were the only family here at the moment, which I felt, was a good thing. Some won't get away from their abusers tonight, she said, while holding her head down. I thought about every time that I left their dad and returned, I shook my head in shame. Make yourself at home Miss Tru, I will come back to check on you and the children before shift change, OK? Also, there will be a form that you will have to sign as well. Alright, thank you ma'am; I replied. She left us to our own devices. I sat down in a chair beside the bed for a moment, taking it all in and watching my children. I could sometimes notice how things affected them in the way they played. Especially my youngest, Darion. He had action figures that he carried everywhere we went and when he showed aggression in one of the scenes, I knew.

I got up off the chair, telling them to follow me to the hall closet, where I gathered bed linen. I couldn't believe that this place had everything that we needed here for us. I came back to the room and she was there waiting for me. She handed the boys their own tooth brushes and tooth paste and put a paper on the dresser and ask that I read it and sign in order to reside here, as she played with the boys. I looked down at it and noticed that it was a confidentiality form, that ask that I not divulge the location of this place. I signed and dated it happily because I was happy to be here. We will go over the rules of the house in the morning, I will leave you now; she said. Have a good night; I added. When she left, I continued making the beds. I bathed the kids, fed them and put them to bed. As the night grew quiet, I couldn't help but wonder if my sister was happy with her decision?

With a cup of tea in hand, I stepped out back to see a beautiful sunrise peeking through the palm trees, dew glistening on the beautiful plants and flowers through out, with the sound of the water falling into the pond next to me, that gave me a sense of peace and serenity. I followed a path that lead to a bench that sit in the center of a gorgeous garden of tropical plants and flowers, this was a true oasis for someone like me to appreciate. My peace was interrupted by a young lady that looked as if she were one of the staff. She spoke softly, as if not to startle me; my name is Mrs. Chi and you must be Miss Tru? She ask. Just Tru, I responded. Welcome, she spoke with humility. I detected a bit of a southern accent, although she looked to be of Spanish decent. She explained, I have to go over the house rules with you when your ready. Will after breakfast be OK with you? I ask, sure; she said. She and I met, she walked me and the boys outside where there was a picnic area, where we took a seat. While the kids sat quietly and played, she pulled papers from a packet, handed me a set and kept some for herself.

She began with rule #1. Confidentiality, it's a must, that we keep all women safe while they reside in this home. #2. all residents have assigned chores that changes weekly, of course if the family makes a mess it is their responsibility to clean their mess. # 3. You are allowed to come and go as you wish, just refer back to rule #1. #4 Curfew is 7pm Monday- Thursday and 9 pm on Friday. Saturday and Sunday, unless you have resided here for five weeks to qualify for a weekend pass. Wow, it felt like I was being read the ten commandments; I thought to myself. #5. You are encouraged to save your money. We supply you with an account and help you to maintain it, to ensure that you attain adequate housing at the end of your stay here; which by the way is for as long as you need. We do not rush our mothers out because we understand. We hope that the rules be followed to maintain peace and harmony along the way. And last but not least, we only ask that 20% of your food stamps be donated towards the house to keep it furnished with food for your family and future families to come. There is a turntable that we[the staff] maintain. I agreed with all of the rules, picked up the pen and signed on the dotted line. Enjoy your stay here Miss Tru; she said. Also, if you need bus token please contact myself or any of the staff members. Thank you so much; I replied.

The kids and I were attempting to settle in around the house. I cleaned to my satisfaction, cooked and helped out on the grounds. I also learning how to care for plants. I thought about where the kids would go to school when it starts. I knew the area because I lived right around the corner with Andy, my boys were too young to remember. The next evening, there was the sound of an angry woman coming into the house which put me on guard. I gave it a moment to settle down but when the noise persist, I went to investigate. Looking back to make sure that the boys were still sleeping, I slowly closed the door and quietly went down the stairs. I stood at the bottom of the stairs just to listen to make sure that all was safe. I heard a heart wrenching cry, that put me in a state of sadness {truly understanding her pain}. I turned and went back upstairs to my children.

The next few days, I kept the boys a bit quieter, out of respect to her. When I saw that she was coming out of her room and moving around, I took it upon myself to better get to know her because in my mind, we were all in this house together and I need to know what type of woman I'm in here with, and are around my kids. My name is Tru; I said. How are you feeling today? I'm better, thanks for asking, my name is Rosa; she replied. Rosa and I continued our conversation. I actually found out quit a lot about her within the small amount of time that we talked. I sit and listened to her situation however I empathized with her but without admitting it, I somehow compared my situations to hers. The phone rang, my name was called over the speaker, saying that I had a phone call. I picked up the house phone, it was Ted on the phone, he said that he was calling to check on me and the kids. I was happy to hear from him but wondered if this was him calling or did my sister put him up to it. He admitted, that it was him, wanting to know how we were getting along in here. I'm doing OK, I guess. I want to know if I could come by and take you and the kids for lunch one day next week; he ask. Sure, the boys would love it. We said our goodbyes and hung up. I was very angry at myself that I didn't ask if my sister was happy about doing this to us? In the days to come, other women were showing up to the shelter, it was a constant reminder that the abuse that caused my trauma still exist. These women came with their anger and emotions that had me feeling some type of way also, it was bad enough that my kids had to deal with my shit but for them to have to be subjected to several different women and their issues just wasn't cool to me, so I began my search for an apartment.

Chapter 10

Mad at the world

The search for an apartment made my heart flutter a bit but like anything else that scared me, I went through what I needed to go through, to make it where I needed to be. I narrowed my search down, knowing that there were certain parts of the city where I couldn't afford to live and then there were parts where I wouldn't live. With the lack of money, Job and no credit, narrowed it down even more. There were postings of apartments for rent on bulletin boards at the center, the social service office, Wic office and hanging in the public library. I picked through and focus on them the most with hopes that one of them would give us a break. We had been there at the shelter for a little over two months now and as far as I was concerned we had overstayed our welcome. The kids and I got on and off the bus for days, walking and looking at apartments, it was truly exhausting. And then I thought about the Greenbrier.

After a nice dinner, a bath and a good nights sleep, we were ready to take on the day. I made breakfast and packed snacks and off we went. It was quite a walk but not far enough that we couldn't make it. My kids played and joked around the whole time. Before I knew it, we were on Grace street. I purposefully walked behind them and watched as they seemed to know where they were going without knowing where they were going. Turning the corner and seeing the street sign{Greenbrier} made me a bit nervous and exited at the same time. My old stomping grounds; I thought. I never imagined I would be back here again but I felt that if there was an apartment to be had it would be on this street where my mamma lived.

We continued walking until we stood at the top of the hill of Greenbrier Dr. It has always been quite a sight to see, for me. I grabbed hands and went across the street to the apartment where mamma lived. I thought that maybe it would be cool if I could get her old apartment but when I walked in the gate and saw the front door, all of the memories came flooding back. I had to keep my composure in front of the boys. I backed out of the gate realizing that this would be a bad idea. Once we were out and on the street, I looked down the hill confident that I will go to each one of these apartment buildings, until I got a yes from someone. I decided to start our journey at the top of the hill and work my way down. I turned to notice a small man and a woman about five feet tall of Iranian decent, working on the grounds across the street from where we were standing. I slowly made my way towards them, careful not to startle them. Good Morning: I said. Would you happen to know who the owners of this building are? I would like to at least get their number to call them in reference to an apartment? I ask. We are the owners; the man said, how can we help you? It was unusual for me to see the owners of a business or apartment building down on their knees in the dirt, I assumed, that they would hire for that.

Yes sir, my name is Tru, I am looking for an apartment for me and my boys Roland, Jamie and Darion. We are here from South Bend Indiana and are homeless at the moment, we are currently residing at the battered women's shelter, that seem to be filling up pretty fast; I said. Well…. follow me young lady; he said. We allowed him and his wife to go before us, they walked through what looked like a small tunnel that lead into an opening on the lower level of the apartment building. Once inside, the sun beamed through the beautiful palm trees that shaded most of the grounds. He sit on a bench that was located in the middle of the complex that allowed us to look up to see all of the apartments above. I have two apartments that are ready to be rented out, one is a one bedroom for $545 a month which is over here, {pointing at a door close to us} and a two bedroom for $645 which is on the second level; he said.

So, which would you be interested in? He ask, with a smile. I looked at them both in amazement. Are you saying that I can rent one? I ask. He spoke; when I saw how well behaved your children were from across the street and your mannerism as you stood talking to me, I knew then that I would rent to you if you needed it, so yes; he said. She smiled and nodded in agreement, so I chose the one bedroom instead, only because I knew that I only had the first months rent and part of the deposit which he allowed me to pay the remainder of, on the next month. We went back to the shelter to thank them and to collect our things, you could see the gratitude in my face. I cried when they offered to pay for a cab for us to get home. With nothing but the clothes on our backs and a few things in garbage bags and two blankets that the center gave us, we were home. Gradually we accumulated things along the way, what wasn't given, I stole from Ralphs supermarket. I only took things like, meat, potatoes, cleaning supplies, just the essentials.

The couple that lived next to me were named Liz and Larry, they were very kind to us. They always let me know that they were available if I were to ever need them. Liz never missed an opportunity to spoil my boys with snacks when she returned from the store. After living in the apartment next to them for three months. I received a raise in income, I went to the couple, in hopes that there may be an apartment available that I could afford in the building. I ask Glenn if I could have it, he says, I have been such a good tenant that he'll show me the two bedroom on the top floor, I was blown away. It was nice, there were two nice sized bedrooms, one being the larger of the two that had a large walk in closet, this one I gave to the boys. There was a hallway with a closet and shelving behind doors for storage, a nice sized bathroom and a door that separated the living room from the bedrooms. The kitchen and dinning room were huge. But what I loved most was that on a clear day, I could see the ocean glistening in the distance.

The boys and I moved our items upstairs piece by piece with pride. I watched my boys as they put their things away without instructions. When done. we all sit on the floor Indian style on our blanket and had a picnic with all of the windows opened listening to the wind come from all directions that made it's way through our apartment. It was nice to hear my children's explanation as to why the wind would be talking to us, way up here. Trying to sleep, I tossed and turned because I knew that I could and wanted to do better this time. I wanted to go to work, I knew that I couldn't work many hours because I had no one to care for the boys but maybe I could find something while they went to school and maybe ask the neighbor to watch my baby. Because, I have no intent on ever having to rely on anyone and become homeless again.

The next day, the kids and I walked to the resource center on Oceanside blvd. to apply for what ever I would qualify for. It was a lengthy process but I made it through. I left with two numbers and addresses to check on that day. I returned again two days later to attain more leads on jobs, getting frustrated each time that I had to return because it seemed, nothing was on the bus line but I was determined to find part time employment. I went back again and forty five minutes into my wait, in walked a long legged caucasian girl. Although young, she demanded the attention of the room and got it. Long dark hair, that swayed as she walked, looking like money from where I sit. With her flawless makeup, freshly painted nails and fishnet stockings that she wore beneath a pleated mini skirt with a silk blouse accompanied with a stiletto ¼ inch heel to match.

I watched men and women, watched her as she walked up to get her number, turn and walk away from the desk. To my surprise she turned in my direction and sit beside me smelling as beautiful as I remembered Joan smelling, which made me sad because I truly missed her so. Upon sitting, she quickly started up a conversation; how long have you been waiting here? She ask. Still in shock that she choose to sit besides me; I slowly answered; I've been sitting here for a while now. And at that moment her number was called, I watched as she walked away and wondered to myself, what it must feel like to be admired in the way that she was. As a little girl, I remember wanting to be white. I had a beige towel that I hid on the side of the dresser, I placed it on my head when playing alone, pretending that I was a blonde. I thought that no matter how poor the whites that I knew, they always seemed to have it better than I. So instead of playing with barbie{ which I never had anyways} I played white. She returned to her seat beside me. By the way, my name is Kizzi, shaking my hand. Before she left, she ask that we exchange numbers and vowed to keep in touch with each other. Go figure.

Job hunting together made it fun. I felt like a kid doing grownup things. We would go to different places putting in applications, while she ran errands when she needed too, which was almost every day. Knowing my surroundings, I always knew where I was on any given day but also like a child I minimized the danger in my mind. Nevada street was where a predominant amount of Mexicans lived. I sit in the car in the beginning which I didn't mind because I was the lookout so to speak, for myself. She made me aware that her boyfriend Armando lived in this house and the cousin Hector lived in the other house, that she frequented just as much. She began to trust me with a lot of information, I took it all in. I saw her whenever she wanted to be seen and that was fine with me because my evenings belonged to my boys.

From the very beginning she trusted me with her car to make store runs. It would be for things that she needed, as well as if I needed something for me and the kids. I would always put gas in it when I used it because she wouldn't accept any money from me. Sometimes while I was out, I would return to the center in hopes of getting a lucky break and finally I did. It was a spot job to cater at a hall the next evening. I was told to wear a pair of black pants and a white shirt and that they would provide the tie when I showed up, and that I did. To my surprise, when I finished my shift at 3am, she was sitting out there waiting for me with a smile on her face. She made me feel as if I had a true friend, she broke down walls that took me years to build up in such a short time, we were inseparable.

It was time to enroll the boys in school and we all were excited about buying school clothes and supplies. I thought that I would get a better deal on clothes for them if I went to the indoor swap meet on mission avenue and then walk across the street to Payless for their shoes. I had it all planned out when there was a knock at the door and in come Kizzi and Armando with four big bags of clothes and shoes for the boys. The crazy thing was, most everything fit them and what ever didn't, I took next door to the new neighbors apartment for her son who was around the same age as my older boys. Her name was Vera, she was a short lady with freckles on her cheeks that stood about 5feet tall, she and her son Kyle moved to California from Chicago to better their life. She had two other children that were grown, one which was a boy that was incarcerated and a girl still back home. She and I formed a sort of a kinship quickly. When I came up, she came up. I believed that it was God that put her next door to me, so I adopted her and took care of her like a good daughter would.

I quickly learned that Kizzi had a hand in a many things to be as young as she was. She would often speak on how much of a drag it was being 18. She let me in on the fact that she boosted all of the kids school clothes and shoes that they brought to the apartment that day. Although I didn't find out everything at once, but as the layers were pulled away, more was revealed. She was also into, checks, drugs, credit cards and a few other things. I told myself; because it wasn't me doing these things, that I had nothing to fear but realistically, I was guilty by association and I really didn't care because I now have found a friend. She ask that I take a ride with her after the kids got on the bus that Thursday morning, of course I was ready in record time. Beautiful as always outside. I stood by the car and watched as she prepared to let the top down and when asked me to flip a switch to secure it from my side, I was happy to do it. As we moved through the streets of Oceanside with the top down listening to {Warren G Regulator}it felt like the best morning I had ever had in my life.

As we drove up a steep hill she proceed to give a bit of information about her parents and their strained relationship with them before stopping in front of a very nice house with a beautifully manicured curb appeal. Of course I was in awe because I had never been this close to a home this nice. She got out of the car and told me to come in. My heart jumped, I can stay her until you come back; I said. Nosy neighbors; she replied. I got out and followed her, noticing that she hadn't locked her car doors or let the top up. When we made it to the door, I could smell the difference from any other home that I had ever been in from of, just standing outside. When she opened the door, what I saw was truly unbelievable to me. From the outside, this house did not look this massive. It's as if the house was built on the back of this hill. There were three levels strategically built to blend into the next and once you reached the top level, there was a beautiful scene through out. I could actually see the wooded area overlooking the terrace that reached the entire length of the home through a beautiful pane glass windows, that also reached across the length of the home. Absolutely breath taking; I said; out loud. There were large oil paintings hanging to my left, some were, of painted lines; I thought; what a waste of paint. A large chandelier hung in the stairwell, with expensive looking art pieces through out the home. A marble floor in the kitchen, I was in awe. Everywhere that I looked, I was amazed. You can have a seat anywhere, I'll be right back, OK? She said. I sat down on a little couch that was in their foyer, sure not to move in case someone who wasn't very nice walked in. I wondered how it must have felt growing up in this house, not ever worrying about where your next meal will come from or if you'll get that toys that you wrote Santa about, or how long you'll go without watching your favorite cartoon due to the electric being off, or just feeling safe within the home.

Tru! Where are you? She shouted playfully. Right here; I said. We rode back down the hill in silence. I wondered why can't all children live, free from hunger, pain, fear of being in an unsafe and dysfunctional environments, why can't we all have level headed parents as I assumed that she had. Where you at girl; she ask. I was just thinking about some crazy shit is all; I replied. I looked up and saw that we were close to my neighborhood already, her house was closer that I had imagined, for some reason. I thought about how trusting she was with information about her and her family, not to mention, her taking me to the family home, which was literally mind blowing to me. Why me? I wondered. Finally, we pulled up to the curb in front of my apartment building, I'll be back later; she said, still clutching that bag that she came out of the house with.

I moved on with my day, realizing that cleaning was so self gratifying to me. I went over to the window to wipe down the blinds and I witnessed the boys stumbling in the gate playing and teasing each other. My oldest appeared agitated, with what the youngest was taunting him about, so I playfully intervened; leave that boy alone and get on up here! As they ran up, I heard the opening of the gate and looked down to see Kizzi coming through looking like a million bucks as usual. I waved and hurried the boys into the door.

Can you come with me? She ask. Well, my boys just came home; I replied. Just come out to the parking lot and bring the boys. I went into the closet {which is where he played with his action figures all the time} to get Darion and signaled for the other boys to follow me. As we walked through the gate, I could see the excitement in her eyes, Tah Dah! she shouted, with a huge smile on her face and her arms extended. I looked over to see three nice and nearly new bikes. I was in shock, I can't take these from you; I said. Yes you can; she added. We went back and forth a few times, finally looking down at the boys, seeing their desperation, I accepted. Anxiously waiting on my OK, I let them go and ride on their new bikes. Please let me pay you back for these; I ask. No! No! Please let me do this for you and your family, you've been so good to me as a friend. She then turned and got back into the truck that she came in, I'll be back later. Thank You! I yelled into the wind. I stood outside for a while and watched as the boys ride in a circles, thinking about how the bikes could have come to be in my possession, I smiled and took the kids in the gate with their bikes.

The kids and I had dinner, bathed and just laid around relaxing and playing games. There was a knock at the door, it was kizzi coming back as she said she would, bright eyed and bushy tailed as usual. I got something I want you to see; she expressed. I sent the boys to their room to play and closed the door with instructions that they play quietly. When I returned, she was going through her large purse and pulled out a book. With a puzzled look on my face I waited, this is a ledger; she said. When she opened it and flipped through the pages there was a lot of writing in it. What's this; I ask. A log of all my transactions; where or who I made this transaction with and how much money it generated and if I made any donations and where. And this is my biggest profit, pointing to a word that I had never seen before. Methamphetamine, it's a stimulant and junkies love it; she added.

So how do they get high with this drug; I ask. They smoke it, shoot it, or snort it up their nose. My heart fluttered a little, listening to her. {I have never told her about my addiction only because I wanted to hide that horrible side of myself from her or anyone else, for that matter}. I'll show you what it looks like, pulling out, what looks like a piece of discolored glass in rock form. I couldn't resist wanting to hold it in my hand to feel it's texture. I rolled it between my fingers, not believing that this was a drug, only because to me it didn't resemble anything that I've seen people getting high off of. I'm showing you this because, I wanna bring you on so that you can make money for you and your boys. It's easy to get off, once you find two good customers they'll be loyal for life. Now, keep in mind you gotta kick them a little something every now and again to keep them loyal but it's well worth it; she said. Now, I'll set you up with your first packages for free; she added. I wasn't ready but, I knew that I wanted to get this money. She showed me how to weigh it, package it, and made me aware as to how much each piece costs because of it's weight. I listened and learned fast.

Three weeks later, I secured two customers that turned out to be very loyal, to the point that one of them allowed me to sell my product out of their apartment across the street. As they say; you don't shit where you eat or sleep, which ever sound best. Business was booming. When someone needed something, she ran across the street to get it from me and I would kick her down something later for it. At that point, I realized that I may need some sort of protection for this line of work because I had heard of numerous people being robbed or worse. So I spoke to Armando in regards to getting me a firearm, he let me know that it won't be a problem. Later that evening, he and his cousin came by with two, one was a 22. pistol and a 38. revolver. They both had black tape on the grip and the triggers as well. I was told that the numbers had been filed off, so that no one could trace it back to where they originated. I knew that I was stepping into territories that I was truly unfamiliar with by the way my heart was jumping around in my chest but I couldn't let that be known. I chose the 22. because of how small and inconspicuous it was. He showed me how to handle it and how to load and unload and away they went.

She allowed me to use her car later that evening. I drove to a vacant spot that I learned about while making a late night delivery. I walked inward a little and shot off a couple of rounds, the power that this small piece of steel had in it, led me to believe that I was invincible. I carried it in a black leather back pack, almost everywhere I went. I tried to treat people like I wanted to be treated when I was selling this drugs, to insure that I would never be in a position that I had to use my gun. Business was good. The ladies remained loyal, I kicked them out a little extra for themselves when they brought me a few extra sales. Reminding them that this is my home and I have a cut off time. It was respected but, there were those other times when somebody came through with two or three hundred dollars. I would hear a light tap on the door as I slept. Emergency, she would say, and I would quietly serve her. Every time that I had to re-up, my stomach churned. I was nervous about coming up too fast and I definitely wanted to stay under the radar from the feds, for fear of being raided because I remembered seeing and being caught up in one. I thought about what would happen to me children if I were to be taken away, so I told myself that I would quit the business, when I made what I needed, to get out.

People had all sorts of things that they wanted to sell, trade or even pond to get this drug. A couple came to me wanting to sell a black leather, living room set with coffee and end tables and a few other very nice items that would go nicely in our apartment, these things were almost new. I gave them a half ounce for it all. I found that if you let them know that you will take items for drugs, then that's how they'll want to pay you and I couldn't let that happen, money only, after that. My personality changed a little, just to keep people from taking advantage of me. I met different types of people along the way who were once people of importance but because of how the drug took control of their lives, what once was, was no more, they had lost it all.

An accountant, was at an address where I made a drop off, who said; I have a service that you need. She and I stepped outside to discuss it further. The next day I needed to see her in action. She instructed that I take her to the bank. I parked up the road a bit after letting her off around the corner in case she was caught doing whatever she was going to do but, when she was done I watched as she casually walked up the street and to the car, from the rear view mirror. When she got in, lets go, she said. I pulled off. I watched as she pulled out an envelope that had a lot of hundred dollar bills in it, she peeled three hundred off and gave it to me for my business and requested two hundred in drugs and one hundred was for myself. She was good at what she did, however I needed to know what this thing was. We all have a story to tell. Lynn, was a mother of two and was a big time accountant, with a business that she owned with her husband. She was highly educated and respected in her world but in this world, it was quite a different story. She knew how to move money around that wasn't hers. She stood almost six feet tall with long beautiful legs, with a thin built and nicely shaped body. She still had her beauty but you could tell the drug was having it's way with her, you could also tell by the way that she carried herself that she was a bad ass white girl in her day.

I moved around while my children slept at night. I would knock on Vera's door to tell her that I was leaving, she would keep an eye on my kids for me and during the day I would sleep while they were in school. The more I sold the more characters I met. Gene was an addict that was a transient. He stayed across the street in a vacant apartment. I would see him coming and going sometimes hiding from people who he thought would bring him harm. He was a nice looking guy of medium built who kept himself clean. I told myself that I needed him in my life to handle a few things and he was happy to oblige. I paid him both in money and dope. We became pretty cool, all he seemed to do was want to please me and I appreciated that about him.

I would have gatherings at the apartment and would invite him, he was so happy to be there just sitting. The nights changed for me, I started entertaining company. I brought a dart board and had Gene to mount it on the wall with a board behind it to cushion the blow of the darts. We gambled any and everything on that board and had fun doing it. Next was my music, I brought a double deck tape player with a small equalizer to play and record music along with two microphones and speakers that were phenomenal. I had to sit them on wooden crates to muffle the base from the neighbors below us. I would have people over and we would sing {karaoke}with music just for fun.

Christmas was moving in fast, I started shopping with no room left in the apartment to hide gifts so I spoke to Glenn about renting a space in the carport to store their toys and he agreed. Shopping this year was much more festive than any other year to me. On December 1st Lynn and I came in from a morning of shopping. We were also waiting on Kizzi to come so I could re-up. She turned towards me and ask if it were OK pointing down at a mirror; yea it's cool; I said, as I prepared to get up. I could hear her chopping the rock up on the mirror and then I heard what sounded like a long sniff, twice, as I turned around I saw her head lye back on the couch as if enjoying the feeling that came over her.

Let me have some of that shit. I said it before I took the time to fully processing the thought. She rolled the dollar up again and held it out for me to take and watched as I took it between my fingers, she then passed the mirror and I did exactly what I imagined that she did and nothing happened. She then held my nostril and told me to sniff what was on the mirror and I did, She held the other nostril and said; again. Oh! MY! God! Everything inside of me seemed to be awakened. I wanted to walk, run, clean up, all at the same time. As I rose from the couch, it was as if there were thrust boosters in my ass. I needed to move around and I did, this was amazing. She watched me with a smile on her face, she knew that I liked this.

If you like it this way, your going to love it, like this; she admitted. I watched as she cut a small piece off and drop it into a pipe that had a small bowl at the end of it. She lit it with a small torch as I watched as the rock turned to liquid. She gently pulled on it, to produce a white cloud of smoke and took it into her lungs until the bowl was empty. Your turn; she said, handing me the glass pipe. I slowly moved my fingers towards the pipe and gripped it, not too tight; she interrupted. I brought it towards my lips and held it there waiting for her instructions. As she put the fire underneath the bowl, I watched as the liquid turned into smoke to dissipate as I inhaled. I laid my head back to enjoy the high, this was different and I liked it. This was the start of something new. The drug became a part of my daily regimen. I felt as if I had found something that made me feel alive and more motivated to succeed as appose to the other drug that brought me down. At least this is what I told myself. All that I needed, was a hit and I would be OK all day. But as the days go by, I found this not to be true. The crash that happened when I was coming down off the drug was truly disheartening. I felt out of it, as if my body wasn't in agreement with anything that my mind was telling it to do. I craved it, this wasn't at all what I expected, so I did more of it to keep this feeling at bay.

My mindset changed, therefore my actions were not my own. I would be out at night making a run and would shoot off my gun, just being reckless. I would leave out, while the kids slept and go up to the neighbors that lived in the loft in our building and get high, listening to the Doors, and wouldn't come out until it was time for them to get ready for school. Saturday night, Kizzi came over to sit and get high with me. It didn't even surprise me because she was always bright eyed and bushy tailed when she came by and I knew there had to be a reason for it. As we sit talking and laughing about nothing. Her face turned serious, she turned to me, your making it hot over here, she said quietly. I looked up at her wondering what could she possibly know that I've done, without seeing me do it? I just couldn't think of what I could have done so outrageous to bring the heat. I have people close, that tell me things, she explained. Enough said, back to business tomorrow; I said.

The next afternoon, I met with the ladies that have been loyal to me. Conversations were had about making serious money. We all agreed and separated. I went home to prepare dinner and invited Vera and her son over. It was nice, I learned a little more about my friend that evening. She has a son in prison by the name of Brock. She explained that he's going to be paroled to her apartment soon. Of course, I wanted to help her in any way that I could because she is my friend turned family. When the young man made it home, I watched Vera be as happy as I had ever seen her in the time I've known her. I made sure that she had groceries and a new bed for him to sleep in. I also provided her with money for whatever she may need it for him. He was 19, handsome and as far as I was concerned, old enough to know better. I set my sights on him early, determined to get what I wanted. When he learned of what I was doing he mentioned that he wanted to make some fast money.

Although his mom was against it, I hooked him up and he quietly did his thing down the hill. I was smitten by this young man. I was thirty years old but age meant nothing to me because I was determined. I made sure that we stuck together by having things to do that I knew interested him. He liked to sing so I started a group called; Voice Control. We had auditions for people that knew how to sing and chose them accordingly. I wrote songs to be sung ocapella. We also practiced using songs from known artists, like Luther Vandross and Secret gardens by Quincy Jones. Sometime, I made songs up from the sound jazz music that I've heard on the radio. We didn't sound too bad with three women and four guys. We practiced every Friday and the neighbors didn't seem to mind. We talked of taking a week off for Christmas to be with family but decided that we all were family and came back together.

New Years Eve was wild, it started out with me being called to the door by a neighbor across the street. Saying that there is somebody walking up and down the Greenbrier calling out your name, Tru! The first thing I did was instruct my boys to go to my room and close the door. I grabbed my pistol and walked out of the front door. I walked down and out of the side gate to a path that lead down the back of the apartments to the next apartment building to exit out of their driveway. I kept listening to see if I could recognize the voice and where it was coming from. I continued to listen as I crouched down beside the concrete wall, preparing myself for the unknown. I looked across the way and noticed one of the ladies crouched down and waiting as well. He called out again, this is Trell! He said. Damn! That's my brother! I shouted. I moved out from behind the wall and made my way to the street to see him walking up the middle of the street yelling out my name again. Stop calling my name, fool; I shouted. He quickened his steps towards me. How did you know where I was? I ask. Your sister {with a smirk on his face} told me.

"I was surprised that they knew where I lived because I hadn't spoken to either one of them since before I left the center." But it was good to see my little brother, he's a man now and here in California. We hugged and walked up the hill together throwing questions and answers back and forth to one another. He looked up at me with a serious look on his face, I saw lil Alfred out in the streets, he's on that shit. I held my head low, because I knew what he was referring too. I said a prayer and nodded at my friends across the street. I'll be back a little later; I shouted. I opened the gate so that he can go in before me, that's different, he said sarcastically. You have never allowed any of us boys to go in before you. I'm still that way, boy, I'm just being nice; I said, playfully smacking him on the back of his head. When he walked into the apartment, he looked to be in awe at what he saw. This is nice, sis. Looking at the large African mask that is made of match sticks in the center of the wall. Turning, towards the large floor model colored television. He sit on the black leather couch, running his hand across it and ask; is this real. Yes it is; I answered. He stood and commented as to how nice the smoked glass coffee and end tables looked in the room. I walked him over to the window although it was night, I had to let him know, that on a clear day, I can see the ocean from here. He turned his attention to the dart board, this is the shit; he shouted.

We all thought so as well, you'll see; I said, with a smile on my face. I walked through the threshold, opened my bedroom door and noticed my boys laying across the bed and the floor playing nicely together. I love you guys; I said and showed them their uncle. The boys looked up at him, with not even a smile. Trell wasn't too pleased that the boys didn't seem to be too happy to see him but I assured him that they will come around, in time. I also told him that he can stay until he finds a job and get his own place to live, he was pleased. I took him back across the street with me to introduce him to some people and to finished celebrating the New Year.

 He wanted to get into everything that I was doing but I couldn't allow that because if something happened to him on my watch, I would feel responsible, also I wasn't sure that he could mentally handle everything that was going on and I didn't want to explain his mental state, to my friends. I don't care about what others think.....but I do, bro. There were times, that I allowed him to go on runs with me, only if it were just me but if someone else were riding along, he couldn't go. Days turned into weeks, Brock became my main focus and Gene wasn't very happy about it, understandably so. Over the course of time, I made Gene my boy toy. He would perform any wild and crazy fantasies that I may have had and came back for more. But on this particular Friday night, this would be the night that I was going to seduce Brock. I told Gene, that I wanted him to leave for the night, he looked me in my face and said; No. You want me to leave when you want to play with someone else, I'm sick of it; he barked. I sucked my teeth. Alright, so leave, if your that sick of it; I said. He continued to speak his mind about it and finally, I was fed up. Look, if you don't like what's going on in this apartment, that I pay rent in...then go across the street but right now I need you to leave this place or we are going to fight; I growled. He said nothing and sit down on the couch and watched me from across the room. A storm was brewing inside of me. I thought about how hot kizzi claimed it was in this area because of me but as I walked over and stood beside him, noticing that he wasn't going to budge, the storm turned to rage. I reached behind him and grabbed the bat that leaned against the wall and as I began to swing, I felt some sort of joy in what I was doing to him. He put his arm up, attempting to block the blows but they were coming so fast and hard until he had no choice but to run. He opened the door and ran out onto the landing and down the stairs. I dropped the bat and picked up one of the kids bikes that were parked on the railing and threw it at him with it landing on his shoulder. He cried out and turned to look up at me. I felt no remorse. I watched as he walked out of the gate looking wounded. I walked back in the apartment to begin prepping for my night with Brock. I thought about what had just happened but the drug in my system wouldn't allow it to bother me.

The candles were lit, the food was done and smelling better than ever. The windows were open just enough to allow the wind to find it's way through, too us. The wine was on chill along with the beer and the kids were next door fed and ready for the bed. I thought about how much time and attention that I was putting into this for a young man that I don't even know, nor have any intentions of being with long term. Although, proud of what I had accomplished. I couldn't help but think; this is something that I would hope to receive from someone, some day before I die. I could see the silhouette of his body walking towards my door through the blinds. I opened the door and let him in, offered him a glass of wine, which he chose beer instead. I fired up a bowl, we drank and laughed………I don't remember much after that. I remember droplets of blood. I also remember being on top, gonna show him a good time; I said. I also remember him gently holding my hips and sliding his body from beneath me. He was wounded, I saw it in his eyes, first. I looked down at where his hand was, clutching his dick and balls. I then knew, where. He removed himself from the bed leaving a few droplets of blood. Are you OK? I ask. He looked away from me and answered; yea, I'm good. I sit on the bed knowing that he wasn't because, I saw the pain in his eyes already. One thing's for sure…..pain shows up as pain, whether you want it too or not, its up to you as to how you choose to express it. He ran out of the bedroom, I then heard the front door open and shut. I was way too high to stay focused. I cleaned the mess and went to retrieve my boys. I wished him well through his mother and came back home.

I wake the next afternoon, the kids were on the floor playing and watching television. I could remember bits and pieces of the night before, what did I do to that boy? I ask myself. I made the kids breakfast and began my day. I went next door to check on Brock. Vera answered the door and stepped out to talk to me. We went to the emergency room last night; she said. What happened? I ask. The head of his penis was split open, he had to wear the condom to the hospital for fear that it would cause more damage and he wouldn't tell me what they did to fix it but I can only imagine, she said. I stood, stunned for what seemed like forever, not quite knowing what to say to her about something like this, finally….I'm sorry for hurting your son in that way, I said. "It seemed to come out louder than I imagined it would" but as I turned to walk away, she admitted, that it wasn't my fault, it takes two to tangle; she said. Dam, I said out loud. I walked away trying desperately to remember what happened last night. I carried on with the plans that I had made, to take the boys to the beach. I told the them to get ready for our adventurous, bike ride. The happiness that they expressed, brought joy to my heart. With backpacks filled with sandwiches, snacks and juices we were on our way. I loved riding with them, I saw in them something that I don't remember ever feeling in my childhood. I was happy to be able to give them this. Crossing the main streets were easier now with my boys being older because they paid attention, remembering what they were taught. "I was having a proud mommy moment" Darion always road on the bike with me on a folded pillow for comfort. Approaching the beach was a beautiful sight to me, no matter what time of the day I went. We continued to ride until I found the perfect spot. I pulled out a small sheet with three small poles, stuck them in the sand and made a makeshift tent to block the sun from us. I watched, as they ran in circles chasing each other. I instructed them, not to go too far into the water as I laid back watching them play. I dug my toes deep into the sand, absorbing the feeling and the memories of last night came rushing in.

 I held his face in my hand, gently kissing his lips, his cheeks and on too his forehead. I moved downward kissing his chest, nibbling on his nipples, making my way down his sides with my tongue in his belly button. I held his shaft in my hand and squeezed and as he jumped. I took it into my mouth. It tasted a bit sour like a pickled pig feet with the same consistency. I eased back from it and continued to stroke it until it had the girth that I desired. I slid out of the over sized shirt, leaving it on the floor. Slowly opening the condom, to slid it on him, careful to leave room for the seamen. I looked up at him, I could tell that he was ready. I held it firm and eased down on the dick taking it all in. I reached around and found the ball sack and played with it while I ride with a steady pace. I could feel him swell inside of me, that's when I quickened my pace becoming more aggressive and then I heard nothing after that. I felt his hands gently grab my hips as he slid his body from beneath me. I stared out in the direction of my children, not being able to control the amount of remorse that I began to feel for him. The more that I thought about it, it felt as if my feelings were swaying. I have never thought about hurting a man in that way and yet I did, a sense of pride came over me. I shook it off and went out to play with my boys.

Three hours later we were home, all cleaned up and ready for dinner. I sent the boys outside while I put something together. Minutes later I heard my children yelling playfully that caused me to go out and check on them, it was Gene walking in the gate, looking up with puppy dog eyes. I smiled and signaled for him to come up. I looked down and waved to the boys and saw a young lady that owed me money from over two and a half months ago. I decided that I would speak to her later, I turned to see him take the steps two at a time, I smiled. How are you? I ask. Sad, missing you; he replied. Are you still mad at me? He ask. I was never mad at you, I just need you to understand the rules of my home, when I ask you to leave, regardless as to what you are feeling, I need you too do just that; I admitted. I will never do that again, please forgive me; he begged. When dinner was done I fixed the kids a plate and then sit a plate in front of him with a glass of cool-aid, he was a happy man, yet again.

That evening as the kids slept, we were having an amazing time. I invited a few friends over while Voice Control practiced their songs. There was a guy that came with Kizzi that had a guitar and he played a few songs of his own and played with us as well. I sounded better than ever. It was still early evening when they all left but we were all high and probably had a few too many. I ask if everybody was OK to drive, walked them out to the street and said my goodbyes. As I walked into the gate I saw the young lady that owed me money standing in front of her door. I moved swiftly through the shrubs and jumped to the lower level that put me within inches of her. As I moved closer, do you have any intentions of paying me my money? I ask. She jumped and "it gave me a sense of control." I was coming to see you on the first of the month; she said. Yea but that's two and a half months too late. I'll tell you what; if you pay me half now, I'll forgive the rest, is that cool with you? I ask. If I had it, I would have paid you a long time ago; she admitted as she stepped in her apartment and attempted to slam the door in my face. I blocked the door with my body and stepped inside. I reminded her of a purchase that she made with another fella outside the apartment building not two nights ago and before I could take in a breath she hit me on the side of my face, yelling for me to get out of her house. She was handling me, throwing blow for blow. I looked down to see a small wooden table, I grabbed it and the leg came off in my hand and I beat her with it until I realized that she wasn't putting up a fight any longer. I stood over her trying to catch my breath and noticed all of the bruises that I left on her fair skin. Your dept is forgiven bitch; I said, as I turned and walked out of the door.

Monday morning, I woke and stepped out to see a beautiful day, the air felt a bit crisp but the sun was shinning bright. I waited for the boys to finish eating their breakfast and I walked them to their bus stop. When they were gone, I walked back in, slowly checking my surroundings and made my way back into the apartment. Darion had awakened, I fixed him a bowl of cereal and led him to the couch to watch cartoons so that I could get a nap in. As I lay with my eyes closed, I could feel a slight rumble in the structure of the apartments I lay still and wait to see if it happens again, in case I have to prepare us for an earthquake. I decide to get up and check outside. I watched as Darion went to his room to play with his action figures. I felt it again, this time with a tinkering sound of steel hitting together. I stopped and stood still for a min. Quickly and quietly, I hurried in to get Darion and his toys from the closet where he play, while covering his mouth with my hand I rushed him to my bedroom. I could see the shadows passing the curtains of the kids bedroom window as I rushed by. I gently put the baby in and closed my bedroom door. I could see that the window to their room was pulled back and I could hear them speaking clearly through the screen. I prayed that they didn't notice it. Boom! Boom! Boom! It scared me so bad, I quietly ran back to my bedroom to make sure that he was OK with the loud noise and wasn't wanting out. He didn't seem phased. I heard their whispers and saw their hand signals but I couldn't make much of anything out of what was being said because of the thumping of my heart. I tiptoed closer to the door of the kids room to get a better listen. Boom! Boom! Boom! Oceanside Police Department! Open up! One of the officers shouted and then it was quiet again. I could hear the door of one of the apartments in the distance. It was my neighbor asking; may I help you? Yes ma'am, are you the manager? Would you happen to have the key to open this door?

Do you happen to have a warrant to inter that apartment? she ask. That's my friend; I whispered. Who are you looking for officer? She continued. I can't release that information; the officer responded. Well sir, I can't open that door without a warrant, she added. They stood in silence as if they didn't know what to say. With my heart pounding, I waited quietly to see what they would do next. I heard a loud thud on my door and then footsteps going down the stairs and out of the gate. A huge sigh of relief escaped my body. I felt paralyzed, I sit Indian style until I could feel that my body was ready to move.

Their radio's echoed throughout the apartment complex from where they stood outside the gate. I didn't feel safe leaving my apartment for a long time after they finally left, so I called Vera and ask that she get the boys off the bus for me when they arrive, she agreed and kept them for a while to make sure that the police wasn't waiting. As the night approached, I felt confident that everything had died down. I looked out of every window in the apartment to see if I noticed anything that looked like a police car, finally I stepped outside, still unsure as to what lurked around the corner. Realizing, that I can't hide forever I walked outside and past the woman's apartment that owed me money. I knew in my heart that she was the reason for the invasion but I kept walking towards the gate to feed my curiosity. When I made it to the gate, I peeped out looking both ways to see if the coast was clear. I took a deep breath and stepped out onto the sidewalk to see if the coast was clear.

Two months had past and all was well. Saturday afternoon, Jamie and Roland ask to go two apartment buildings down the street to play with their friends, giving instructions on what time to check in, I allowed them to go. Forty five or fifty minutes after they left, Jamie ran in the gate screaming at me, telling me that Roland was at the bottom of the pool in the apartments at the bottom of the hill. I couldn't run fast enough to get to him. My mind couldn't fathom what I heard him say. But when I made it there, he wasn't there. He had already been taken away by helicopter. The people that stood around told me, that it happened an hour ago, no one knew where the little boy belong, someone called 911. I became unglued! The officer offered to give me a ride to Try-City Hospital after noticing how out of touch I had become. As we drove over to the next county, I tried not to think the worst, I found myself making false promises to God. I lied to myself and I knew this because I was an addict, I couldn't stop just like that. But I knew that I loved my son and I wanted and needed him to pull through and that he did. We were there in the hospital for three days, he fully recovered. I attempted to bring a Lawsuit against the apartment building for negligence but it was to no avail. I had my son and that mattered most. I slowed things down a lot for a while after that, to get a handle on things.

I hadn't learned my lessons on life as of yet. I purchased another firearm from an old man that had this beautiful treasure, for many years and really didn't want to part with it but he wanted the drug. And when I saw this beauty, I selfishly didn't want to leave it with him either. It was an old smith & Wesson hand gun, with a pearl handle, it didn't matter how many shots I could get off, I just knew that it was something that no one else that I knew, had. He knew the value of it but I didn't and I didn't care but I lead him to believe that I did, so I gave him a bit more than what we originally agreed upon so that he wouldn't feel as if he was being taken advantage of. It was nice, really nice and when I had it in my possession, I did something that I should not have done, I went across the street to shoot it off on the hill. That same hill that I sat on that overlooked the beautiful vegetation below, many of mornings ago when I stayed with my mom.

Three times, I shot it off in the air and on that third time my hand felt as if it was on fire. I was so high that the heat from the gun burned a little but I thought very little about it. I was mesmerized by the skyline, so I didn't notice the blood dripping down my hand but when I did, I turned to walk back across the street to find my neighbors waiting outside of their apartment as if they knew it was me. I walked in the gate with the gun in one hand and blood dripping from the other and they jumped into action. She went into her apartment and grabbed a white rag and wrapped my hand and guided me into their apartment, where she sit and doctored me up. He on the other hand, admired the beautiful piece that I had in my other hand and I felt proud about it, although the backfire from the gun could have killed me I later found out.

The next two months were filled with sheer chaos, I am aware that I'm the one that caused it. If crossed, I lashed out on those that I felt were in deserving of it, although sometime the punishment didn't fit the crime. It felt like the thing to do, the more that I did the drug the less I valued my life. I was responsible for a many incidents that happened on the Greenbrier. I believe that my neighbors knew that most of what was going out there, was me but never said anything. Things were moving so fast, that I created a game for the boys, called; lock down. No one was allowed to come in and no one went out. We did what ever the boys wanted to do, while we were in game mode. I was also able to sleep without interruption while the boys played. If someone knocked on the door, they knew not to even ask who it was, they knew the rules. When I finally decided to surfaced, I walked out to see the landlord downstairs working on the landscape and when he noticed me, he signaled for me come to the table below to speak to him. I put my finger up indicating, that I'll be down in a minute. I decided not to smoke a bowl before heading out, I closed my door and went on down the stairs. I need a favor of you? He ask, right away. I need you to do something for me off of the books. I understood right away, he knew that I would do almost anything for him because of what he's done for us. Can you take care of something for me, he ask. "I knew why he would ask things of this sort of me, it was because of the things that I do and the people that I know". When he was done explaining what he needed, I said, YES. I am happy to oblige, I replied. For obvious reasons of course.

Three weeks later he and his wife came to my apartment, to have a sit down with me. Never has this happened, at least not on the inside of the apartment. They both seemed concerned as to how this information may affect me. They must know, that I care very deeply for them; I thought to myself, they need not worry about my feelings. I received a letter from the police Dept. Stating, that if I don't relocate you soon, there will be a fine issued that will increase with each passing month; he blurted out. I almost gave him the look…he had to have known that I wasn't falling for this, however I sit in silence waiting for the rest too emerge. Don't worry, I will take care of everything; he added. With a raised eyebrow; I said OK. "I feel, that if a man goes through all of this to make up a story to get you out of his house, you need to leave and that's what we did.

Two weeks later, Glenn and I drove over too Oceana Apartments on Oceanside Blvd. He had already spoken to the apartment managers. I have no Idea as to what he told them but I was in. All I had to do was sign the lease. He transferred my deposit and rent from the old apartment to this one. I was shown two units that they had available and I chose a nice two bedroom across from the pool. It was a nice apartment, not as big as the other one but nice. The living room was small but cozy, there was a dinning room off to the left and kitchen next to it. You could walk through the kitchen to get to the first bathroom and oddly enough up the hall a bit was a second bathroom and then the master bedroom which wasn't as big however it had a sliding glass door that lead out to a small fenced in patio. I loved it, he was pleased of that.

We began the move that next week. I had enough friends that the truck was filled and emptied fairly quickly. I was grateful that most all of those that I ask to help, came through, even my brother, who had been gone for weeks. After we got everything in and put away, it was time to celebrate. I turned on the music and hooked up the mics and the party was on. This move truly gave me an opportunity to make a change in my life and yet, I chose to continued on the path, chosen. My ability to make rational decisions most of the time were distorted by irrational thoughts. I knew that help was needed however pride would not allow me to speak out on it. I was a mother during the day and a pistol pack'in mamma at night. All of my business was my own, no one ruled over me and yet all that I had to show for it was five thousand dollars, so I told myself that I had to step up my game. I needed to meet and get in good with the king pen that I heard lived close but when I was finally able to have a meeting with him; I'm not interested love, only because of the reputation that you've made for yourself on the Greenbrier; he said. "I stood before him embarrassed and prideful of even knowing that he knew who I was."

One week later, I made the slow walk back to the apartment from the store, to see that my blinds were wide open, I could see throughout the entire apartment. I walked in and yelled at my brother for leaving them open and warned that someone could come in a rob us. I closed them and walked back to my bedroom. As I extended my arm to close the bedroom door. There was a knock at the front door. I stood in silence, to see if I could recognize the voice, I couldn't. But, what I could hear, were muffled voices along with walkie talkies. My heart began to pound. I also heard them ask my brother if it was OK that they come in and take a look around. This fucker, said; YEAH. I quickly and quietly closed the door and grabbed my backpack from the bed as quietly as I could, opened the glass door and tried to jump over the fence but I fell down. I tried again with no success. I looked over in the corner and saw my sons big wheel, I stepped up on it and lifted myself over. I attempted to run but, slipped and fell on the ice cycle plants. They were all over the place. I fell forward, sliding and tumbled down the large hill in the dark. When I landed, I knew that it was a creek with curved cement when I felt pain shooting down my arm, from the landing. I got myself together and started to run and noticed that there was pain in my leg as well. I knew, that I had to push that shit to the back of my mind because I knew that I had worse things to worry about, if I got caught. I looked up to see flashlights moving around in the night. I crouched down as far as I could and rose up to steady myself to began my run in the middle of the creek with no shoes on as my socks made noises as if, the clapping of hands. So, I took them off and kept running the length of the apartments until I found an opening in the gate near the front. I slowly crept through the hole in the fence to see a lot of people standing around chillin. I walked around them, to make it back to the apartment that I left earlier. The place was full of people, I made my way through the crowd to chill along with them.

I watched people come and go from this apartment for at least an hour and a half. I wondered, if my apartment looked like this, to those outside looking in. I vowed to try harder to straighten my life up once and for all, once this shit blows over. "I can't keep this way of living, up". I finally decided to start the slow walk home. I looked around every corner, watching for anyone that looked like a cop. Finally, making it to the pool area. Slowly, I crept, making my way around to see if all was clear and when I felt confident, I made a mad dash into my apartment. My brother looked up in total surprise. What were you thinking? I ask. How could you just let the police into this apartment? How could you do this to your own sister? I continued. I waited patiently for him to say something, anything that could explain why he did this. But all he did was shrug his shoulders and say; I don't know, {looking stupid as hell}. What did they say? More importantly, what did they do? I demanded.

They ask if they could come in and search the apartment. You didn't know that they needed a warrant to get in here? I ask. No; he said. They walked around in the living room, moving shit around and then, walked in the kitchen looking in cabinets and down the hallway until they made their way back to your bedroom. I heard a lot of rustling and glass breaking. And you said nothing? I interrupted. No; he said. They were in there the longest and when they came out, they had a gun in their hand. In passing, the looked at me and said; "nice doing business with you" and they were gone. "So they came for the old man's gun" I thought to myself. Your a child! I yelled. I looking in the living room and then, walked back to my room to check the damage. It was in bad shape back here, I checked to make sure that the gun was gone, and it was. I sit on top of the clothes that were pilled up on the bed to check my wounds. I decided to clean them right away. When done, I walked back in to the bedroom and stood in silence. My shoes, clothes, books, everything was thrown all over the place. I sit again to catch my breath before cleaning up this mess.

I woke the next morning having an eerie feeling about the day ahead, it may have been from the night before but it was there and I knew I had to shake it off. I went to the bathroom to care for my wounds that now looked irritated to me. I came out and looked in the direction of my brother and thought about whoopin his ass real quick but I went into the kitchen to fix breakfast for my sons. I needed to know how they were they feeling after last night. There was no better way to get information, than over a good meal. We thought that it was y'all having fun, out here ma, says Roland. OK; I said. I laid down after breakfast and went to sleep and slept the rest of the day away. The thrill was gone, there was nothing more that I wanted in these streets. I'd been scared straight and vowed that I would calm things down in my life. I went to sleep that morning and didn't wake up until 8:30 pm the following night. I was awaken to a knock at the door. It was my friend, Mando. He hurried in and ask to use the bathroom. While I waited for him to come out, I sent the boys to their room so that I could talk to him about getting out of the dope business. When he re-entered the room he began cutting off my weight in drugs. Before I could say anything he ask if I could go out and park his car in a parking space because he didn't want a ticket; I agreed.

It was a beautiful night, I could smell the beach from where I stood in the parking lot. I should take the kids tomorrow and make a day of it; I thought. I made it to the car, got in and started it up. I looked around and found the parking space that I wanted to pull into. As I began to accelerate, a bright light shinned on the hood of the car that forbid me too see in front of me. I immediately heard a lot of shouting, that sounded as if it were meant for me. Hands up! Put them out of the window! Now! A man shouted. The lights were now shining directly in the car. I couldn't see a thing but I could hear the helicopter flying overhead loud and clear. The shouting continued and was coming from all directions, now. It took some time to get my thoughts together but once I did, I knew what this was. I began yelling; this ain't my car! This ain't my car! I could hear many footsteps running towards the car, the door flung open, I felt hands on my arms and I could hear voices but the lights were so bright, still I couldn't make out any of the faces. I was thrown up against the car and handcuffed immediately. I heard the voice of a woman behind me; I'm going to frisk you now, do you have any weapons or any drugs on your person. I was put into the back of a police car. As I sit, watching as they searched the grounds looking for what ever. They seem to have special interest in the car, I watched as other officers searched, it. I couldn't believe that this was happening, to me. The ride to the police station was the worst. All that I could think about were my kids, being home with my brother and this guy, whom I thought was my friend. I felt helpless but I knew that if given a chance, I could get out of this because they will see that I'm not the person that they are looking for.

Chapter 11

The victims

March 3rd 1995 at age, 31. I was standing in front of a judge looking at 9 felonies and I was scared as fuck. All of the legal mumble jumble had my head spinning. All that I could understood was that I was being transferred to a place called Las Colinas detention facility in Santee California for women, shit got real... real quick. I knew, in my mind, that this charade wouldn't last much longer because my court appointed lawyer was going to straighten this mess out. My wrist and ankles were shackled. The chains that were placed around my waist were connecting me too and another person. When we made it to the van, we were released of those chains around our waist to be shackled to others that had joined, two at a time. It was a long ride. The only thing that I worried about, were my children. I remembered speaking out in court in reference to where I wanted them to go, although I knew there was no guarantee that it would happen. I said a small prayer for them and myself and road the rest of the way in silence.

When we arrived at the facility, we were herded into the building through an enormous bay door. When on the inside, I noticed that it was as bright in there as it was outside. We were all separated immediately to be body searched and later brought back together to be given the rules and instructions of the facility. We were finally allowed to shower and were separated once again. I was told to go into a large room with 40 or 50 bunk beds in it, with just as many bodies as well. I wanted to come unglued at that very moment but I knew that there was a time and a place for everything. I wouldn't dare let these women know of my pain. This room was where they held me for two weeks, until I was processed, I hated it. There were fights, funk and fucking and more funk and I didn't want anything to do with none of it. I just wanted to know if my boys were good and when I was going home. It was hard being in this place with all types of women who had committed all types of crimes. This was a mistake, I shouldn't be here; I thought to myself.

Two weeks later, I was finally transferred right next door from where I was being held. It was a big module, with a steel gate that stretched from the ceiling to the floor that also stretched across the wide space, It was a fortress inside of a fortress and I was trapped inside of it. There were 12 cells that held two ladies each. The guards were in the center of these modules ruling with an iron fist. I was guided into the gate, another inmate took me to the cell number that was on the paper that I had been given. She introduced herself but I said nothing and went into the room and attempted to close the door and realized just how heavy it was and decided to leave it alone. When I turned to look at my new home, I could tell that there was someone in here with me who had the bottom bunk, so I found my way up top and put the sheets over my head and laid down. Moments later, I woke to someone yelling out; CHOW! I slowly rise up to see what this "chow" was all about. I saw the same young lady that brought me to my room, pulling a large cart inside the gate, and begin to hand out covered plastic trays and a juice to each woman that walked up to get one. I jumped down, looking at the toilet and the sink noticing how some genius welded the two together and put it in this small space. Suddenly, I realized that I was hungry but didn't want to interact with these people. I felt that I wouldn't be here long enough to get to know them. I quietly walked up to get a tray to return to my room, someone shouted out; we can't eat in the rooms. It took me a second to comprehend what was said and the fact that it was said, to me. I slowly turned to search for a vacant seat away from people at the table. I walked over to sit beside a woman who looked as scared on the outside as I did on the inside.

Two days had past, I hadn't heard anything about my kids, my apartment, nor my case, I was angry about it. Trul'ee Benevolence! The guard yelled out. I walked up to the large gate to take the letter from her hands, from your lawyer; she announced. How does she know! I shouted in my head as I looked down to noticed that it had a perfect rip across the top of the letter. I looked back at her and rolled my eyes before I knew it. Aside from all of the mumble jumble that was written on the paper, what mattered most was that he was coming to see me in three days to give me information. I counted down until the time was here. The same guard called out my name; you got a visitor, be ready in thirty min; she shouted. Get ready? with what, how? I thought. I have no clothes, shoes or a comb to rake through my nappy hair, I was angry that this was my life. I walked into the bathroom and brushed my teeth with a washcloth and used my hands to wash my face and arrange my hair. I came out and sit on the bench and watched the timid young lady get bossed around by what I assumed was her girl friend. Benevolence! Front and center; a guard called out! I stumbled to my feet, feeling exited that I was just a little closer to getting out of here. After having my hands cuffed in front of me, I was lead out of the gate. As we walked, the guard looked down with a stern look on her face; you feel better today, inmate? Without looking up, I answered; yes.

What I felt must have been written all over my face. We walked the rest of the way in silence. We made it to a well lit cubical with windows and a wall that separated the two sides with a phone on both sides. I was ask to step in and put my hands out of a small opening. She removed my handcuffs and walked away. I paced back and forth feeling very anxious but positive about what I was going to hear today. I saw a guy coming in my direction, the closer he came, the more my anxiety rose. When he touched the door, my heart nearly jumped out of my chest, Miss Lane? I stood in silence, feeling lost, that this man ask for the wrong person. Someone grabbed the door behind him, Miss Tru'lee? Hi, my name is Douglas P. The P...is for Pursuit. And that's what we're in...the pursuit of justice; he chuckled... ha ha ha.

He was of medium height, blonde haired guy with a nice smile that you could trust, or at least I wanted too. When he sit, I could smell the freshness of him. First things first; he started. Your children are in good hands with your friend Vera as you ask, the District Attorney allowed them to remain there until their father Jamie, comes from Indiana to pick them up. Now, how are you; he ask. I'm OK, I just want to get out of here; I said. Well, it may take a little while but we are going to get you out of here; he added. He began to put paper after paper on the table for me to see. It all seemed a blur but as he began to explain, I felt as if I were in real trouble. Each sheet defined a trumped up version of each crime and a determined sentence for each offense. What does all this mean for me? I ask. There are nine counts here, four of which we can say goodbye too, if we play our cards right, however you may have to take a plea on the rest but we will discuss them at a later date; he added. Let's discuss it now, I want to go home; I demanded. I have to file paperwork for your case, I wish it were that simple, just sit tight and I'll do what I can to make it sooner than later; he said as he rose to his feet. You have a good day and try not to worry OK? Thank you, I said sadly. I waited an hour for the guard to come back to get me, which wasn't a bad thing because I was mad as hell, that I couldn't get out of here when I wanted too. I just wanted to go back to my cell and take a nap, not be bothered. However, when I made it back, things were in an uproar. Apparently there was a woman that had been brought in that was sick from drugs. I didn't understand how drugs could make you sick like this, she was shitting and throwing up and shaking as if she was freezing.

She was finally taken out to the infirmary. It took a while before things calmed down. I stayed my distance from people, still hoping that my name would be called to get out of here but as days turned into weeks I slowly opened up to a few of the women. I watched and learned things that were not taught on the outside of these walls, like how to make a tampon, hooch, a tattoo gun and nameless others things. I knew nothing about how this system worked. Women ordered groceries, perms, hair grease and other items from money that were put on their books. For those, like myself, who didn't have money, we hustled to get what we needed from the woman who had it. I had a gift for gab, I could talk my way in and out of anything that I put my mind too. I mastered the use of my fingers as well and after all that I had been through as a child, I kinda picked it up along the way. Now seemed a perfect time to utilize it. I offered to do a woman's hair for free, so that she would be a walking advertisement me. I was a jack of all trades. I waited and it wasn't long before I was able to make my stores from other people in our small community. It was just that, women were making the best of their time in here, they were communicating, creating, teaching and learning and I was observing. I noticed that the timid young lady {Sarah}was still being harassed by [Brenda}. I found that they weren't in a relationship, just one person dominating the other, I knew all to well what this was. It was saddening to see but what was worse, no one intervened.

That next morning we were told that we were going outside. I so needed this, I hadn't see the outside since I'd been locked up and it took a toll on me. I waited for just that and finally we were outside where the sun shined bright and the grass grew green, oh my and the flowers were just as beautiful as I remembered. I sat on the bench took my shoes off, and watched the inmates. I took fresh air into my lungs. It seemed to be over as soon as it started. I found myself secretly protesting about it. I didn't want to come in but when I did, I chose to lay down to alleviate the stress that I was feeling, I was angry that I was not able to relieve it while being outside. Dinner was called an hour later. I awake still feeling angry, I washed up to join the ladies, only to witness Sarah being bullied again and watched as no one intervened, I didn't get involved either because I didn't want anything to do with anyone else's bull crap. There were women coming by the table to make appointments for their hair. I made those appointments and continued to observe the madness from a distance.

Monday morning turned out to be like any other morning in here, with the exception, that I was going to court today and I was very optimistic about the outcome. I was going home today; I told myself. I was called to the gate to be handcuffed to walk through. Those of us that were going to court, were put in a holding cell together. There were other women from other pods that shared a cell together across from where we were as well. Finally, one hour later, most of us that were brought from our pod were handcuffed and shackled and led to a van. I wondered where they were taking us but I dare not ask. We road for a long time on the highway and when we got off things looked a little familiar. I ask one of the other inmates if this was near Oceanside, yea, this is vista; she said. We were herded into another facility to be put into yet another cell and held there awaiting our time to be heard in court. I waited and waited. I looked up at the time, realizing that it was now 4:30 in the afternoon and something inside of me, indicated that I wasn't going before the judge today. It was 5:40 in the evening when the lawyer came in to speak to me. He had no new information, just that he filed the paperwork today. So why did I have to come here? I ask. They have to bring you here for your court date although it may be me, that goes in for you because unfortunately this is how the system is set up; he said. He continued to tell me about my case and then he was gone.

The ride back seemed even longer than the ride there. I was angry and disgusted that I had to remain in this system for something I didn't do. I needed to go home to my children and nobody cared. Finally, we're back to this hell hole. I noticed that there were two more ladies added to the pod. I was livid because they were loud, talking back and forth to one another, laughing out loud and just having a good time. To avoid it all, I went to the cell to check out for the night. I walked through to notice Sarah sitting outside of her cell on the floor with her face swollen. She had been crying, she looked so helpless to me. I moved swiftly, before I knew it, we were nose to nose, why don't you fight somebody your own size? Bring your ass own; I taunted. The two ladies that had just came in, suggested that we lock down in one of the cells to fight, so that the guards won't know what's going on, she added. If your caught fighting, that's another charge tacked on to your case. Enough said, I said out loud. One of the girls ran to her cell to return with a small jar of Vaseline and proceed to rub it on my face and arms. Brenda walked over and the door was closed behind her. It was just her and I going at it. She was strong but I was stronger, I let all of the pent up rage inside of me come out on her. Careful not to get too loud, to bring attention to ourselves, I could hear her whimpering beneath me, I slowly and cautiously let her up.

We stood in separate corners and got ourselves together before I called out to ask the guard to unlock the door, as I was instructed to do. I walked out first, so that the guard could see me, since this was my cell and when the coast was clear I told her to come out. Every since that episode, Sarah was allowed to move to another cell, not to be bothered by Brenda again. The temperature between Brenda and I was cold but I was fine with that because, I made a friend for the remainder of my stay and the level of respect that I gained was above all else, the most important. The next week was yet another court date that I wasn't allowed to attend. The brutal ride there and back was enough to send me over the edge. Not being able to get out and go home was even worse. This lead me to finally call Vera, collect. I talked to the kids, which I had avoided for quite some time because of the pain that I imagined that it would cause. The first thing that the boys wanted to know was, when could they visit. I wasn't in favor of them seeing me locked up like an animal, so I made up a story that a child would understand...

I ask the guard if they could summon my lawyer for me because I had a plan. Two months had gone by and I was loosing hope that I was ever going to get out of here. As the day passed, I could feel anxiety building inside. Benevolence! I heard the guard yell, you have a visitor; she added. Wow, that was fast I told another inmate. I went back into my cell and paced around in the small space, while waiting for them to call my name again. Finally, my name was called. I was handcuffed and taken to the same type of cell that I met him in before. As i waited for him to come, I constantly watched to see if anyone were walking in this direction. Finally there was a silhouette coming through the sea of officers that were standing around but as he moved closer I realized that he wasn't my lawyer. Coming even closer, I knew that I had no idea who he could be and this made me a bit nervous.

He stood next to the door waiting to be let in, I could see his whole body through the window of the door and what a nice one it was. He had dark wavy blonde hair about shoulder length, a nice built with a large bulge in his pants. When he stepped in, I couldn't help noticing how his leather jacket touched his upper abs. I gave him a 10 right away. Miss Benevolence? He ask. Yes; I responded. My name is Detective Spears. I'm here to inquire about an incident that happened in front of the apartment building where you lived on Greenbrier avenue. I'm sorry' what incident, sir? May I record our conversation; he ask. I have nothing to hide but no you can not; I said. Let me refresh your memory; he added. "There was a young lady who says; that it was you who slapped her with a large wine goggle across her left cheek that left her needing seventeen stitches across her face. My nerves felt like volts of electricity running through my body. I knew that I had to concentrate on my facial expressions. Only because of all the movies that I've seen in the past, suggest that this was the way they got their man. I found his eyes and locked in and admitted; I was there but it wasn't me. But she was sure who her attacker was, she repeated words that you were known by others to have said; he added. Again, I found his eyes and locked in; I was there but it wasn't me, sir.

He rose up from his seat and turned; by the way? I was also told; the same evening, you were seen shooting at a guy that goes by the name of Butcher; what do you know about that? Holding eye contact, I have no idea what your referring too, sir. Alright ma'am, I'm sorry for wasting your time however I am still investigating these cases and if any one of these point back too you, I'll come back and slap a few more years on too what your already facing, I promise; he snarled. His threats did not fall upon deaf ears. I heard him loud and clear. He scared me. The accusations, the threat, it made me feel as if one of my layers had been peeled back but with every fiber in my body I held it together. See you soon…. Miss Benevolence; he said, as he exited the room. I watched as he walked out and looked back at me, as if looking for a sign of weakness, that I was too afraid to reveal. I sit in that cell thinking about these things that he was accusing me of. It felt as if the air had left the room, all that I could do was put my head down and close my eyes.

Two days layer…Benevolence! You have a visitor; the guard called out. It was my lawyer this time. He had a brake in the case finally, the DA was offering me a plea. They suggested that if I cop to the lesser charges, than I would have only five years to do as oppose to the 10-20 that came with the full 9 count. What? "they can't pin that shit on me" The nine counts ain't mine anyways because it wasn't my car nor were those my drugs that were found in the car. The police knows this, the assault with the deadly weapon, possession of a firearm without a license to carry and having paraphernalia on my person. Was all that they had on me, I agreed to the plea. I was confident with my decision but in the meantime, I wanted and needed a transfer to a facility close to my children so that Vera could bring them to see me. I knew that he was the man that could make this happen. Benevolence! You have court, she yelled. I dreaded the whole process, it was literally an all day affair. When I made it there, the lawyer came in to tell me that I will stand before the Judge today and boy did that give me the jitters. I was shown the DA from across the room. I was actually grateful to see the guy who helped me, by placing my children with Vera, which was the best because their dad never came to get them. They were going back and forth in reference to the car that I moved. Soon, things got quiet and they began to whisper among themselves and then the DA ask for a continuance and the judge granted it, he also granted the transfer that we ask for.

 I was held in a cell with three prostitutes that had been drinking and talking loud between them. Finally, the next morning, I was relocated and taken to a place that resembled a giant spaceship inside. The two tier guard station were lit up behind the tinted windows like a large control station. From where I stood, I could see the small illuminated lights on the control panel. There were three large two tier modules surrounding the guard stations that stood as tall as the ceiling above them. Myself and two other women were escorted to the gate, when inside we where taken to our cells and the door were closed and locked behind me. I was alone, finally able to loose my cool and that I did, quietly of course.

The next day was clearly a new day for me, all that I needed was a shower; I told myself. I looked out of my cell and saw a curtain to my left, I looked down and saw water on the floor in front of it and knew that was it. So I grabbed what was given to me and made a mad dash. I could hear someone speaking about a fight that must have happened right before I made it here last night, that's the reason for the lock down; I thought. It was a beautiful Friday morning. I could partially see the sun through the small windows at the top of ceiling. We were told that we were going outside today which was amazing timing. I so, looked forward to feeling the sun on my face and taking in the fresh air. Later, we were given instructions as to how we should act and what is expected of us. We were also told, what would happen if we got out of line. An hour later, it was finally time to go out. There were five guards there to escort us out without hand cuffs. We were told to put our hands behind our backs and clasp our fingers together. We were all instructed to cross over on the right side of the room and stay close to the wall. We were also told to walk on a green line that had been painted on the floor beneath us. When we took a few steps, there was a voice heard on the guards walkie talkie and then we were told to stop. There was talking heard in the line behind me, no talking got dammit! The guard yelled! I waited, and listened to find out why we were ask to stop. Suddenly from around the corner they came, we watched as other inmates walked by us in silence, with their hands behind their backs as we are. I paid close attention as they walked in unison on a red line. When they passed, we were told to continue. I could see the outdoors in the distance through huge triple pane glass windows. There was a door that had pane glass in the center but had steel all around it, that gave you the understanding that "you ain't going nowhere."

We were herded past a huge guard station and told to stop again, the guards in the station buzzed us in. When I walked in, all that I saw were four walls of concrete, it felt as if I were in a big cardboard box. There was no grass, trees or a place that the sun could seep in, this was because of the catwalk above blocked all signs of life, out. I was very disappointed, there was nothing to do in here but walk around in a square, shoot at a rim with a basketball that was flat. I hated being in here, more that I did being in the other facility. I sit in silence, waiting to be taken back to my cell. To my surprise, the women in here were a bit different than I expected. More compassionate, nurturing and giving for the most part. As the days pass, one after another were coming to me introducing themselves and wanting to know who I was. At no time, was I made to feel uncomfortable, as I settled in to my new norm. Most, had shown me a part of being a woman, that I hadn't experienced in a while now, this made my stay here, tolerable. I was involved in many different activities before long, with writing being. I continue with my singing and writing songs while being locked down. Poems became a thing with me because of my experiences throughout my life. When I traveled back in time, my memories became overwhelming to me, so I needed a way to cope with them. Including a {jailed house}relationship which was quite an experience as well but due to my inability to connect emotionally; {is how she explained it} it didn't last long.

Going to court this morning put me on edge. I worried about things that I couldn't control but there was one good thing, the time it took to get there was cut in half because it was only a short drive away however waiting in that holding cell was still the worse. I stood in the courtroom watching the two lawyers go at it with no resolution in sight. I went back to the cell feeling as if all hope was gone. Elizabeth held my head in her hands, looked into my eyes and told me, too trust the process. Two days later she was released on a time served.

Although happy for her this made me sad. I moped around in my cell all day. But, once I started to sing, I couldn't stop. The more that I sang, the more I wanted to continue. It was beautiful, I had created a beautiful lullaby for my children. Later that evening, I was finished and I tried it out on the ladies….They loved it. My joy had been restored. I thought, that I had written a song that voices would never sing.

Two days later, my lawyer came to inform me about the case. Here I go, worrying about things that I can't control again. The 7counts has been dismissed, he said, they couldn't prove that anything in that car belonged to you. However, the deadly weapon charge and the drug paraphernalia found, would be yours if you decide to take the plea bargain, along with that you would be given three years probation as well. OH, one other thing; If you decide that you want to move this to a trial, in other words, try to fight it and you lose, you will have to do a ten year stretch. I looked into his eyes…. if I take it, when do I get out of here; I ask. Well, if you take the plea, I have to go back to let them know. We then go back to court to get a release date for you. Where do I sign; I ask, with excitement. I watched as he left the small cell, remembering what Elizabeth said, trust the process.

Three days after his visit, my children came for a visit. They had grown so much in 6 months. I was elated but saddened that I couldn't hold my babies in my arms. They were here and I listened to everything that they had to share with me in the short time that we had together. When the visit was over, I told them I wanted them to hear something and I proceed to sing their Lullaby to them.

Rock-a-bye babies

Rock-a -bye loves

Giving the praise, too him up above

> Mommy will love you, no matter what
>
> Rock-a-bye babies, from heaven above
>
> He's there to watch you, when I'm away
>
> for you I pray, every day
>
> you'll feel his presence, like the morning dew
>
> Just think of your mommy, cause I'm thinking of you....

Short and sweet; I said, as I watched the smiles grow on their faces. I turned to Vera and thanked her, kissing my boys through the glass and watched them leave my sight.

One week later....Benevolence!! Your going home! A male voice shouted. I couldn't control the tears, nor did I care who saw them, I yelled out loud but quickly remembered that there were women in here that weren't getting out as of yet and some were awaiting life sentences, so I kept it quiet. This was the day that I had waited on for six long months. This was quite a journey, one that I never want to repeat again. I walked through saying my goodbyes. I came back to the cell to say a special goodbye to she who lay next too me. My mind wouldn't allow me to think about what I would do when I got out, so I just sit smiling looking like a crazy person, waiting for them to come and get me. The process of release was long and drawn out. The walk was slow but steady and when I made it to a room where I was given back my street clothes to put on, they didn't fit. I had gained a massive amount of weight and I hadn't realized it. I was given a rope to run through the belt holes of my pants, I tied it and pulled my shirt "which I found to be smaller as well" down over the pants, it didn't matter because I was ready to go.

 I was walked around to another room with a window and given my backpack and all items except those that were confiscated to build their case against me. Finally, through too a room to wait to be joined up with another inmate that was being released as well. After twenty minutes or so....the door opened too freedom. The first thing that I noticed was the sun on my face. I could hear the door close behind me and deciding not to look back. Goodbye and good luck, I said to the lady that was released along with me. I kept walking in the direction of the sun, until I reached the front entrance of the parking lot. Not knowing what direction to go, only grateful to be going. I saw a car ride past me as I begin to walk towards the main road in hopes of coming up with a plan to get me closer to my boys. It was quite a walk down the hill, as far as I could see. I could see the city below which pushed me to walk faster. The car that I saw back at the jail pulled up beside me, it was the young lady that was released with me. Would you like a ride? She ask. I'm going to Oceanside; I replied. That's OK, Get in, she added.

Pulling up in front of the apartment building brought on an array of emotions. I thanked Lori for the ride and said my goodbyes and wished her well. When they pulled off, I stood there in front of my old apartment building on the Greenbrier remembering my past life, here. I dried my tears and walked through the gate. I took several steps and heard a child cry out, it sounded as if they were hurting. I heard it again and realized that it was my child and then I heard another chime in...Ma!! As they all came running towards me the tears began to flow profusely. I was finally able to hold my children in my arms, this seemed to bring life to my soul. I held them until the pain inside of me subside. Finally, letting them from my grasp, my two youngest grab a hand each and guided me toward the stairs. As I walked up the stairs, I looked in the direction of my old apartment, it looked unoccupied to me and I couldn't help remembering how lived in it looked when I was there. I walked into Vera's apartment to see that everything was as it was before I left, with the exception of the two extra large boxes that sit in the corner of the dinning room. I gave Vera a hug and sit down holding all of my kids on my lap at once. Her one bedroom, one bath apartment was packed with her and her son, my kids and now me. This took something out of me, we were homeless, yet again. She cared enough to allow us to camp out at her home until I got on my feet. She and I sit and caught up on current events in her life. I finally ask, what happened to the rest of my things? My son told me that you had been taken by the police that night. In the beginning, no one knew how long you were in, for. The police brought the kids her, they thought that I was a relative, you knew that I would get the kids? She ask. Yes of course, I said. After thirty days had passed, I talked to Glenn to see if he could help and he did. He found these big boxes to pack your things and we all moved you out of the apartment, together. Glenn stored your larger things in a storage on the other side of this building. I could see that she had my stereo equipment up here in her apartment however I wanted to go down right away to take a survey. She and I walked down, talking and laughing, while I played with my boys. We opened the large door to notice that my furniture was gone right away. All that I saw were boxes and the frame to my bed and nothing else. I slightly looked through my things and closed the door behind us. When we made it back to the apartment, I called Glenn to inquire about my furniture, he admitted to having it all. What was I to do? I had no home to put it in, so there was no need to protest, I thanked him for his help and hung up.

That evening, I offered to cook dinner for us, sent the boys outside so that she and I could talk. I quickly admitted to her; that it was hard for me to come here to stay, being homeless felt like the end of the road for me. If it wasn't for my children maybe I would have come out a different person than when I went in. I also told her about the fight in jail and why. You risk your freedom for another person? That was honorable but stupid; she admitted. I was pissed about my own shit as well; I admitted. I needed to know, what was Jamie's excuse for not coming to get the boys? I know that it was a big responsibility for him; I said. But, the kids could have went into the system. As a matter of a fact, they were supposed to go, I have no family here that they knew of! I yelled. I wouldn't have dared relied on my true family, I can't remember them ever being there for us. Jamie said, you knew that he didn't have a job. That's not what he told the DA. I just thank God that they allowed them to stay here with you. Thank you, Vera. I called all four of the boys in for dinner and we ate laughing and having a good time.

Three days later, there was a knock on the door, her son looked out and whispered; it's a white man. I had a feeling that this would be for me, so I made my way to the door to answer it. Hello; my name is Michael's, Mr. Riley Michael's. I am an officer of the probation department of San Diego County, may I have a word with Miss Benevolence please? This is she; I answered. With a stern voice, have you been using drugs today? No; I replied. Surprised at how he started the inquiry. I want you to pee in this cup, he said as he handed a small plastic cup with a lid on it, in my direction. If you have used any mood altering substance, the officer outside will handcuff you and take you right back to jail where you will serve your full sentence. Every word that he spoke after that, was followed by a threat of taking me back to jail. If there was a point to be maid, he was there to make it. I was scared shitless and he knew it. He walked through Vera's home looking through drawers, cabinets and closets. He even looked under her bed. He made sure that I was beside him every step of the way, as he held me captive with his threatening conversation. I looked at my children's frightened faces, feeling helpless. He turned to face me, open your eyes....wide; he said in a harsh tone. I did, as he ask of me. He looked into my eyes as if looking for evidence that I had been getting high, he paused and pulled back taking the small plastic container from my hand and walk towards the door. He turned in my direction, when I come back here, I better not find anything fishy or I will, lock your ass up! He spoke in a tone as if he were talking to everyone in the room. When he walked out, my lungs didn't want to cooperate with what my brain was telling it to do. I just couldn't breath, Vera walked over, gave me her inhaler, and a hugged me until I was finally able to relax and breath. I held my kids tight, telling them that we are OK, now.

Pulling myself up by my boot straps seemed a long way off for me. I had been going in circles for two weeks after that. I was starting my life over and I couldn't help feeling sorry for myself. Yes, my boys had their mother back but I had yet too find myself. Early Sunday morning as I sit at the window that faced the parking lot, looking down at the dumpster, I felt empty inside, I was a person with no purpose. I knew that I had to shake this feeling inside for my boys, so I did what makes me feel better and that was to clean for now. As and I began wiping off the counter and cleaning out her cabinets, I was startled by a loud thud. I turned towards the door to see the shadow of several bodies outside of her window. Damn! I said to myself. I watched as Vera ran from her room, feeling the thud as well. Then there was another, she swung the door open to see Mr. Michael's standing with several officers that proceed to walk past her to enter the apartment. Mr. Michael's stood firm and instructed them to turn the place upside down.

Vera and I watched helplessly as the officers did as they were told. They began pulling out the kitchen drawers, dumping them into the sink. Another officer was pulling out the silverware, pots and pans from the cupboards. I couldn't believe what I was seeing, there was nothing that either one of us could do about it but sit where we were told, to watch. I looked over to console Vera in some way and saw the tears running down her cheeks, it made me sad to see her like this knowing that it was my fault as to why this was happening. They were all over the apartment, now moving into the bedroom and the bathroom area, which from where we sit made it hard to see them and what they were doing. We could here things being gone through and thrown about in the bedroom and then it was quiet.

I was tuned in, curious as to what made them stop. Suddenly, three of them walked out with something in their hands observing it closely. One of the officers signaled for Mr. Micheal to come over to where they stood. I never took my eyes off of the prize, I wondered what this could be that has them so intrigued. When the officers dispersed, I was able to see that it was, a medium sized machete with a decorative black handle, is that all? I questioned. I watched as Micheal's turned around to face me but as our eyes met, another officer walked towards him with something in his hands as well that broke his gaze. I watched as he looked down to examine what it was, when his eyes rose to meet mine again, he seemed to have a look of anger in them. Didn't I tell you; if something smells fishy, that I am going to take you back too jail? He shouted. Afraid to speak, I responded with a nod. I'm waiting on an answer; he snarled. Show me your arms; he ask, as he reached for me, my body began to involuntarily shake. He checked my left arm and then my right, do you take it between the toes? He ask aggressively. I don't know what your talking about, sir; I said. Are you shooting up? He shouted. Careful of my tone; No, I answered. He turned to the officer standing behind him and reached out to receive the machete and turned back to me; is this yours? Since we all know that you like fighting with deadly weapons, get up! Put your hands behind your back, your under arrest, anything you say will be…..Those are my syringes! I'm a diabetic! Vera yelled. And, as far as that knife, it belongs to my oldest son….this girl ain't done nothin' since she got out. With the handcuff's on, I was walked outside to the beginning of the stairs and he stopped, turned, ask for the keys from one of the officer's and set me free. I'll be back; he said. He walked passed me and down the stairs, I felt the tears escape my eyes and tumble down my cheeks.

Once I got my head together, I called the lawyer in charge of my case to see if there was something that he could do to stop this harassment. I waited for his response most of the evening. The next day, I wanted to call him back but didn't want to seem too aggressive. it was hard concentrating on anything else without thinking about that call. However, I did think about how grateful I was that my kids weren't there yesterday to witness that horrible shit. Vera and I had to rush to get the apartment back in order before the boys made it home from school, it was just short of a miracle, the time frame that we had to do it in. It was 7:30 in the evening, when I finally received a call from him. Miss Benevolence, so sorry for the delay; he said. I have been in and out of court all day but I received your message. Thank you for returning my call sir, as I slowly began to explain the reason for the call, tears began running down my face. I'm sorry that you had to go through that; he said. I've heard that he does this scare tactic with all of his parolee's, however there is a program that each states offers that will allow a felon to do their probation in the state where they are originally from, it's called an interstate compact. I will have to file this motion in court, I see no reason as to why they wouldn't allow it, unless there is another case pending. I remembered, at that moment, the detective coming for a visit while I was in jail. I slowly drug my words; there was a detective that came to visit me in jail; I explained. I know; he said. Well he hasn't filed any motions to have you detained as of yet, so lets move forward with this; he exclaimed. It didn't put my fears to rest but he made me aware that Mr. Micheal is well within his rights to inter the home if he feels there were probable cause. It was just a waiting game.

Chapter 12

Do or Die

Being home seemed more intense this time than any other or maybe I was just out of sorts after riding two and a half days from California. We rested most of the day on Sunday after making it in late Saturday night. The boys were a bit hesitant around their father who was attempting to restore lost time in a day. I appreciated that he allowed us to come back to his home. There were no assigned duties, nor were their any discussions of us rekindling a relationship. I was grateful for this because I had changed internally and he was not a priority any longer. My priority was to find the probation department and enroll my children into school. It took me a while to find the probation department, I thought that it was in the county city building but it was across the street. Once inside, I was introduced to a Miss Davis, who turned out to be a nonchalant type of woman. Everything was done by the book, which made it a lengthy process. All of the paperwork, the phone calls to California to check this and that and to finally be ask to pee in a cup. I was told that I would have to report once a week and take a random pee test for three years. To establish a rapport, you must come on time and gradually over time, you will be allowed to come every other week; she replied. When I walked out of the office I felt bewildered and powerless. After I finished with her, my job search began. I wanted to be enthusiastic about about my journey in life but the fact that I was back at square one only depressed me even more. I would sit and go into deep thought about where I'm at thus far, it was pretty pathetic. It's definitely time for a change.

But of course, that change didn't come right away for me, as a matter a fact, I knew that it wouldn't be for a while because I still wanted to get high. The craving was as it had always been, intense. When I found out that I was no longer required to give them a urine sample, something clicked inside, that put me on a search for methamphetamine. It seemed as if everywhere I looked, I couldn't find it, which landed me back to what's familiar. I hadn't been home three months now and I was out of control. I saw myself with that gun that I'd stolen, threatening with the appearance of it, for what I thought I needed.

Coming down from the high, logic started kicking in. I called my cousin Roland to come and get me again, from off a shady side of town, in a shady house that's on a shady street, where I chose to hide out. He dropped me off at the ER, as I ask and pull off. I'll be OK from here; I told him. It was there, that I remained for 30 days, Detoxing. It was not easy for me this time. I suffered through out this process. After being in for 26 days, there was talk of me being released. I knew in my heart that if I went home, that I would surely use again. I begged and pleaded with the three social workers that were assigned to my case, to please, find me a facility too continue my treatment in.

At this point, nothing else mattered more to me than staying clean. I shared with Miss Eva, that going home was a trigger for me, I'm not sure that I'll survive; I added. From the look on her face she heard me loud and clear. I can empathize with what your going through, she whispered. I knew that there was not a text book made, that could help her to understand just how powerful this drug is or what it kills inside of you. Regardless, if she was in my corner or not, I had no choice but to trust her. Two days before my release, she walked in grinning from ear to ear; I have good news; she quietly shouted. There is a place in Indianapolis called, First Step. They have an opening for you. I then noticed her smile fade away as she mentioned... the bed will not be available until the 20th of next month. That's only four weeks away, I believe in you; she spoke with compassion. I could feel the tears rolling down my face.

I went into survival mode and began begging and pleading for my life. Please find me an alternative place until the bed becomes available. Can I stay here at least? She quickly reminded me that I was poor, by telling me that medicaid would not pay for an extended stay. I'll go back and speak to Tom in hopes that he knows people that I don't, OK. Dan was another case manager who actually came to us with an alternative. There is a bed available at the Salvation army, Harbor lights facility there in Indianapolis; he says. It's co-ed however, you can stay until your bed becomes available at First step. The only problem is, that it won't be available for two weeks. We believe that you will take all of the precautionary measures to stay out of those sticky places, we believe in you, Trul'ee. I appreciate the fact that they believe in me but I need to believe in myself in order for this to work. I bowed my head and thanked them for all of their efforts.

The feeling that one has, just being released was overwhelming. The unfamiliarity of your surroundings, the newness that's felt about the faces that you've seen before. Well, I didn't feel that. Instead, I felt an abundance of fear, anxiety and paranoia. I walked over to the chair and I sat down for what felt like only a minute and turned to Jamie, I need to talk to you please. Alright; he replied. I let out a sigh before speaking, I'm scared; I admitted. I'm scared that I'm going to use drugs again, looking into his eyes, I continued... I want to do better, so that I can feel better and be an even better mother to my children. I don't want to live like this anymore, this has to work this time because if it doesn't, I will go to prison or surely kill or be killed. So what does this have to do with me? He ask. I need your help; I pleaded. With what; he snapped. I have two weeks to remain here before I can go to Indianapolis for treatment. I'm begging you not to have anyone in here that does drugs or have them in their possession....please; I begged. Like I've told you before, this is my house, girl, you and nobody else gone tell me how to run it! OK; I said. I rose up slowly and walked to the boys room where I sit on their bed and cried silently. I remained in there all day to avoid any communication with him. When my kids came in from school, I interacted with them in the bedroom as well, until bedtime. They bathed and we all laid down telling stories until we fell asleep. Later in the evening, I was awaken by rustling and the sound of people attempting to whisper. This took me back to a time when I tried to stop using drugs in the past, it scared me to tears to think that I could travel that road again. I laid still, holding my youngest in my arms, waiting for the storm to pass. Finally, they were gone and sleep didn't come easy. I tossed and turned, trying to fight off my demons with desperation. By morning I was exhausted, I got up and got the boys ready for school. I really didn't want them to go because, I would then be here alone in my thoughts. I looked around and decided that I am going to conquer my fears. I've always found peace in cleaning and because I was allowed to have most of my day uninterrupted by him or anyone else, I took my time and did it well.

When I lived here before, I was the type that stayed too myself. Mainly because, the friends that I acquired when I was young, were chased off or stop coming around due too my circumstance. I had no real friends and my family was never really close, so this made it easy for me to digress back into the person I once was. As the day came to an end, I felt that if only I could remain within these four walls for the two weeks, I will be OK. Finally, the day came that I needed to go to the store for food, my heart sunk. Shopping with Jamie was not an option for me, we have never shopped successfully together without something being said or done that made me feel like snatching his head off his shoulders. I found the strength to go alone, still, I feared that I would see someone that I knew that sold the drug or smoked with me. So, I decided to wait for the kids and take them shopping with me. Turned out to be a good idea, the kids enjoyed it and it was very therapeutic for me as well.

Finally, the day was here. It was time to leave. I stayed up most of the night playing around and loving on my kids, which left me tired but for a good reason. All of the hugs and kisses helped me too realize that this was the best thing for us all. I said my final goodbyes and jumped on the bus. My thoughts were all over the place…what if this doesn't work? What would be that thing that would set me off, to make me want to storm out? My negative thoughts were consuming me, I had to redirect.

When the bus pulled into the station in Indianapolis my heart fluttered. I stepped off slowly to see a woman that seemed to know who I was just by looking at me. I guessed that all of us addicts have that look about us; I thought. She walked up to me; are you Trul'ee Benevolence? She ask. Yes I am; I replied. She and I walked towards a mini van. I stopped and thanked her for coming. Your welcome dear. I've been where you are now, trust the process; she said, as we got in and drove off. I remembered hearing that same saying in jail, trust the process. Driving for what seemed like a short distance, we parked and I followed her in. She and I walked into the foyer where there were quite a few people there doing what looked like going through donations that had been brought in. I was told to have a seat and that someone will be here to get me, soon. I sit a little longer than I'd hoped. Finally, a tall dark skinned man with a mustache and a full beard came into my view. He introduced himself as Howard, one of the directors here at the facility.

Hello Trul'ee, how was the ride here? He ask. It was OK; I answered. Thank you for allowing me to come; I added. This is what we are here for, follow me; he said. He led me through a dimly lit hallway that opened up into a large sitting area where several people sat around reading and talking among themselves. On the other side were offices on either side of the hallway. He stopped in front of one of them and opened the door and told me to have a seat. With a smile he sat in his chair and pulled out a manila envelope and began with a whole slew of questions. The more he ask the more irritated and uncomfortably worthless, I felt. I couldn't wait to be done with this torture. Forty minutes later, finally he's done. He wrote something on the envelope and filed me away. I watched as he stood to his feet, follow me, please. He announced that he's taking me on a tour of the facility. We walked in silence for a while, We walked through the outdated but clean building. We passed through a lunchroom that looked to be converted from a gymnasium that might sit about sixty people or so, I thought to myself. We continued to walk through, to a room with book shelves loaded with books and board games and then on to the laundry room that was just off to the left. Last but not least, was where I was too sleep. It was outdated as well but clean, I could see that there were three other women that shared the room with me, although they themselves weren't there but their things, were. You will have too get your own bed linen from the laundry room; he said, most everything that you need are provided here however, those things that you want, you'll be responsible for them yourself.

The first week was uneventful, my roommates showed me the lay of the land so to speak, they tutored me as to what was expected of me during my stay here. There were a number of N/A and AA meetings that I was responsible to make in and outside of the building. As I approached the second week, I began to feel agitated about everything, as if I were loosing my coping skills. I needed someone to talk too however this took a while, by then it was time to move on to First Step For Women.

The ride up Washington street wasn't long at all. We pulled up to an ordinary two story brick building, that I later learned was the residence for nuns back in the day. Knowing this, made it special to me right away. When we walked up to the door, it was quiet and the further in that we went, I could feel the presence of peace. I was told to sit and that someone will be out to get me. Finally, a lady came out and guided me to a large room with three desks inside. Hello, my name is Amanda, what brings you here, Miss Trul'ee? She ask, as if she didn't already know the answer. The question took me so much by surprise, that I couldn't find the right words to say. Everything that ran through my mind had a bit of sarcasm attached to it. I'm here to learn how to live without the use of drugs; I finally blurted out. Well, your in the right place, she added. As the questioning began, I felt myself drifting off in thought. I couldn't believe that I had the chance at a normal life, I just knew that I would die out there in those streets. You can find the rules placed through out the house, she said, breaking my train of thought. but here are four that are very important that you should know to remain in the house, she added. # 1. No violence # 2. Be respectful of others and their property. # 3. Be polite to all staff. # 4. Report too all scheduled meetings. # 5. Make at least two meetings a day, if you have no job and one meeting, if you do. # 6. Do assigned chores. # 7. Meet with your counselor once a week with updates. You will fit in perfectly, most of the ladies here have jobs and cars and will give you a lift to meetings outside of the house. There are nine rooms in the house with two beds a piece in each. As far as food, you are allowed to eat what ever you wish as long as there are no names written on them. The house will apply for food stamps on your behalf, while you reside here. You are required to find employment in a timely fashion however we make allowances for detoxing time. You are also required to save at least 60% of you earnings each week towards after care,{an apartment, etc}. Do you have any questions; she ask. Yes, are there any therapist available for us? We have counselors on sight however, if your in need of one, we can set you up with one within our network; she answered with a smile. I don't know why but I felt like I ask the wrong question. We have someone here around the clock if you were to ever need someone to talk too, OK; she added. Thank you, I said. Now, let me take you up to your room and show you around. When we made it upstairs, I stood waiting for her to finish getting linen out of a closet near the stairs, she then walked me to a room that had the number nine on the door and announced that I shared a room with a young lady named Veronica who was at work at the moment I watched as she turned and left me alone.

I noticed that this young lady loved art because of all of the small paintings hanging on the wall over her bed. I stood admiring each piece from my side of the room. I looked up at the bunk and thought; I'm home for the next few months. I began to make my bed and in she came full of life, hello! She said, with enthusiasm. Hi, I said trying to conjure up a smile. I'm sorry that I can't stay and get to know you, I have somewhere to be, I'll get at ya later, OK, as she smiled and ran out of the room. I smiled and continued to make my bed. I then put my only picture of my boys over my head. When I finished, I walked downstairs in hopes that no one was in the kitchen so that I could get a snack and get back upstairs to be alone. As I looked around, it seemed that there was no one in the house but me.

By 6pm that evening, I heard the door open and people talking and laughing. I could tell that there were a few of them. I wasn't sure if I were ready to get up just yet, so I decided to stay in bed, covering my head attempting to go back to sleep. I could hear the sounds getting closer and finally they were at the door, knocking. Are you asleep? I heard a voice call out. I quietly eased out of bed and went to open the door to see three women around my age or slightly younger standing on the other side waiting to see my face. Very politely, one of them ask; will you come down to meet the rest of us? I agreed; give me a minute; I said. When I finally built up the nerve to go down stairs, I felt a bit nauseous. I stood there at the top of the stairs in disbelief that

I was going through all this over... people. I pulled myself together and slowly walked down the stairs into a room full of women with big smiles plastered all over their faces. I could immediately tell that these ladies had taken the time to develop friendships here, which is something that I hadn't done with people without the use of drugs and those friendships weren't lasting. As I move around the room shaking hands and introducing myself, I couldn't control my hands from trembling with fear. And then she touch my hand, looked me into my eyes and told me that my feelings were valid. For some reason those words made it all seem better instantly. As I sit quietly watching all of these different personalities interact together, eating dinner, laughing and swapping stories of how their day went, somehow gave me a feel of home, which was nice.

The next morning, I was alone again. I put on clothes and ventured out walking, in hopes of finding employment. After turning a couple of corners I finally found the main road. I stood on the corner looking around to check my surroundings. I noticed what must be an airport in the distance to my left. To the right, were businesses, so I began to walking in that direction. I walked a mile and a half and noticed that there was absolutely no places that I wanted to work. But on my way back, I stopped into the goodwill store just to look around for things I may need for my room when I had the money. The thought of stealing entered my mind but when an elderly lady walked up to me too ask a question about a piece of merchandise, I decided against it. I explained that I didn't work here and when she walked away, a gentleman walked up and did the very same thing. I then decided to find the manager to ask for a job. I was hired on the spot.

Happy about the fact that I was able to provide for myself and to contribute to the house as everyone else had, made me feel a bit empowered. When I gave the staff the news that I was working and where, there was no need to tell her what I made because she already knew how much I was making. She made me aware that many of the ladies had gone there for employment, it's a life line for a many of them, she explained. I would like for you to turn in your check stub every week, they'll cash it and disperse money to you, she explained. I was OK with that, there was nothing that I needed but toiletries anyways because the house provided everything else. As time passed, I moved around even more, the further that I ventured away from the house the more empowered I felt. Learning the lay of the land was exciting. I would find myself in the downtown area where the bus rides through Indy was quite amazing. On occasion I would get directions to where the meetings were being held and catch a bus there, if it were earlier enough in the day that is. My first meetings, I sit and just listened. I was amazed at how their stories matched mine however there were differences in our experiences of course. There were meeting held at the house as well, people from outside were allowed to come and sit in. After attending these meetings several times, I realized that I was the only black person in those meetings, as I was the only one that lived in the house also. However, it didn't bother me at all…..in the beginning. "She" would come in and sit near me or sometimes, next to me. She always smelled as if she had just gotten out of the shower. I smiled letting her know that I see her and put my head down, feeling shy.

When the meeting were over, I would retreat to my room only because I felt like the odd woman out, so to speak. I was OK with that as well because "she" would sometimes come up and say a few words to me, before turning in for the night. This time she sat in my room on the floor and told me a bit about herself. Her name is Sasha, she and her family are from Germany, her accent wasn't thick but when she mentioned it, I noticed a hint of it. She told me some pretty personal things about herself, as I listened with a smile on my face. One thing that raised my eyebrow, was that she was in real pain, the type of pain that was on the inside; she says. And when she feels this pain, she admits that she cuts herself and as she proceed to show me, I immediately wished that she hadn't. This was the type of thing that when you've seen it, it couldn't possibly be unseen. As I continued to listen to all of her sadness, I began to feel her pain as if it were my own. I kept seeing all of the places that she had sliced on her body, noticing the fresh ones as well. She finished by saying that this conversation was held in confidence. I thought to myself; why would she entrust all of this information with me? She doesn't even know me. But, I agreed.

The next day I couldn't get her off of my mind, I just couldn't believe that someone so beautiful could be so sad inside. But then it wasn't about the beauty or the ethnic background. I found that in life there were many different factors that tied into depression as it had with me. After that night we didn't do that flirting thing that we had done in the past. We seemed to be avoiding each other. However, the next weekend, I noticed that she seemed to walk a little different, I stopped her, to ask was she OK. She looked at me with a look that I hadn't expected and walked away without uttering a word. I didn't quite know how to receive this behavior from her because I did nothing to deserve this. When I saw her again it was later in the evening. I noticed, what looked like smeared blood on her pant leg, my eyes immediately fell to her shoe that had droplets of blood on it as well. It had to be blood; I questioned myself. But what held my attention was the contorted look on her face as she walked by, she looked as if the devil had taken a hold of her; as the old folks use to say. I was worried about her, so much that I wanted to save her, from herself. After another failed attempt to talk to her, I went into the counselors office to let them know that something appears to be wrong with her, and could someone please check on her; I ask. A counselor, name Theresa and two others that were there for shift change, left the lower level to go upstairs, where they stayed for a while. There was no conversation heard, nor was there any commotion. Finally, they all exited the stairs with items in their hands that they took to the office. Sasha came down and sit in the middle of the floor and began telling her secret to all of us that were in the room. I looked on in amazement and thought; she's spilling her guts? She admitted to everyone, that in order for her to heal from this, she must first reveal the monster inside, as she put it. I was wrong for expecting Trul'ee to carry my burdens alone and for that I am truly sorry; she added, looking in my direction. I nodded in her direction, feeling like a deer caught in headlights. I watched as she apologized to all the women for bringing this behavior in the house. She rose up and everyone hugged her and told her that they were here for her. It was a type of love that I had only seen on a sitcom or a movie.

As days moved to weeks, my existence in the house remained as it had from the day that I arrived. The ladies and I had nothing in common with the exception, that we all were there recovering from one drug or another. I tried desperately to blend in but it seemed to be in vein. When I needed a meeting they would offer to give me a ride but it felt awkward because of the silence while in the car. When in the meeting, I wanted to share about my experiences with my drug use but I thought against it because our paths that lead us here were entirely too different and I just didn't think that it would be understood around these tables. So I sit in silence and listened. I would take in what I needed from what was said in the meeting and the rest I would leave there and that's how I preferred it to be.

Back at the house, things were quiet, a little too quiet I would say. I noticed that the ladies would speak but weren't very sociable, although Sasha apologized she stopped speaking to me all together. I felt ostracized but I continued on my journey. I worked two jobs now and made my required meetings. I held my composure until the Saturday night meeting at the house, the topic was anonymity. I learned that the ladies of the house, felt that because I went to the staff weeks earlier about Sasha, that was breaking her anonymity. The words didn't bother me as much as the looks that I endured. The fact that no one spoke up for me, spoke volume about those that I shared a living space with. I thought that I was saving a life. At that moment, I thought that I should've, let the bitch kill herself. I removed myself from the meeting after listening to most of the comments on the matter. The counselor came upstairs too comfort me. I believe, that she came up to see what I was doing and how I was handling what was said about me. Her questions were sharp and full of accusation. I was very careful to answer calmly; I meant no harm, I only wanted to help her; I explained. There was silence between us, no more words were spoken after that. I watched as she left the room and waited to make sure that she was gone, my emotions got the best of me.

The next morning, I pulled myself together and went to work. When I returned to the house, I was asked to step into the office. We, believe that you may be harboring resentments; Miss Sheila said. I looked up at her in disbelief, how did you come to this conclusion? I ask, in confusion. The ladies of the house felt that you have been detached and unapproachable since you've arrived her. Not true! I said, swiftly. I have always tried to be open and receptive to the ladies here, we are all still fairly new to one another due to our schedules being as conflicted as they are; I admitted. I was ask to sign a plan of action. That entailed; that I would engage more with the people living in this house and participate in more activities. What if….. "they" don't want to engage with me? I ask. She looked at me as if I spoke a foreign language, finally, this is part of your agreement you can agree or disagree, she added.

I was furious when I left her office and there was nowhere that "I" being who I am..could defuse. I walked outside and around the church grounds crying to myself trying to find a place to be alone. I noticed a crowd of people coming out. I turned and made a path to the empty lot on the side of the house, I walked until I reached the trees that were on the far side of the property and away from anyone or anything that could hear me and screamed out in pain. Twice more, to file out all of the hurt and anger that I felt inside about my life in general. I paced in a circle, when done, I stood in one spot to decide my next move. Do I stay or do I go, was the question.

Once I calmed down, I was able to breath a sigh of relief. All negativity had been dispersed from my body. I slowly began to make my way back towards the house while wiping all evidence that I had been crying away. As I moved closer, I noticed what looked like police officers in the distance standing at the back door of the house. I continued walking and thought about Sasha and actually hoped that she was OK. The closer that I came to the house, I began to realize that their focus wasn't on anything in that house, it was on me. My heart skipped a beat, although my fight or flight instinct was heightened, my feet kept it's stride. When I made it too the back door. I stepped up on the first step, attempting to ease by everyone to go into the house, while, pretending as if I didn't see them looking in my direction moments earlier. Hello, Miss Trul'ee, my name is officer Rise and this is officer Brick, we were called because the director believes that you may be a threat to yourself or others. I looked into Theresa's eyes searching for something that I knew wasn't there. With the lack of empathy showing, I knew that it was her that called and not the director. I then turned my attention back to the police waiting patiently for them to finish. I have no intentions of hurting myself, nor will I hurt another human being, I said, sternly. I only went out near the trees where I thought, no one was paying attention, to let off steam; I added. Boy, was I mistaken; I said, while cutting my eyes in her direction. So, you are OK, he ask. Yes officer, I was taught in the meetings, how to channel negative energy; I admitted, slightly looking in Theresa's direction again. The both of them turned towards her and the three of them walked away talking among themselves.

I walked past everybody that stood outside, went in and closed the door behind me. When I made it to my room, I was able to relax and in that moment I made a decision that I was going home. I had been here almost four months now and I convinced myself that this was all that I needed from them. I will be OK until I am able to connect with recovering addicts, locally. The temperature around the house had definitely changed after that day. I put my name on the list today to be seen by the director on Wednesday. Her name is Lauren, a short caucasian woman with freckles on both cheeks and dark hair to match. I would like to withdraw all moneys that I have accumulated to buy a bus ticket too return home; I told her. She looked surprised, as if she had no idea as to what happened here a week ago. I chose not to reiterate, I just sit and waited for her response. When she finished looking in the computer; it will take two days to get things in order for you, alright? Thank you; I said, surprised that it was that easy. I couldn't help remembering how I felt when I came here as appose to now, big difference.

I found a peaceful place in my head, sit back in my seat and enjoyed the ride home. Jamie was there to pick me up. I felt as if I had some sort of an armor of protection around me. I made it home to a place of peace with the kids being at school. I wanted to go up there to surprise them but I decided against it. I figured that I would get some much needed rest instead. Before I headed for the room, I ask Jamie if I could talk to him. What now! He ask. I'm begging, not demanding; I said. Can we please keep those that are doing drugs or in possession of them out of the house? I sweetened the plea by adding; if "WE" could only stop the traffic, I think that we can afford so many thing in life, for once…. we could get our self esteem back and move on from there.

He stopped moving, stared past me and turned to looked into my eyes. Like I told you before, girl, this is my house! I do what I want to do in here; he added. Some time passed, and then he shouted back into the room…. I'll keep'em out, while still holding a look of authority. Thank you; I said, hurriedly. As days passed, I was in an uninterrupted state of happiness being with my boys. It was nice to cook dinner for them, sit at the table and watch them eat, it was the small things for me.

Making meetings was a must for me, it was a part of my survival. I would catch the bus to every meeting or if at a meeting I would catch a ride with someone to another meeting. The sad thing, was that I wasn't able to trust anyone enough to truly connect with them. I watch as friendships were made and sometimes, wished that it were me. There were times when it rained, I'd ask Jamie if I could use his car but that was a no go, based on what ever he said was wrong with the car. There were times that I had enough money to get there but none to get home. It was wearing me down, I felt alone, although I was in a room with many other people, people who say that they have been where I am.

Sitting in a meeting one night, it all poured out, I couldn't hold it in anymore. I spoke on how hard it was to continue on this road alone. I have no money and no support system and….. I stopped speaking because of the lump in my throat. I felt the sting of that tears that slowly fell to the table in front of me. I sit in silence after that, remaining, until the end of the meeting. There were a few that hugged me, telling me that it was going to get better. I watched as most of them came together talking loudly about their next destination. I moved towards the door, when a man walked up to me and ask if he could hug me. I sadly responded; yes. When he released me he held my hand and replied; it going to be alright, keep coming back, more will be reveled, and placed something in my hand and walked away. I looked down and saw a folded twenty dollar bill. I walked out into the parking lot and cried, thinking that I can make it here tomorrow.

You think your better than me, don't you! He yelled! Since you've been going to these meetings, letting these people fill your head with all that bullshit. You still ain't shit! Say's the alcohol that spoke through him. I listened but, said nothing. His rant went on for what felt like hours, I knew this guy, oh so well, I knew not too challenge him when he's like this. When I realized that he had calmed down, I felt that it was safe to go into the boys room. I lye down on the bed. I talked and played quietly with them until it was time for them to go to sleep. I loved on them, said goodnight and closed their door and went in the other room and quietly closed that door. When I laid down, it tickled me, to think that I had to tiptoe getting myself ready for bed. I knew that there had to be a change made. I thought about the changes that I needed to make until I fell asleep. It was 3:30 in the morning when I was awaken by the sound of the front door and 7am when I heard it again. I didn't say a word, because he knew that he wasn't holding up his part of the deal. As days turned into weeks, I knew that this type of behaviors was putting my sobriety in danger and I had to do something. As much as I knew that I needed a job, I believed that I needed to find somewhere to live first. I waited for the right time to talk to him and the boys, frightened that my words may come out wrong, I waited even longer. A week had passed and on the night that he and his friends decided to drink to get drunk in the house, I knew then that the next day was my time to talk.

Afraid but determined, I took my thoughts to a meeting that morning and threw them on the table, attempting to open up and receive feedback. Regardless, of what was said, I knew in my heart, that I had to go. That afternoon, I sat in the chair, watching the kids as they stumbled in the door from school, smiling, as one after another came over to greet me. When they were all settled and given their snacks, I called them all into the living room for a talk. I rambled a little in the beginning until I found what I wanted too say to them all. When I had all of their attention. Jamie; I called out, feeling as if cotton was in my mouth. I know that I've gotten on your nerves, wanting to go too all of these meetings, begging you for your car, calling you when I got stranded at one of the meetings. Well, I apologize for all of that. What you trying to say, girl? You know that the car ain't been workin good: he snapped.

I'm just saying, I know that I'm aggravating you and I don't mean to do that. So, I figured that I would find somewhere else to live. I don't know what you up too girl, just do what you wanna do, I'm gone be alright, with or without you, he replied. What you gone do with these kids? He ask. Well...what do y'all wanna do, guys? I ask, with a smile. I don't have a place to stay yet, nor do I have a job but you know that I will get one, right? You can go with me or you can stay here with him. A look of confusion came over their faces, as if I had ask a trick question. I watched as they turned, looking at each other as if searching for the answer in each other's eyes. Little Jamie's face was contorted in a way that I had never seen before. But as he spoke, I could hear the vibration in his voice. I want to stay with my daddy, ma. I was shocked to hear my babies transition from calling me mamma to ma. All of my friends, my school, my granny and my cousins live around hear; speaking in his little man voice. It stung, however I understood, he was done traveling into the abyss with me.

I tried to harbor the pain that I felt inside to the point of shaking. Finally getting my composer; are you guys sure? Looking around to find each one of their faces. Darion, was still young, I wanted to make him feel as much a part of this as the others. You know that it won't take me long to get it together, right guys. Yea ma, I know but im'ma stay, he said, without hesitation. I looked over at Roland, what about you? I feel the same, mamma. All of my friends live over here on the Lake too; he said. I immediately looked over in Jamie's direction to get conformation as far as Roland was concerned, he nodded his head in agreement. I held my arms out for Darion, I whispered; what do you want to do little man, I ask again? I wanna stay with my brother; he admitted.

My boys and I talked every day about do's and don't's and if there was anything that they needed too call me. They wanted to know where I was going, I explained that I had no idea at the moment and that they will be the first to know when I find out. By instinct, I called my cousin Roland, who I had called on for years only because he was my enabler during my addiction. Now, clean and sober, I loved and appreciated him but his home was no longer a safe or healthy place for me to be, so I hung up the phone right away and called the shelters around town. As the days passed, I guess I wasn't moving fast enough because my presence seemed to irritate Jamie. It started with him nit picking about everything, then the insults and along came the arguments, until one night he grabbed me by the neck and begin choking me because of a remark that I made that he didn't like. He let go, when he felt the piercing of the knife in his leg. He yelled to the top of his lungs; get out of my house, Bitch! I had been put out of his house so many time through out the years that I had lost count. I slowly added the knife back to the spot where I had found it and scrambled to get my things together and took them outside and put them on the side of the house to wait for my cousin Roland, who I had no choice but to call, to pick me up. I thanked God that the boys weren't there to witness yet another scene between their father and me.

On the third day of staying with my cousin, Jamie drove up in front of my cousins home with my son Roland in the car. He told him to get out and go to your mamma as he walked to the trunk and pulled out a trash bag and a white laundry basket that he set on the ground in front of my son, closed the trunk and drove off without saying a word to me. I walked up to Roland, holding out my hands to him, grabbing him and proceed to hold him tight in my arms without speaking a word. I felt all of what he could have been feeling. I was responsible for this and I would make this right with him. In the meantime, it was becoming very challenging for me to remain in their house, for obvious reasons that I choose not to mention. So I had to make a change for my sobriety.

Chapter 13

Breaking the cycle

Hope rescue mission, was the best option. I called the Homeless center, however they wanted me too be unemployed for at least 18 months or more so that I can go through their housing program for mothers and children. I couldn't do that of course because I was determined to get on my feet as soon as possible. The Hope Rescue Mission, was my hope of having a better life. It was a co-ed facility that housed women and children on the second floor behind a locked door. All of the men were located on the first floor, dinner was served on the lower level and as long as we all followed the rules we were allowed to stay. It was a big building that housed people of all different walks of life. That lead me to instill different types of rule for Roland now that we were surrounded by these types of people. He was instructed to stay close too me, when I move, you move, just like that, I said. My son and I were given our own room with two beds in it, nothing fancy but it was a place to lay our heads.

My son was settling in nicely. There were programs for the kids that lived there, that were in different age groups. Roland played the trumpet and he seemed to pull it out more while being there than he ever did at home. I could see the difference in him, there were people that were asking him to play that actually sit and listened. I loved seeing the pride in him, when he played. He and a couple of kids were ask to play in the Holiday event for Christmas. Of course my son was elated, this was his time to shine. He would practice everyday for this event. There were several different school buses pulling up taking kids where ever they went to school, when Roland's bus pulled up, I was ready. I said, my goodbyes and began my journey towards downtown. I put in applications in the few restaurants that were down there and then noticed three ladies with the same uniform on. I followed them into a car garage and through a receiving area that lead to a laundry area. I ask if they could tell me where I could fill out an application? I walked through a small door on the right as instructed and came out an employee of the Marriott Hotel.

I strive to be the best housekeeper that I could possibly be because my name was on the card that I left on the tables in each room and because of that fact, made it all the more important to me. I met some pretty nice and helpful ladies, that would assist me if I got behind. This, in time, taught me what time management meant. I began to miss my boys, I would attempt to get them on the weekends but Jamie had a reason as to why they couldn't come on this weekend or that. It angered me but I chose to channel my anger by putting in more hours at work. When I made it back to the shelter, I was happy that there were meetings being held there twice a week, because there were days when I was so exhausted, I just didn't feel like traveling on the bus to make a meeting outside.

I saved my money and took advantage of what ever there was, that was free but, fun to entertain Roland. As time passed, I decided to take another position at the Marriott. I applied and got the position of the head dishwasher that paid more money, with more responsibilities that

I could add to my work history. On occasion, I was allowed to assist the Sous-chef with plating up and preparing for large banquets, which was pretty cool. I learned quite a bit, about organization and food contamination. I was enjoying what life had to offer so far, being sober. I had my job, a roof over our heads and we are safe from harm, the only thing missing were my boys. This was a challenge for me, I didn't want to believe that he was trying to keep them away from me but yet another weekend came and went with claims that they were not available.

I worked long hours and continued to save my money in hopes that one day soon, things would turn around for us. Two weeks had passed since our last argument on the phone about our boys and finally he allowed them to come for the weekend. When I spoke to the kids, I could hear in Jamie jr. voice that he did not want to come to the place where I was staying due to the stories that he had heard from his dad. I assured him that I will protect him from all monsters and boogie men. Saturday morning, Jamie dropped them off in front of the building and pulled off again not saying a word to me. Why is he so angry about this, we spoke about this several times, which gave him the opportunity to change the outcome. I looked down and grabbed the boys, holding them tightly together in my arms, until I felt them squirm to be let go of. We walked into the building and went upstairs to the room so that they could put their things away. I noticed the discomfort in Jamie Jr's face as he looked around the small room. I could tell that he was uneasy. The other two were playing fine together. OK guys, I said loudly; you did bring your swim trunks, right? Yea! They screamed. We all changed into our swim suits and put our clothes on over them and walked downtown to the Hotel. As we walked, I could see that they were themselves again, running and playing together. They couldn't wait to get in the water, they were very patient as I signed in. When in the door, they jumped in the water as if they knew how to swim. I looked on, knowing that even though I didn't either, I would have jumped in to save them as if I knew how. They had a wonderful time, we showered and I took them up to show them where I worked and introduced the to my co-workers. I felt as if I had made an impression on them by the looks on their faces. We walked around to the restaurant to have brunch before the walk back. It was an awesome day.

When we made it back to the Hope, I took the boys on a tour of the building and collected snacks from the kitchen to take upstairs when we were done. There was a family room upstairs, that had all sorts of toys that I allowed Darion to play with, while the other boys and I played board games until we were bored. We had a very interesting conversation about things that their dad was saying. Some were pretty bad things about me. I wanted to stop them but I wanted them to feel as if they can vent about what was on their minds. I know that it might be hard to ignore, but he's saying things out of anger, and you have to try, OK? I suggested. Focus on school and before you know it, we will be in our own place, we are going to be OK. I added. The next day was sad watching the boys leave, this made me even more determined to get on my feet.

The Christmas program was slowly approaching and Roland was anxious about his debut. This made me happy to see him as excited as he was. He prepped and practiced everyday until, finally, the night of the program was here. I brought him a black vest, pants and shoes with a white shirt and cut his hair for him. He looked handsome and happy. There were three churches that were invited there to preach their sermons and my cousins church was one of those chosen. When he saw me, he had a surprised look on his face. I walked up to him, we reached out to one another to hug each other, he held me tight while whispering in my ear, you didn't have to come here, you know. Yea, I know but I had to do this on my own; I said, you have always been there for me, I thank you but it's my turn now, I added.

The program went on without a hitch, my son played beautifully and he gained a lot of recognition for a job well done. I could see how proud he had become. As time passed, the director by the name of Charlie was very helpful with our journey from that point on. She had taken a personal interest in me and my son, took us under her wing, so to speak. I thought to myself; there goes my Father, looking out for us again. I signed up for programs that she suggested that I get into, I increased my meetings because, it was hard living life on life's terms without the use of drugs. Since the staff change, things seemed a bit tense around here but she showed me the program to choose so that I may keep my job and remain in the building a bit longer. I also thought that it would a good time to reincorporate family. I loved the idea of having a real family, people to call our own, although we hadn't been very close in the past, maybe that's why it wasn't such a difficult decision for my mother to relocate to California, I wondered.

I began visiting my cousin Roland and his family, trying to form a bond with them which was difficult for me to do because of past experiences with him, however, I continued to try.

I often stayed the weekend when I requested a weekend pass from the hope. Never being deceitful, I made my cousins aware that there was an event going on at the recovery house that I wanted to attend that evening or the next. While over there, I met a lady named Rosemary. She sat on the side of the road near my cousins home in tears about her truck breaking down. I sat and listened to her share about what ever was on her mind. In time she and I became very close friends and soon lovers. She was the most sensitive woman that I had ever met. She cared about everything, from people, nature, the ecosystem and the mammals in the sea. She was such the opposite of me, which turned out to be a great thing for me and my boys. I learned things from her that I never thought I would, she was a walking book of knowledge for me and I loved it. We both agreed that we would get a place together, and that we did. We found a place on the South East side of town on Donald st. Which was awesome because, it was right across form Riley high school. I knew that this was where I wanted the older boys to graduate from because I had once went here myself.

It was a nice small two bedrooms, on bath home with a small room in the basement. The indoor porch had windows the length of the house.

She and I put our love into this house, making it our home. When all was completed it was time to move in. I talked to the new director of the Hope Rescue Mission and made them aware that we were leaving, thanked them for all that they had done for us and we were gone. I quickly found that living with a woman was pleasing. There were times that I believe that because of our ethnic differences, we may have struggled at times but by talking things out, we were able to work through them. We also had our deeply rooted issues about ourselves as well however, communication helped us through them, also.

As time passed, I felt that it was time that I had the talk with the other boys about her and how she will become a part of our lives. I was finally allowed to get the kids after yet another argument with Jamie. When I picked them up, I took them all out to lunch for a briefing on the current events. I began with her personality and how nice she is. How I believed, that she would become a great asset to our lives, not to mention, how much they are going to like her. I think that she will be good for all of us, are you guys ready to meet her? I ask. As we pulled away from the restaurant, I felt confident that all would be well. As we approached the house, I see her standing outside watering a plant that I had previously called a runt, looking as beautiful as the day I me her. She noticed that it was me and smiled, it made me smile and I knew that all was good in our world. Is this the house? Darion yelled out, as I began to slow down. Yes; I said, as I pulled into the driveway. That's her? Jamie ask. Yes; I answered. Darion yelled; she's white! Quiet son, she can hear you, that's not polite. I whispered. OK OK, he complained.

As they exited the car, they started to run in the house but I stopped them in their tracks and introduced them to the lady of the house. Hey guys, this is Rosemary. They both gave a half smiles and said hello. She politely said hello and off they went leaving us alone to join their brother. I hugged her, reassuring her that it was going to be alright. As the day progressed, the boys seemed to open up to her and by night, we all were sitting down to a hearty meal laughing and talking together. When the time came to take them home, Darion hugged her, I was surprised and so was she. They said goodbye, and off we went. The whole way home they were excitedly talking about what a great time they had at our new home. I loved it, I let them off at their dad's home and waited for them to go in, it left me feeling a sense of pride.

My son Roland was now old enough to work for the summer programs around town, so I went to my supervisor and ask if he could come there and work for the summer, he agreed. They allowed him to work in the employee cafeteria which was located on the same floor in which I worked, which was a good thing, I could walk down to check on him from time to time. I was so very proud to have him there with me, he looked so handsome in his white uniform and white chefs hat, I bragged to all that would listen. His duties included; serving food to the employees, provided by the kitchen, wiping down the serving line, stacking trays, wiping down tables, filling salt and peppers shakers and moping floors at the end of the day. I communicated with him as often as I could, in an attempt to help him manage his first job. He was proud of himself and then there was a change in him that showed that the job was no longer a good fit for him. It was OK because he is still young, I told him.

My boys came over again and when they returned home this time, they told their father about the good time they had at our house and he blew a stack. What the fuck; Tru!! Why do you have my kids around that nasty shit! I told you about that the last time; he shouted in the phone. I just listened. When I had the opportunity to jump in, he hung up on me. From that day forward, he made it even more difficult to get the boys. When I spoke too Jamie jr. on the phone, I told him that he can come home when ever he wants. It saddened me that he wasn't ready as of yet. Although Jamie Sr. never said the word No but the excuses that he came up with were too much.

Meetings were more important to me now because of all that was going on, I needed to share what I was going through to prevent a meltdown and possibly flying off the handle. There are things that I spoke to my sponsor about that I felt, which was a bit too personal for the meetings. I also informed her that I wanted to inquire about a new job, she didn't think that it would be a good idea right now with all that was going on in my life, new job, new relationship, the kids, the ex, it was all towering in. She thought it to be a good thing to work on my steps instead. I understood her way of thinking, however, Christmas was coming and I needed to make more money for the boys too have a better holiday than they ever had from me this year. This was to make up for the life they've had in the past. So I inquired at Holiday Inn downtown and got the job on the spot. It was swift, I went in made my money and came out with what I needed for the holidays. With the two jobs together it felt as if I were more stable financially and felt that it was time to buy a car of my own, as well.

It was a rose colored Oldsmobile with a beige rag top, it was very nice, something to be proud of. I began making my transition at this time as well, so the style of the car, mattered. When I decided to become a full fledged lesbian, I didn't take the decision lightly, let's just say that I knew what roll I wanted to play. I took off the makeup and lipstick, cut my hair into and Afro, changed from a women bra too sport bra's, panties to boxers and the clothes and coats that I wore were of a style of what a man would wear. I didn't just wear any clothes, they were suits, dress shirts and stylish shoes with hats {DOB}, the color were of what ever suite I chose to wear. Rosemary didn't understand what was going on, although she was very happy to help. I believe she became aware of it all when she noticed all of the attention that came with it, so this caused her to step up her game, so to speak.

She went shopping for dresses that would match any occasion that arise, she looked stunning. I also noticed that there was a bit of jealousy forming with her. The more that women paid attention to me, the more on edge about it, she became. So much to the point that she didn't want me to go out to party without her, her wish was my command because I didn't want to worry or upset her. The change and attention had affected me as well, made me feel a sort of confidence that I hadn't felt about myself and it felt good.

Sea Horse Cabaret, was owned by a little lady by the name of Doria Frank, whom I met on my first visits there. After stepping in with my lady. I walked in to see an amazing sight. It was nice in there. There were lights and the stage and a nice sized dance floor. I looked down to notice an extended hand, your looking mighty fresh; she said, with a smile on her face. I returned the handshake, Thank you; I answered, smiling from ear to ear, not knowing at the time that she was the owner. As I frequent the club, I learned about her and how passionate she was about the establishment and to the patrons as well. The bar became a focal point for many of us who had been searching for a home, somewhere to belong and be ourselves, I found that place, here. This was the place to be for me on the weekends when I wanted to unwind, see my friends and just watch a good show. As time progressed I knew that this was the place to be because I once traveled to Illinois and Indianapolis to their establishments, someone on stage would ask people in the audience, where they were from. When I mentioned South Bend there was talk and laughter of memories had at THE SEA HORSE. Which was a pretty awesome feeling.

I broke a promise to Rosemary, that I wouldn't go out without her. We conversed about it and in my mind, I felt that as long as I wasn't drinking or doing drugs nor hanging out with people that I should not have, she should trust me, until she was given a reason that she shouldn't. But she never did, as a matter of a fact things were getting worse. I wasn't able to do anything without first calming her to a point that she was comfortable with me leaving, this was no longer cute, it was an annoyance. I felt that the sex was the reason for the behavior change, so I stopped giving it to her as much and this created another level of issues.

Meanwhile, at work there was yet another employee change, this time it was my supervisor, this guy rubbed me the wrong way from the very beginning. He not only got on my nerve but everyone else as well. He was a real jerk and all of us had an opinion about him. My issues with him had somehow became so deeply rooted over the course of time that I became defiant. Not outwardly so much but inward. There were times that if he sent a message that there was something that he wanted done and didn't assign my name to it, I wouldn't do it, although it should have been me that got it done. With all that was going on, old and new, I thought that I should seek help, because I wanted to hurt someone. I felt the most pressure with Jamie, about the boys, yet again I had to argue about getting the boys that weekend and I was overly angry. More so, that I was having unhealthy thoughts about what to do about this situation. I found that our job had a program that paid for 8 free visits to see a professional and I looked into it. Still not sure because, it is still my belief that black people don't actually go in to see a therapist and it actually work for them. I struggled with the day to day, although I worked on my twelve step program, it seemed to still overwhelm me. As I struggled mentally through out the week, still finding the strength to stay afloat without an angry outbursts. I finally called and made an appointment after Rosemary hit me in the top of my head with a plastic flower pot, I laughed to shrug it off but in reality I wanted too grab her by her face and throw her to the ground. It wasn't pain that almost put me over the edge it was the rage inside.

The first couple of visits were quiet because, I had no idea what I should talk about. I heard her say; start wherever you feel comfortable. However, when I think about my past, I knew that my childhood would be off limits. I didn't want to think about it, never the less talk about it with another human being. That would indeed push us past the 8 free visits. Although, the pressure of only eight visits, my thoughts were all over the place. I started slowly, with just current issues being careful to keep the deeply rooted ones out of conversation, surprisingly I felt better in time.

Three weeks into my session and my son Jamie, was dropped off at our home by his father with his belongings. I watched as his dad drove off without a word, yet again. Leaving me wandering what happened or what was said. Although, I'm always happy to see the boys when they come, I couldn't help but feel confused. I reached down and gave him a playful bear hug and ask what happened? I don't want to live there no more, ma; he said, as he strolled by me. I chose not to question him at that moment. But, two days had passed and I noticed that he wasn't going to talk about what brought him here, I then decided to pull him in the sitting room alone and attempt to pull it out of him. Now, what happened over there that brought you to the point where you didn't want to be there anymore? I ask. He looked up as if he didn't want to tell me but I interjected his thought; come on and tell me son; I said again. Well....all he talks about is you, he gets mad at us, cause he mad at you; he admitted. I sit there looking at my son in disbelief. A part of me found this hard to believe but an even larger part, knew it to be true. He was angry with me for leaving him however, I continued trying to be his friend this whole time but he wouldn't budge on the idea.

It's OK son, he'll calm down one day and we'll be alright, OK? He looked up at me; yea, OK ma, and left the room to go out and play. I went to a meeting that night, feel a sense of deja vu, yet again. I shared what had happened in hopes of finding some clarity. It was hard dealing with an angry man all of the time when I needed to see my kids. I called him on the weekend to see if I could get Darion on the next weekend and yet again there was a big argument about it. Without thinking, I jumped into my car and drove over to the lake to demand that I get my baby. With my hands shaking, I pulled up, opened my door and demanding that he let my son out of the house. His mother came out first, to defuse the situation. But his voice rose above hers and the things that came out of his mouth about me, were so harsh that I looked around to see if there was anyone walking by, had heard. I became insanely angry and reached in the trunk for the bat, my thought were to silence him forever. Larnice yelled; Y'all stop this, now! I looked up at her, feeling sorry that she was in the middle of this. So, I returned to the car to put the bat back into the trunk, I looked back up at him and saw that his face was beet red, I turned and got in the car and left with out my son, telling myself that I will not go through this again....Ever

Monday morning after making sure that the older boys were off to school, I called off from my job letting them know that I won't be in today. I drove over to Harrison Elementary, walked in and withdrew my son out of school. When I made it to my house, I called both him and his mother to let them know that I have Darion and that he will not be back to live with them. He complained about his toys being left behind, I will buy you new toys and clothes; I said. How would you like that? The smile on his face was all I needed. I enrolled him into a school in our district and once that was done, I made a conscience decision to eliminate all things that were stressful in my life. I stepped out on faith by quitting my jobs and going to apply at Notre Dame University for food service. I was hired on the spot and assigned to the North Dinning hall, where I remained for one year and met some pretty interesting people and made good friends. Because of long hours that kept us there till three and four in the mornings, I thought I would find something more stable. I went to a place called specialized staffing, that sent me to another place called Nylon Craft where I worked for two weeks being a temp and was hired in on October 16th in the year of 2000. I had never worked in a factory before, I was grateful and quickly became a proud associate.

I chose to work third shift, so that I could have my days available to manage my kids, Dr. appointments and school activities, which was perfect. My relationship was going sour, toxic would be the correct understanding. I had to deal with her leaving anytime that I wouldn't conform to her liking. Boundaries were being crossed and disrespect was prevalent. Five years that she and I had been together, we even had a commitment ceremony to confess our love to each other and it was now coming to an end, this was painful to me. The last straw.... she stormed out, not to return that night, she kept me up all night with the constant phone calls, taunting me. No More! I shouted. It's over.

The next day I proceed to pack up all of her belongings, getting them ready for pickup on the upcoming weekend. She was hysterical but I reminded her of how long this bad behavior has been going on. When she and her friend came that weekend to retrieve her things, I offered to help and was told, no. I couldn't describe my feelings at this point but there were many. Over the next few weeks I mourned her, my life seemed to be in limbo. With my sponsor knowing this, she had something that she wanted me to do and thought that I was ready to do it. I believe it's time that you give a lead...tell your story, she said. Give back that, which was so graciously given to you. I'm referring too the tools to sobriety, she admitted. OK, I said. I then began preparing what I thought that I wanted to say, however those things that happened to me seemed too personal at the time to share with anyone. While starting over several times, feeling that what I may have written before may have been too much to share. Finally, deciding on what I will disclose of my life, I then felt that I was ready. I was scheduled for the next Sunday, which was cool with me. Between work and the kids settling in, I had my hands full, which made the time fly by.

Sunday, felt different than any other day, I knew that it was because this was the day that I was to share a bit about myself that I had never shared with another human being. Stepping in front of the mirror to check everything and have a pep talk with myself. Once I was satisfied, out the door I went. You Got This; I said to myself, again in the car. Stepping inside the door brought on a wave of fear however, I continued on until I was at the top of the stairs. I paused, to catch my breath. To finally take in air as I walked in the door where there were at least forty people sitting around talking. I scanned the room looking for my sponsor while waving at those that I knew. Once I spotted her, our eyes locked and she rose to her feet and walked to meet me. We hugged and she whispered; are you ready? Yea; I guess, I replied. I watched as she made her way to the podium and grabbed the mic to speak. As she began to speak, I couldn't believe how important she made me sound. As the words filled the room, I could feel the adrenaline rise inside of me. When she finished, the clapping began, there was no turning back now. Stepping up to the podium, hugging her, I then stood in silence, to gather my thoughts.

Can we have a moment of silence for the addict who still suffers, followed by the wee version of the serenity prayer; I ask the crowd. After ten seconds...God, grant me the serenity...Thank you. My name is Trul'ee, Tru for short and I am a recovering addict and alcoholic. As I began telling my story, I listened to the laughter of their voices while watching the sadness on their faces as I made them aware of my journey that lead me here. I could only pray that I was spreading hope and not madness. When I ended, I received a standing ovation and for that I was truly humbled. That night was truly a memorable one, although, I worried that I had given too much of myself away. But the feeling soon passed, in the days to come. Living clean and sober day by day was a task that I didn't take lightly. My boys and I were all together again and it felt good. I promised, that we were free from all of the negativity. We will start taking family trip every year together, if it's Gods will. The first was to Michigan City beach, I couldn't believe that I had never been there or too any beach in my whole life and with this one being so close, I couldn't resist. The boys loved it and so did I.

Life seemed to get better for us, so much, that it scared me. I made a decision that I would look into ways to purchase a home, it wasn't easy for me because I didn't have people in my life that I felt would guide me in the right direction, so I ventured out on my own. I found that I had things on my credit that I had too get off and I did. One year later, with perseverance, I found a small two bedroom home with a living room, dinning room, a finished basement, {which was where the boys lived} with a second bathroom, with a shower in it. There was also a back room for laundry and storage. It was enough space for the four of us to live comfortably and then I attained custody of my sister's child, we continued on with love. I stayed consistent with the boys, making sure that I was able to keep my word and not make any rash decisions that would lead to doubt. From the look of things, I was building the trust that I had lost in them. I curbed the angry outbursts, that I knew where due to stress and the use of drugs. I incorporated more playful encounters, which made a happy home, not perfect but happy.

As far as my love life was concerned, I had a few encounters. I had issues connecting with women due too what I believed were trust issues that stemmed from my childhood. I felt that if I were honest with them, that I shouldn't have any problems and for the most part I hadn't. There was always more than one, which for me was within my comfort zone. I never dealt with women that were know to be loud and over emotional. My business was my own, I always apprise that little tid*bit before hand. I was good to them both and although they lived in separate homes, there were times that I would bring them together on the holidays to share Thanksgiving and Christmas together with all of our children, it was nice. I enjoyed things as they were however I still wasn't quite satisfied. I wanted to be normal, what ever that looked like in the gay community. So, in the months to come, I told the ladies that I needed a break to focused on my sobriety. I beefed up my meetings and my step work when I was able to focus. I also decided to take a break and began to plan a trip for the boys to Indiana beach for the upcoming summer. I invited my sister-in-law and her children to come along. The longer I stayed clean and sober, the more of life that was revealed to me. I was proud to be a single mom, raising four energetic boys that were heavily involved in sports, they gave me purpose.

I began to meet people in the gay community that were really cool. I was invited to their homes and different events going on within the city. I was also invited to go to Chicago, to the gay parade which blew my mind. I knew at that moment, that I was coming back the next year. After the club on a Saturday night early Sunday morning, about a dozen of us would go to a restaurant called Toasties and let it all hang out, we would have a ball, talkin shit and laughing, true connections. There were those of us who were friends with a barber, {that was in the lesbian family} by the name of Macy that lived in the apartments out near the airport. I was told about how good she was, I got her number, set up an appointment with her and that's where I was going from then on. It was awesome how there would be four of us standing around sometimes, talking and laughing waiting on our turn to be cut.

Chapter 14

Establishing A foundation

June of 2005, I came for a haircut and ran into my friend Nick hanging around Macy's apartment shootin the breeze with another fella. When I was done getting my cut, she and I stepped outside and noticed there was two people coming in having a rather loud conversation, we both looked at each other, gave a bit of a chuckle and continued to my car. Two hours later, I received a call from Nick asking if I wouldn't mind if she gave my number to a lady who could use my help. After thinking about it for a couple of minutes I said, no. I explained that I'm not ready for that type of commitment yet. A few days later, she called back expressing the urgency. I told her that I needed to make a call and that I will call back. After peaking to my sponsor, looking for the reassurance. She gave the OK that I'm ready for sponsorship. I then returned the call and told her to pass my number on.

Her name was Grace, she was a stud from around the way that says she wanted help and knowledge on how to get and stay clean and sober. My first suggestion to her was to abstain from the use of drugs and that she make meeting until they make sense. I told her that I would make the first meeting with her. She agreed. I picked her up on that Friday and took her to the Friday evening meeting. We pulled up a little early to sit and talk, or for me; just listened to her telling her story. For the most part, I feel we all share similar stories as addicts, however I chose too humbly listen. I noticed, that she repeatedly mentioned a young lady who she was obviously was in a relationship with. What does she have to do with your sobriety? I ask. She is in my house and is a part of the problem; she said. I think, that you should have a conversation with her about what you are doing to better the quality of your life and that you should establish boundaries between you two. Says me, who is finally learning what boundaries are. She and I got out of the car to attend the meeting. Which was a good one, incidentally, the topic was about boundaries, she and I looked at each other and smiled.

After the meeting, I drove her home, turned my car off so that we could talk for a bit but she insisted that I come in. Just for a minute; I said. I watched as she unlocked her door. I walked in behind her, she immediately started fussing at what I could tell was a woman, about the condition of the apartment. I quickly excused myself and said my goodbyes and returned to my car. Later, I called to see if she wanted to get a meeting the next day but there was no response. I contacted her the next evening and still, no answer. I waited two days to call again and no answer, so I contacted Nick to see if she had seen or heard from her. I told Nick that I was worried about her, she then made me aware that she was getting high again. Hearing this, made me sad but also made me aware that the devil is still busy out here in these streets.

I started dating again after that day, her name is Wendy, she lived in Illinois and was cute as a button. She had a body on her as well. A nurse by profession and I was up for the task. I had known her through her cousin in the years previously but there was something about her now, that sparked my interest. She was a part of something that was called the "chase" a cat and mouse game that we human beings played with one another weather we admitted it or not. The bad thing about this game was… the chase ended. When the cat caught the mouse or you were no longer interested. However, she and I ran in circles and it was fun for a little while. I would travel to Illinois most times to visit my friend, knowing that she would be there. The crazy thing was, I hadn't even kissed her as of yet. And then one day I slowed the pace and she did not like it very well. I made her aware that I needed more and that next weekend, the cat got the mouse. That same evening, my phone rang, it was Nick. What's up man? I ask. Man, there is this woman that's in need of you to sponsor her and she's serious. She's got a kid that she needs to stay clean for; she said. Not this time, man; I said. She continued on, she's cool people man, I know her, she could really use your help; she added. Alright man, alright; I said. I hung up and finished talking about what I wanted for my life. She admitted to me that she didn't want to be domesticated, as far as I was concerned...it was the END.

I found that we were working overtime which was a big deal to me, being a single mom, I needed to be home to make sure that everyone of my boys were where they needed to be in the mornings. I got lucky finding someone to work for me, there were always people that wanted that overtime. One morning after work, I walked in the door to hear the phone ringing, Hello? The voice on the other end sounded like a bill collector. I was ready to hang up but when she mentioned, Nick's name, I relaxed and continued to listen. Her name was Yvette. I'm originally from Chicago, I now live in the suburb in Illinois with my family; she said. As I listened to her story as to how she hit her brick wall in life, I couldn't help feeling sad for her situation however I had to excuse myself to get my boys ready and out of the house to school.

When I called back, she picked right up and we continued our conversation. She and I spoke well into the day about which avenue's to take in order to stay clean while in her city. I informed her that I wasn't entirely sure that I would be able to sponsor her however I would reach out to someone who possibly could. But until this happened I suggested that she check in with me every day. There wasn't a day that passed that she didn't check in as she was instructed. We had long sessions of conversations daily, about everything and then nothing. Sharing about our children, our hopes for them and personal things about ourselves. As time passed, I looked forward to hearing her angelic voice on the other end of the receiver. You lead me to believe that I'll be in safe and secure company, with you being my sponsor; she admitted. As I said, I'm not sure as of yet but I will let you know, when I know. As the days turned to weeks, I could feel a little of myself gravitating towards my wanting to remain clean and sober and a desire to find someone that matched my energy. I couldn't help but think about her. As the following weekend approached, I had to come to Illinois, I needed to find a place called Chicago Heights. After two failed calls to my friend, I realized I had no idea as to where I was going but I knew that she did, I called her and she was up for the task.

After two phone calls to her, making sure that I was headed in the right direction, I finally made it to where she lived. I pulled up and she walked out. Tall, light brown skinned, thin with a very frail build. You could tell that the addiction had been on her for some time now but she was beautiful to me. I could tell, that she had her hair freshly done in a way that brought contour to her face. Her small lips were perfect on her slim face and when she smiled she revealed the gap in her teeth. I thought to myself at that moment, she's a liar, as the old wives tale would have it. But the voice matched the beauty. I introduced myself again and opened the door for her to get into the car. As we were riding, the conversation was flowing so freely that I almost lost sight as to why I was there in the first place. I had to pull it back a bit and get back on track. When we returned to her home, I purposefully left the car running to keep the goodbyes short.

However she was all that I could think of, on the drive home. All of the what if's, were bouncing around in my head. I know that I couldn't allow my wants to get in the way of my needs, so I slowly pulled away from her, attempting to direct her to meetings in her area. The more I attempted to pull away, the more transparent she became as to how much she needed me in her journey. I guess I'm a sucker for a damsel in distress. Remembering myself being in that same place once upon a time and needing someone who cared enough to help without strings being attached. But, was I being honest with myself, I wondered.

I accepted a phone call from Wendy that seem to suggest that she still wanted to play the game, although I made it perfectly clear that I wanted and needed more. As weeks passed Yvette was in my other ear asking if she could come to Indiana for a visit. In the mean time, I would ask if she made a meeting today or will she make one in the evening, to divert her but the excuse was always, no transportation. However she was persistent about coming and bringing a baby. Finally, I said yes, and prepared my home for them to come for a visit. Today was the day that her train was on the way. I was anxiously waiting for their arrival. When the South Shore pulled up to a stop, my heart jumped, then I saw her and the baby exit. I walked up to help with her bags, she fell into my arms with her child in hers. Hey, how was the ride; I ask. It seemed longer than usual; she said. I spoke to the little one and swooped her up in my arms and carried her to the car, noticing that I could still smell the scent of her mother on me. Once in, she and I continued with the small talk. Before I knew it, we were home. I pointed at my small abode and in we walked. I was intrigued and wanted to know more about the woman that sit in front of me, however I didn't want to appear to eager, so my questions were very vague. My attention was on the little chocolate drop that was on the floor playing in front of us, most of the time. Would you like to go out to eat? I ask. We can stay in and I'll cook for you if you like; she admitted. I couldn't let on that her comment blew my mind. I thank you but I don't have anything thawed out, so we can go out where ever you want, OK. Because of the way she thought that she was dressed, she suggested burgers. I was cool with that.

 When I wake, I noticed that the little one was awake as well and seemed to be OK that mom wasn't. So I knelt down to ask was she ready to eat. I gave her something to chew on until I finished making breakfast. By the time I finished, mom came into the kitchen with her hair all over her head, I laughed and said; girl you need to do something to yo hair. You said that to me the first time you saw me; she said. Turning up my eyebrow, where was that; I ask. You were at Macy's, getting a haircut, you passed me on the way out saying those very words. I felt embarrassed, while a smile grew on my face, I apologize for my behavior; I said. But, you were right; she exclaimed, I went back to her house after you left and did my hair as you suggested. Her house? I ask. Grace's. It was me there when you came in with her after the meeting; she added. I remember that day, I left because I didn't want any part of what I saw; I said. I had no Idea that was you...are you two still seeing each other? I ask. No! She yelled. I left her home that evening and caught the South Shore back to Illinois and have been there every since; she said. I looked her in her eyes and then realized that I didn't know her well enough to know if she was lying or not. I don't want any part of yawl's madness; I said, jokingly. {but I was serious}I promise, nothing is going on; she admitted. That night, we cooked together while laughing, talking and just having a good time listening to good music.

The next day, she told me that she had a wonderful time and that she appreciated my hospitality. My pleasure; I replied. I kissed the little one on the cheek, hugged mom and watched them get on the train. On my ride home, all I could think about was her and the fact that I didn't kiss her. For weeks, we talked every day, sometimes well off into the night, except when I had to work and then she let me know that she would be up around my break time {at 10pm} and she would call. It had gotten to a point, where I looked forward to hearing her voice. I tried to keep the focus on recovery at times and still the conversation would drift back to us. On two separate occasions, I reminded her as to how important recovery is to me and my family and if there was ever anyone that attempted to sabotage it, I would end all communication with them. I understand completely darlin, she said softly. I liked how each word was properly enunciated. I listened to everything and learned. Before, I knew it, I had ask her if she wanted to come for another visit. Yes, I would; she said, happily. I knew that I was smitten with her and her daughter, the idea of family continuously popped into my mind, no matter how many time I tried to push it out.

When the train pulled in, my stomach fluttered, yet again. I knew that I was excited but not to this magnitude. As they exited, the feeling intensified. She again fell into my arms and it felt nice, I then reached around her and grabbed the little chocolate drop from her arm. It was early evening, I decided that we stop and get dinner and go in for the night. After dinner, I played a few games that I found in the toy box that would suits a 16month old, hoping that she would get use to me, after a while, it worked. She followed me everywhere, watching everything that I did. I looked up on occasion and saw mom watching me as well. I guess, she was gauging how I interact with her daughter, I smiled each time. When it was time for bed, I showed her and mom to the bedroom, she turned to face me; I'll see you in a minute. I walked to my bedroom, pulled back the covers, lit candles and turned on the music. I could hear her singing, Freddie Jackson's {you are my lady} playing softly in the back ground as she passed to go into the bathroom, we caught each others eyes as I slowly walked past her gently touching her thigh. When I returned, from the kitchen with grapes and other edibles, I found her laid across the bed looking inviting.

I gathered my things, walked towards the bed to kiss her already moist lips. I rise in attempt to leave, she playfully pulled me too her asking, that I do it again. Slowly and passionately I kissed her while finding my way to the very top of her already perky dark brown nipple. Her moaning and gyrating gave me the feeling that I was in the right place at the right time. I then took my time, making my way to her hips, where I suckled and toyed around noticing that she was sensitive in that area, I smiled and continued to her sweet spot where I hovered over, breathing and teasing. With the very tip of my tongue I slithered and slid my way through, too her abyss. When I finally released her, the wetness amazed me, I moved the creamy substance between my fingers while softly massaging her clitoris. I listened as she seductively called out my name, I smiled and slowly rose up and went into the bathroom. When I returned, I noticed, with the candle flickering behind her somehow made her look angelic. I moved closer to the bed feeling the fire rising inside of me and finding her lips kissing her passionately once again, this time a bit harder to express my feelings of being with her. We made love well into the night till early morning.

We were awaken by the sweet sounds of Trina's voice wanting the attention of her mother. I could also hear one of the boys come in from being at their dads over night. I planted a kiss on her lips, ran in and got the baby and excused myself after bringing her to her mother. As I walked through the house, memories of last night came swarming in, I really knew that I was smitten by her. I went into the kitchen to talk to my son about his night, looking at him and realizing he is getting so big, almost taller than I am, I thought. I have someone I want you to meet in a little while, OK? So go down and get yourself cleaned up, I'll call you when she's ready. The door opened again and it was Jamie jr., I told him the same and returned to the bedroom and began playing with the baby.

She got dressed and ready to meet two of the boys, unfortunately my oldest didn't live with us anymore due to conduct issues. Finally, the boys were able to meet her, I sit and watched their interactions with her this time and smiled. When the weekend came to an end, I could see by the look on her face that she didn't want to leave. I watched the playful pout on her face and smiled. I wasn't entirely sure if I wanted her to go either but I had to work in the morning. On the way to the train station, she made it clear that she didn't want us to continue seeing each other this way. What would you suggest, honey? That we become exclusive, a couple; she answered. I smiled because I didn't know what to say at the moment. As I pulled up to the station, I looked back at the baby and gave her a smile, Yvette interrupted and ask; are you ignoring me? No dear, I'm just not sure how to answer. I just know that I enjoyed you last night and I reached over and kissed her goodbye. I watched as they got on the train and I pulled off with thoughts of how it would be if they lived there with me, it frightened me, only because nothing good ever last; I thought. I couldn't help but envision her body beneath mine being ravished in ways that she swore, no one ever had.

As I maneuvered through the weeks, all I could think of was her and the baby. Thoughts of what it would feel like having her close to me every night, excited me. I think of her so often, I've made the mistakes of saying her name when speaking to someone else. Surprisingly, I let it escape my lips, that I am in a relationship, too Miss Wendy. She was not happy to hear this news and showed it in a way that I never thought she would. From the time she hung up, she called my phone every day, sometimes twice a day, to just hold the phone and say nothing or she would just hang up, this went on for approximately 31 days. This behavior was disturbing to me, I didn't know what was next with her. However, I chose not to add fuel to the fire, I said nothing to her about how this shit made me feel. Meanwhile, I called Yvette and explained that I would like to meet and talk. I offered to drive to Illinois this weekend and she agreed.

We pulled into the parking lot of the restaurant, I couldn't resist kissing her, she was looking truly amazing to me. I took her hand and we walked in together, with me stopping to hold the door open for her. After careful consideration, I think I would like for you and Trina to be a part of my family; I said. I paused and waited for a response. She smiled and let out a screech, I would love that; she shouted quietly. There are just a few things that I want for our relationship and that's, honesty, communication, commitment and meetings. Because, we as recovering addicts have to have a foundation in order to stay clean and sober. She also agreed. Well... she started...I mentioned that I had other children and I need them to be a part of my life as well; she said. Absolutely; I said, in shock. What type of person would I be if I didn't want that for you, I wouldn't have it any other way, I said. She confided that; Grace didn't want the kids around. In that case you should not have been with her; I added. I need to ask; where will they all be staying? I don't have enough room to house four more children, dear: I added. They are with my family; she admitted, they are OK where they are. Sorry that I had to ask; I said. But you understand? Yes, I do dear. She replied. We continued on with our date and I returned back to South Bend alone afterwards. When I made it home to tell the boys that she was coming to live with us, the response was as if they already knew. The two, that met her were all for it, the others were like, OK. She was due to arrive on the next Friday with the promise that she would maintain abstinence from drugs and alcohol. I fixed up the spare room for the baby, made it perfect for a little girl and cleaned out drawers in my room so that Yvette would have space, in my life.

When the train pulled in, my anxiety rose high as I stood across the street leaning up against my car trying to catch a glimpse of them walking out. There is a rule, that I can't leave my car unattended or it would be towed away, so I stayed still, and patiently waited. When I finally saw them coming through the last window near the door, I noticed that she only had one suitcase and it was old and tethered. It didn't matter to me because she wouldn't need it anymore after this day anyways; I thought. I loaded them in the car and took them to the house. The next morning, she and I did inventory of what she brought with her. There wasn't much in there and what there was, it was old and warn. I then assured her that I would help. We went shopping for the essentials, first for the baby. I brought new shoes, clothes, socks and her first pair of underwear and a new potty chair. Next was mom, toiletries, panties bras and a couple of outfits. I was happy to have the money to help her, who I obviously had feelings for.

Things were going wonderful for us all as a family, she made things much easier for me around the house, while helping with the cooking, cleaning and on occasion, laundry. I loved watching her do whatever to make the house her own. Wendy was still calling and hanging up and Yvette handled the situation as a woman should. I was proud to have her and it showed in every way. If there was something that I thought that she or the baby needed, I made sure that they had it. I was stern when it came to going to meetings because I didn't want any slip ups between the two of us. I went to a meeting every Wednesday, Friday and some Sundays and attempted to take her with but eventually she started making up excuses and before long she wouldn't go at all. We had words about it but how can I be angry, the reasons for missing meeting were because she was doing things around the house that benefit the family, most times.

Three months, I felt as if we had been together much longer than that. On May 4th we were preparing to celebrating Trina's birthday, she has turned, two. I made a big deal about it because she was the first girl child to be raised in this house and I was overly excited about them both being here. Everything was ready, all we needed was the cake and Ice cream. Yvette, said that she would go and pick it up as soon as she was dressed. I looked her in her eyes, falling deeper for her and kiss her passionately, wishing her safety before leaving. Forty minutes later, is when I realized that she hadn't returned yet. I called her cellphone and waited for a return call, nothing. One hour and thirty minutes had passed and I was beginning to worry. Countless trips to the window to see if she had pulled up, but nothing. I then ask Jamie jr., if he could come over for a bit, to let me borrow his car to go out and look for mine. I had just brought the Jeep, it was red with black interior, with black and red floor mats. I had installed an amplifier with a large speaker in the back, she ask that I trade my Oldsmobile in, due to it being a whore magnet, she would say. I had no Idea as to which way to go when I started looking, so I ask myself, if you were still in your addiction, where would I be? I hit those spots that I thought, one being, Lincolnway. Which is where she lived with her ex, Grace, but nothing. So I turned and went back home.

Two days had passed and still no sign of her, not even a phone call. I worried that something bad had happened to her, out there. It was hard trying to stay positive while keeping a small child entertained. With hopes that it minimized her wondering where her mother was. I called off work, still hoping that she would pull up however on the evening of the third day, I felt that I had to call and talk to my supervisor, Cara. Only to make her aware that I had a situation. With having no transportation and a small child, I wasn't quite sure what I should do, which was hard. She listened to me as a friend would and suggested that I not stress about work and to believe that all will be well. On day four, I called my son back over to use his car again. I drove back up on Lincolnway, too look around, and...nothing. When I made it back home, I thought that I would just call around to see if anyone has seen or heard from her, I didn't want to involve others in my business but I needed eye in those streets. So I called, Nick, to see if she had heard or seen her...nothing. She informed me that she would call a few more people that may have seen her as well but in the mean time I knew that it was time to call Illinois. I called her friend of 30 years by the name of Mel, in hopes that she had seen or heard from her. She began rattling off names of people here, that she may be in the company of, however I didn't know them nor their numbers. Where is Trina? she ask. She's here with me; I said. Why don't you bring her here to her family; she ask. Well, I really don't want them to know as of yet; I said, also they don't know me and I'm hoping that it doesn't come to that. Good luck; she said, and we hung up. Reluctantly, I called non emergency and reported my Jeep missing.

My mind was all over the place, I took a seat where I stood and watched as the baby walked over to me. I placed her in my lap, reached over and grabbed one of the books that I began reading her earlier. She looked so sweet anticipating the story. As I read, my mind was still drifting, I never skipped a beat though. I was great at changing my voice for the stories that I read to her. When she smiled, I noticed that as young as she was, she was self- conscience about her teeth, she knew that they were rotten in the front and she didn't like it, it showed each time that she smiled, or half smiled. I knew that was something that a dentist could fix for her and before this thing happened with her mom, that was a plan of mine.

When I finished reading to her I got her ready for bed and called my son to come over. She looked so precious that I began to sing to her, Rock-A-Bye baby Rock-A-Bye loves….. I said goodnight, walked out leaving her door cracked. When Jamie showed up, I explained my intentions, told him to eat what's left on the stove and I left the house. I hit a few corners, hoping to catch a glimpse of her anywhere, even if she's without the Jeep, I just wanted to know if she's alright. There was a crowd of people standing outside of a small corner store, I slowed down but none of them were her. I made it to the stop light and made a left on Lincolnway. I noticed a lot of lights flashing way in the distance from as far away as I was. I proceed with caution. The closer that I came to the commotion, I could tell that there were all police officers and no ambulance, so no one is hurt; I thought. I'm almost up on the incident now. I can't clearly see because of all of the bright light they have shining on this person that they are putting in handcuffs. I look closer and notice that it's her. My eyes seem to flutter trying to keep the tears at bay. She's OK! I shouted throughout the car, I then searched the area for the Jeep, as I made a U-turn with caution. I noticed it parked on the street behind them with the drivers door still open. I could feel my heart beating as I watched her do the walk of shame, as I call it. She had on the same clothes that she did when she left the house four days earlier, her hair was messy and those brand new white k-swiss tennis shoes that I brought her, were filthy.

I pulled to the side, making sure to be in view of the police officers. I got out with my hands up announcing; I'm the owner of the Jeep! I called you guys days ago; I shouted, still watching them walk behind her putting her into the back of a police car. My heart raced yet again. I wasn't sure if I should allow them to take her as a punishment or attempt to save her, I was conflicted. After showing my license as I was ask to do. I was allowed to go to the jeep to retrieve my registration, I looked in and saw the pioneer stereo still there, looking further inside and saw that the everything else seemed to be in order as well. I could tell that she was getting high in here because of the shake (small pieces of crack) that I saw on the rug and in the seats. Before walking back to them, I quickly looked in the back to see that the speaker and the amp was still there. I looked down to see the babies birthday cake sitting back there untouched.

I walked back to the crowd of officers, that by this time were just standing around talking. I gave my registration to the nearest officer standing beside me and reached for my drivers license and waited for validation. When he looked up; your free to go ma'am. he said. Thank you all for your help; I yelled. I could here men in the distance yelling, no problem and your welcome, as I turned to leave. I stopped, this felt wrong, I had to do something or at least try; I thought. Officer! I called out. Is it possible that she could be released into my custody? I begged. Once we put the handcuffs on…. I think a couple of nights in jail would do her good..don't ya think; he said sternly. I looked away and back again, without hesitation; with all due respect sir, what she needs is a drug and alcohol treatment center. I stood there frightened by the words that I had just spoken, that could have been taken wrong by this man standing next to me. While he stood thinking; sir I can get her off of your streets and take her home to Illinois in hopes that her family will get her the help that she needs; I added. He kicked a rock, that was on the ground and shouted; McBride! Set her free. All of the air came rushing out of my body at that moment, breathing a sigh of relief realizing, that a higher power was at work her tonight. I looked over in the officers direction to see the confusion on his face as he lifted both arms in the air, as if to question the decision made. Without further fuss, he reached down and opened the back door and held her arm to help her out. He turned her towards the car, to take the cuffs off. At that moment I called my son to tell him the good news and to be ready. The officer mouthed something to her and stepped aside. She slowly crept passed him in the direction of the street. The officers were all looking in my direction, I shrugged my shoulders because I didn't know what she was doing and then, it was apparent that she had her own plans. She stepped out into the streets, we all watched as she walked off into the darkness. I walked over, locked my Jeep, thanked the officers again and drove off in my sons car, to be brought right back.

As I lay in the bed next to Trina, I wondered what I could have done differently to bring her mother back to her. As I replay the events of the evening in my mind, I realized that as an addict, we are in charge of our own destiny, not our loved ones. I was heavy in thought, when I heard her ask for her book, I reached over and began reading until we both fell asleep. It was 1:45 in the morning when the phone startled me awake. This was one of many phone calls from Yvette, pretty much doing a feelings check on me. This was a behavior that I knew all to well. I remained silent and allowed her to question and attempt to antagonize me into showing that I care for her in that way. Finally, ready to tackle the situation, I spoke in a solemn tone, reminding myself that there is a child here that hasn't seen her mother in almost five days. She now wanted to do what ever it took to remain together, she even offered to go to meetings for the ninety and ninety,{ninety meetings in ninety days}as was suggested of me in my early sobriety. I continued to listen and finally, I said; let me come and get you and bring you here, so that you can take a shower and sleep. She agreed. There was a long pause… I'm over to Grace's house; she admitted. I'm on my way; I said, and hung up the phone.

I sit, staring off into the other room, remembering, that her house was part of my search. She must have had my Jeep hidden from me all of this time. I pushed all of the thoughts aside, got up to get the baby ready to go. When we pulled up in front of the apartment, my thoughts were all over the place. I watched as she walk out and got into the Jeep. Hello, she whispered, in a low tone. Mommy! the baby yelled out. She turned and gave her a smile. The ride home was quiet, the tension was thick, the baby must have known because she didn't utter a word, either. As we walked through the door; go on and take a shower, I said. I watched as she reached down to pick up the baby who had desperately tried to get her attention as we walked up the walkway. I sit on the couch and watched as thoughts of what I should do with this woman, came towering in. Soon after, I could hear water running along with Trina jumping and playing coming towards me.

Come here little girl; it's too early in the morning for all of this, go get a pamper. I watched as she happily ran off and then it was obvious what I had to do about mom. As I laid the baby down, I could hear the doorknob of the bathroom door turn. I proceed to sing my lullaby to her, covered her and said goodnight. As I exited the room, Yvette stood in the mirror looking at herself. I couldn't resist stepping inside the door. We stood face to face, I'm sure that the anger that I felt, reflected in my eyes. She looked as if everything was OK. I grab her face and pulled hers close to mine to find her eyes and just squeezed. YOUR GOING HOME! I whispered in anger, sure not to disturb the baby. I released her face and walked into the living room and laid on the couch.

The next morning, I woke up feeling refreshed and ready to hit the highway. I fix breakfast for the family, fed the baby and got her looking cute. Yvette, finally came from the bedroom still in her pajamas and wanted to talk to me. I insisted that there is nothing to talk about, you betrayed my trust, I said; calmly, not wanted to alarm the baby. Soon after, we were on the highway heading to the aunts home. The ride was quiet, with the occasional plea for our relationship every now and then. One hour and twenty minutes later we were in front of the aunts home, I turned off the ignition and sit in silence waiting for her to get herself together to get out of my Jeep and my life.

I pulled the baby up front with me, to say my goodbyes. I hear Yvette on the phone but can't quite make out what she's saying and then she hung up. As I'm playing with Trina, I see her children, coming out by two's. She's rolling her window down and two of them are poking their heads in smiling at her and Trina. I wait for an introduction of who I believe are her children. Tru, these are all of my children, she says. This is Ashten, a tall thin built cute preteen. Tower, who was tall and thin framed as well with a handsome smile. Here is Justin who is the oldest of them all, who seemed shy, and then there is Josiah who is the baby boy, who had a sweet look on his face, she said. I politely said hello to the children and then turned my attention towards her, giving her the look{she knew what she was supposed to do}.

She looked at me, opened her door and without skipping a beat, told her children to tell me about them selves. As she exited the car, they all filled in and one at a time begin to talk. I looked past them and saw her walk up the side walk without turning to look in my direction and walked in the door. I could feel hell rising up inside of me. I stopped them from talking, trying not to sound rude, I told them that I had to go, what was strange to me, was that they alternated going in and out of the car as if it were all a part of a plan. Finally after forty minutes of this shit, I raised my voice {although I knew it wasn't them doing this} I got to go, now! I said loudly.

At that very moment she appeared out of the house wearing another set of clothes and shoes with her hair slicked to the side. She opened the door and sit back in the spot that she left and joined the kids in conversation. I watched in amazement as she conversed with her kids without looking in my direction. I grabbed my keys from the ignition, got out and walk to the corner. I stood there watching them, trying to calm myself. My mind, told me too grab her by her neck and drag her out of my Jeep but my heart made sense of the matter,{you are of value to her and she knows this and does not want to let you out of her life}. I looked up to notice that the kids were no longer in the Jeep. I slowly walked back, thinking about what I would say because violence was not an option. I sit in and noticed that she had already turned on the tears{which is, what I would have done if in her situation}to plead her case. I patiently listened to her plea, finally fed up with the shit; I need you to let me leave, go on and do what ever you need for you and your children, please; I said calmly. Your actions were way out of line, girl. I need this! She cried. I know that I need you in my life! She added. I know this! I will die, she cried. If this is true for you, why would you do the shit that you did? I ask. The drug; she said. Get out!

I shouted. I will do what ever you say, I need what you have; please help me…..PLEASE.

On my ride home I thought long and hard about my decision back there, how it would possibly affect my life in the long run. Things already seemed unbalanced but as I look in my rear view mirror to see the little chocolate chip strapped in the seat belt behind me, I believed at that moment that she would help keep the balance. I looked over at Yvette and chose not to speak because as far as I was concerned, there were no need for words, only action. When we made it to the house, she began with conversation about the 90 and 90 { meetings}. No exceptions: I said. Reminding you, that you said that you are willing to do whatever it takes to get and maintain this relationship; I shouted. There was tension between us for a couple of weeks to come. Although she never said anything, she wasn't happy that she had to catch the bus. This is what consequences looked like in my world; I said to myself.

Finally we decided to leave our past where it belonged. Our communication grew stronger, we were able to tell one another what we needed from each other. Our aspirations were meshing, she spoke of getting a degree under her belt, we were in a mental state of working towards those goals that I heard, held most marriages together, she was becoming my queen. I was proud of her and how she was maturing and settling into her own. I loved watching as she went about her daily activities. I was happy to hold things down, while she made her climb up the ladder. Her daily phone conversations with her children and other family members in Illinois showed me how the connection between family should be. In a quiet moment of the day, I watch as she sit on the couch looking absolutely beautiful to me. Do you want the other children her for a weekend? I ask. Yes! She shouted. Arrange it on that end; I said. I'll go there and pick them up and bring them back for you, OK? She was as happy as I had hoped she'd be.

I prepared myself for the ride to the suburbs, I got lost but found my way, quickly. When I pulled up, in front of the aunts home, there was a very tall man standing outside. When I got out of my car, I noticed that he begin to walk towards me, he held out his hand to introduced himself as Tower Sr. I noticed the resemblance of the middle son of theirs. Your name is Tru, right? Yes. These are my children, I pray you'll be responsible for them as if they are yours, if I allow you to take them; he ask.. He proceed to call off their names and they moved front and center. I assure you that I will care for your children as if they were mine, Tower; I replied, sternly. He stood for a minute looked at the ground and then, ask if he could see my drivers license. I need to make sure that you are who you say you are; he said. Absolutely, I answered, while pulling the ID out of my back pocket. Once he had a good look at it, he nodded in a way that indicated, that we were all good too go. The kids began to walk up to him giving hugs as I opened the trunk and waited for them to put their things in. I assured him again that they were in good hands and pulled off. As we made our way up the highway, I could hear the excitement in their voices. Finally, we pulled up to my home, I could see her standing in the doorway looking through the spot where she wiped the condensation off of the window. The kids jumped out of the Jeep running to the door trying to be the first to make it to her. When I was able to make it past the kids, I yelled for my boys to come up and meet them, before long, there were a total of nine children in the living room handing out names and swapping personalities, it was nice watching them interact together.

Make yourself at home guys; I said. Boys sleep downstairs and Ashten your upstairs with your sister; I added. I looked over to see that Yvette was in bliss. She got on the phone to notify their father that they had arrived and that was my Que to exit. I went downstairs to get blankets out for the boys and came up to help her with dinner. I honestly felt that things between us were good, real good. I was experiencing all of these feelings about our situation/relationship that put the fear of God in me, however every time that I looked at her or walked past or just slightly touched her, it sent a surge through me that I had never known before, that gave me a sense of peace. I couldn't keep my hands off of her, I just had to touch her, my favorite was walking up behind her as she stood at the stove or the sink and wrap my arms around her while gently kissing the back of her neck and shoulders with a nibble of her ear. Not to mention the occasional smack on that ass, as I walked by.

 Taking the kids home, was much different than it was coming, we all were engaged in conversation now. When I pulled up, the dad wasn't there but their great aunt was. Her name was Emi, short for Emily. I was told, it was she who cared for Yvette's children often and loved them as if they were her own. She stood in the doorway waiting for them to cross the threshold and when they were all in, closed the door. I thought nothing of it because I knew that she didn't know me as of yet. After that weekend, I came to get the kids pretty often for Yvette. I would also bring her to visit with her family as well. The kids dad, would have the kids there for her, in advance. I was finally formally introduced to the aunt who stood about 5'4 with a stern look on her face. I smiled a lot too soften my appearance but it was to no avail, she would not smile back for nothing. That same afternoon Yvette took me around the corner to her brothers home, which was nice as well. She told me to get out playfully and come on in, I followed her into the house where there was no one present. We sit around talking, I could see how comfortable she was being there. I heard someone coming through the door, it was her brother. She introduced us, however he had things in his hands that prevented him from speaking, I guess. I watched as he put the items on the counter and proceed to have a conversation with Yvette. I moved towards the front door, quietly whispered to her, I'll be in the car, she attempted to stop me but I was out the door. She came out an hour later to check on me but we didn't leave for another three hours. I didn't mind because she was spending time with her children and they all kept me company throughout.

We made it home late at night and while at the door I could hear the phone ringing. I opened it and went to answer, Yvette, it's for you; I shouted back. Not ten minutes after I handed her the phone, I could hear that she was in a heavy discussion. She wasn't loud but, she was somewhat forceful with what she was saying, however I stayed in the basement getting clothes from the dryer. Minutes later I could tell that she was getting emotional, so I made my way upstairs to see what was going on. I stood near her signaling for her to hang up and take a break from who ever she was talking too. A few words later, she did as I ask and sit quiet with tears in her eyes. What's going on, baby? I ask. The phone rang again, I need to get this; she said, and then I'll tell you; she added. I could tell that this person was someone different because of her tone. I raised up from the couch to go into the bedroom to give her privacy. She came in the room an hour later and ask that I turn the television off, I did. He face looked as if she were sad, I reached over to console her, whatever it is baby, I'm here for you; I said. I have always allowed them to control my relationship with Grace; she explained, with an angry look on her face. She was never allowed to come around my family because they didn't want that. I sit, with thoughts of confusion, although I understood. I couldn't believe it but, I understood. I sit in silence, not knowing what to say to her and waiting on her next words. It's not going to happen this time, raising her voice indicating that she meant it..... I love you and I want you in my life and that's that; she shouted. I grabbed her in my arms and held her while kissing my little soldier, passionately.

We went on with our lives, Yvette got herself into college and although I worked third shift I was home being domesticated as usual. I fixed breakfast and got the boys off to school and made sure that the baby was fed and changed and she went to bed with me so that I could sleep. I loved feeling as if I were doing my part to better us. Soon, she landed a job at a mental health facility in the area. I was so proud of her and from the way she walked, I could tell, she was proud too. That weekend, she wanted to go to Illinois to see her friend Mel, who lived in Chicago. I was happy to take where ever she wanted to go. I picked up some food and snacks to celebrated her success, we were on our way. We had an awesome time. We made it home around nine pm, still happily in our bliss from the day. When we make it in, the phone is ringing again, she makes it over and pick it up and whispers that it's her mom, I say; OK and made my way with the baby to the bathroom for a potty break before bed. I could here that the conversation was stressful from the very beginning but because it was her mother I remained at a distance. An hour had passed, by this time I had put the baby down and I was in the bed relaxing and watching television. She walked in telling me that she needed to talk. Of course, she had my attention.

My mother is having a big birthday party; she announced. Well, that's nice; I said, happily. Her parties are usually very nice; she added. Cool; I said, smiling and patiently waiting for her to get to the point. She wants me to come but she doesn't want me to bring you; she blurted out. Time seemed to have stood still for me when I heard this. I could hear her calling my name, I looked in her eyes, are you alright, she ask. No, I'm not; I replied. She doesn't want me there? Why? Because I'm gay? I ask wildly. Yes; she said. Your being gay doesn't fit into her idea of what a family should look like; she added. Yvette! I have never been up against such homophobia in the whole time that I've been a lesbian, until finally meeting your family; I shouted. I'm sorry Tru; she said. I knew this about them a long time ago, this is how they treated Grace. As I've said before, for years I've let her control our lives and Grace didn't seem to care, as long as she had me; she admitted. Well, the ball is in your court on this one dear; I said. I left the room and went into the living room to sit to further think about what had actually happening. As much as black people have been through pertaining to racism in this country and around the world, you would think that we, as a race should love and support one another more and not profile each other because of our differences, I thought. She walked out too sit in front of me and held my face, too tell me; I'm not going; she said firmly. But that's not going to go over well with your family; I said. I don't care, I'm not going without you; she demanded.

If that wasn't enough, the ex girlfriend, Grace was sitting outside, across the street from my home the next day, just parked. I walked out to the car, what's up, man? I want to see Trina; she demanded. How did you know where I lived? Yvette came out and gently pulled me back in. You can't be here Grace; she said. I want to see her now, she demanded. You have to leave or I will call the police. And, when the police showed up, they made us aware that she was on public property and there was nothing that could be done unless she was deemed dangerous. We walked outside too see her sitting, stalking us daily. It had gotten so bad, that I wanted to fight her but Yvette warned that she would call the police and prosecute to the fullest. This went on for two months and then it stopped, which was an act of God, as far as I was concerned. She on the other hand was going through with her family after telling them that she was not going to show up to her mother's birthday party without me, it was just unheard of for her to stand up against them, I assumed.

Three days later, Trina and I woke from a morning nap, I went to the door to check for mail, there was a paper rolled up attached to the screen door by a rubber band. I was almost afraid to touch it for fear that it was something that would harm me. I removed it, unraveled the paper and I read it. I had to read it again because I couldn't believe what I was seeing. It was a summons to court, Grace was suing me for threats made towards her. I thought that my eyes were deceiving me, I read it again and then called Yvette at work to make her aware. I was hot, I wished at that moment, that I would have whooped her ass when I started too.

The next three days were spent working hard, trying to keep my mind off of what was going on, the fact that I had to find a lawyer that I could afford that would take this crazy case. The search and find was real for me... his name was Mr. Marks. He was a short white male, that appeared overworked. However, after meeting with him and assuring him that I never put a gun in her face nor did I threaten her life, he agreed that he would work hard to get me off. That was all that I needed. Yvette's mother's birthday party was quickly approaching. I couldn't believe that she was actually standing up to her parent on my behalf. The birthday party had come and gone, I admired her for standing firm. But I had more important things going on before me. My court date was in two days and I worried about things that I had no control over. I tried to prepare my mind for it however, all of the therapy and meetings that I had gone too wasn't kicking in at this time, so I prayed.

The feelings of anxiety seemed to subside a little, until I stepped into the courtroom and seen that girl sitting there, all ready to go. Fear shot through my body so rapidly that I hadn't noticed how tight I was gripping her hand. She whispered in my ear that everything will be alright as she and I sit in silence watching and listening to the charade. She lied and then was caught in a lie by my lawyer, she was making a spectacle of herself and I really don't think that she realizes it. Yvette was ask to come up to the stand to be questioned on my behalf. I watched as she walked up and sit with poise, looking as beautiful as ever. I couldn't have been more proud to have her as I was at that moment. When the questioning was over, it was my turn and without further ado, I was freed of all charges. I thanked Mr. Marks and was on my way. When we exited the building, we saw Grace on the next street in passing, I could tell by the look on her face that she wasn't happy with the outcome. There was a question floating around in my head as I watched her ride by, how did she even know that I had a gun? Or was it a coincidence?

As weeks turned to months, it was now time to prepare for the Holidays. This was the best time of the year for me because this is when my light shined the brightest. I'm able to give back by sharing what God has graciously given me. I've brought and prepared Thanksgiving and Christmas meals and provided gifts for my family, friends and siblings for years and all whom I knew were coming to our home on those days, and now I'm able to share this with her. In the midst of making the list for the food, another Aunt of hers by the name of Jasmine called to invite us to her home in Chicago for Thanksgiving. This was a traditional event that their family had for years, I was told. They all met the eve of Thanksgiving so that everyone could be home with their families on the actual day. She turned to me to ask if it would be OK for us to attend, of course; I said.

Fast forward…to the day of the gathering. We have driven out to Chicago to an area where there was a parking ordinance, making it difficult to find a parking space due to the high volume of cars already on this street. I could see other cars pulling into this street slowing, to look for a space as well. Although dark out, I could see that there are people walking into this large home wearing very nice attire. I assumed that this must be the place. Finally parked, I could feel the acceleration of my heart as we walked closer to the house. I looked over at my baby Trina who looked like a princess and smiled at me with her new teeth. When the door were opened, I looked past her to see more people in a home, than I ever had without their being a funeral. My heart seemed to beat even more as we made our way down the stair to the lower level of this massive home. Once we made it down stairs, the amount of people there, seemed to surprise my son as well from the look on his face. We followed Yvette over to her aunt to be introduced to her. She was as beautiful as her niece, she wore her hair cut very short, which I had never seen on a black woman on purpose, she made an impression on me right away. Her kindness was at an overflow, as was her daughter Tia. She seemed to have the same aura as her mother. Have you heard from my mother? Jasmine ask. Yes, I have; she replied. I listened as she spoke with proper English. She isn't coming; she added. I saw the disappointment in Yvette's face and it saddened me to think that there was nothing that I could do to help her at the moment.

Your brothers, their families and your aunt Emmy aren't coming either, she said sadly, while holding Yvette's shoulder. This was the saddest and unprovoked incident that I've ever witnessed. Well Tru! Make yourself comfortable and have a good time; she says to me with a smile on her face. Thank you; I said, as followed Yvette upstairs to take the baby to her siblings who were up there as well. When I finished talking to the kids, I walked over to the window and stared out, wondering how was I given all of this power over these people to keep them from coming to a traditional family gathering. I watched as Yvette turned her emotions off, it was a truly amazing sight to see{I thought that I was good at switching and hiding emotions but she was better}. She turned too face the crowd before her, I watched as something turned on inside of her that was recognizable because that was what I saw in myself. As she begin to work the room, it was like something I'd never seen before. It was an amazing time, I met a slew of family members and friends of theirs, it was a beautiful time had.

The ride home was spent talking about the night. Before bed, she and I sit in silence, I knew that she needed to voice what happened back there. It was a lot to process for me, so I knew that it was much more for her. All of the air in her body seemed to rush out, as she began to cry while explaining the matrix of her and her mother's relationship. After a while of listening, I felt selfish, thinking about me and my mother's relationship as she spoke. I worked hard not to think of the things that I went through with mamma, to the point, that I entirely blocked her out for a minute or so. I snapped out of my thought when I heard her blow her nose. I listened for as long as she needed me too.

The morning brought on a whole other set of issues when the phone began to ring early. For the first time since I began dating Yvette, I heard her mothers voice. Hello. May I speak to Petty? Yes, you may; I say. Petty was a nick name that her family gave her as a child. I handed her the phone with a smile and left the room.

My priority was to create a sanctuary of success for my children. Surrounding them with an abundance of encouragement, words of affirmation and countless speeches of empowerment to ensure that they thrive in this world and to remember..{ take care of your business or your business will take care of you} to stay focused. I went down to make sure that clothes were in the washer, homework that was assigned for the weekend was done and beds were maid and the space that they lived in, was clean. Everything that I did or said, was a teachable moment, I made sure to say it when ever possible because the world is a hard place to learn lessons in. When I made it back upstairs, she had a look of satisfaction on her face. I smiled, believing that what ever their conversation was about, must have ended well. She begin to explain, her mother felt remorse and that she didn't want this thing between them to go on any longer. She wants us all to come to her home on Christmas Eve. I looked at her, surprised at what I just heard. No; I said calmly. I do not want to be around people who feel this way about people like us; I continued. She looked down too the floor and then back up to meet my eyes. All that I've gone through with her about this, will not be in vein; she insisted. For once, I needed her to finally see that she is wrong about something that's truly passionate to me. Standing up to her meant that I was not going to allow this to happen anymore. Now, what every brought her to this point, we! I say. We, are going to forgive her because, she is my Mother! she added sternly. I felt driven by her words. Enough said, I'm with you; I said calmly. She held both hands out and embraced my face, placing a soft kiss on my lips. I love you; I whispered.

December 24th was a day of dread for me, I scrambled around making sure that Darion and Trina were looking most impressive as ever. You won't get a second chance to make a first impression I said; out loud, while chuckling. Yvette came out looking as elegantly casual as ever, I was proud to be a part of her world. It was time to go. We had two big garbage bags full of gifts in the trunk and more inside the car, front and back for everyone that mattered. It was an hour and twenty minute ride. I noticed that we past Emily's home, she instructed me to continue on around this winding street until we made it to an opening. Turn right, she said. I could see that everything about this area was different and when I made the left turn I couldn't help but admire the large beautiful homes along the drive that were lit up with Holiday cheer. I looked over at her to see if I could see emotions erupting in her face but I saw none. Shit, I was about to jump out of my seat. She then instructed me to make another left into a culdesac. There were so many cars parked, that I couldn't find a park for myself. She instructed me to double park in front of a very large but beautiful home, so that we could take the gifts out. She then called her kids outside to help. Everything was moving so fast, I just wanted to sit there and catch my breath. I could see my son out the corner of my eye getting out to help the kids carry things in. I did as my mind told me to do...sit there and catch my breath.

I watched as the kids carried gifts into this beautifully decorated mini mansion in front of us. I noticed the strategically placed lights that shined around the house, I couldn't help think that I have never seen a house like this up close and now I'm about to enter one. As I walked up the walkway with Trina in my arms. I quietly pointed out the Christmas decorations to her. I stood at the front door wrestling with my nerves, trying to get them under control. I followed Yvette through the front door to stand in a foyer that separated three rooms, a living room, sitting room, and dinning room, which were all beautiful in there own right. As I walked in further, the tall ceilings, had my attention. I attempted to put Trina down so that she could be with the other kids, but she wouldn't budge. She seemed to not be familiar with her surroundings. So I had to pay attention as I walked, careful not to stumble over her. When I stepped down, I inhaled when seeing all of these people down there. There were folks passing me that were speaking to me, that I met on Thanksgiving and others were just being polite. I continued to walk behind her, looking for a place to sit. I found a space at the end of the couch, as I begin to sit, I locked eyes with what must have been her mother. I could tell by the way she watched me. I could see a slight resemblance, I gave her a nod and continued to sit down, choosing not to look in her direction again. I watched as everyone in the room moved around, to my left I noticed Yvette walking towards me with people that I didn't recognize coming with her. It was her brother Raymond and Troy, they were quick to say hello and walk away. I admired her for that because, if she hadn't done it, I don't believe that they would have. Those just coming in that met me on thanksgiving, came right up to me and spoke, having pleasant conversation, I loved the attention that family and friends showed me.

Sitting, while playing with the baby, telling her how adorable she looks, I could feel a presence walking in our direction. It was Yvette with the mother, the same woman that was watching me earlier. Ma, this is Tru; Yvette said. Tru, this is my Mother Miss Carrie McDeer. Hello; she said, conjuring up a smile that made the contour of her face appear distorted. I watched as she walked away, thinking that her heart wasn't quite into that. I quickly tuned my attention to others in the room. As the night progressed, I noticed that Trina would not leave my side, she wouldn't even go to play with her cousins. Her siblings, teased her in a playful way but, she didn't like it and showed it by crying; y'all better leave my baby alone; I said, playfully.

I picked her up and took her to the dance floor to spin her around to make her feel better and it worked. When I slowed down, I see Yvette's mom sitting on the couch across from where I was sitting, watching me while holding her other grandchildren in her lap. I looked away emotionless and played with Trina once again. It was soon time to call out the gifts. It was nice watching everyone in the Christmas spirit. Every child there received a gift, even if they were forgotten, they received money. When all was done, the music was turned up and sounding good. I picked my baby up again and began to dance with her while watching as Yvette walked in close to dance with us as well. I had a nice time, it was getting late, it was time to head home. Getting them in the car was a task with everyone saying their goodbyes. I walked over to Miss Carrie McDeer, to thank her for an amazing night. {I now know what nice and nasty looks like while co-existing in one person now}. The ride home, we conversed about how nice of a time we had and what we were going to prepare when we get home for tomorrows meal for my family. I reached over and gently slid my hand under hers and held it all the way home.

She and I prepared our holiday meal together, when things were almost done, I left to pick my sister, brother and my oldest son up to bring them back for our holiday celebration. I wouldn't have had it any other way, being with my family meant everything to me. My sons and my nephew were settling into their own with school and sports. My oldest, was with his father and doing well. After being with Yvette for a little over a year, I thought that I would ask her to be a part of my recovery journey. I ask that she take a ride to Indianapolis with me, which is where I've gone on my anniversary date for the five years that I've been clean. She agreed, I explained that I re-visit because this is where I feel that my life began. I go to a meeting and I visit the house where I lived and hit the mall on occasion and if there was an event or two that I was interested in. She was excited because she's never been there. I'll show you the city; I said. We had a nice time.

Fast forward…..there were changes happening at her job, her friend/supervisor had gotten fired and the position was quickly posted. Management thought that she would be the best candidate to fill the position from within. I was elated for her, this meant that she would be responsible for all of the front desks throughout the entire facility. She's on her way; I thought, She is one month shy of receiving her bachelor's degree as well, the sky is the limit. I loved her and I showed it in anyway that I could, once she settled into her new position, on occasion I would stop at the store to buy roses, candy, balloons and stuffed animals to celebrate her, sometimes just because. The security guard would let me into her office to set things up for her and then I would go on home to share more love with her before she left for work. I loved knowing that she was happy, this brought me joy, as well.

It was the week of May 4,[th] again. her friend Mel came for a visit. We decided that we would have a small celebration for the Trina's birthday. That afternoon, knowing when her lunch break was. I thought that I would surprise her with lunch. I parked in front of the door closest to her office, leaving my car running, I ran in and ask the young lady at the front desk if she was back there? No, she's already out to lunch; she answered. I walked back out to my car and realized that the car had locked, I had no way of getting in, other than calling her. My phone was in the car as well. I had to go back into the building and call her, to come and open my car for me. The first four tries, went to voicemail. I hung up, waited for a moment and tried back, after twenty minutes, she answered. I was happy to hear her voice, I explained what had happened and ask that she come to bring the keys to open the door. She agreed and said that she'll be here shortly. I stood outside to smoke a cigarette, after forty minutes had passed and she hadn't made it, I went back into the facility and called her back. She informed me that she was on her way again. I went back outside, walked around and waited some more. After fifty more minutes of waiting and still no her. I worried that something bad had happened, I went back in to call her, yet again and there was no answer. I worried even more. Two hours and some change, way past her lunch break she finally pulled up explaining that she was caught in traffic. I was so happy to see her that the time hadn't mattered to me, anymore.

The baby had a good time at her party. Mel returned home that night. A week and a half later. I was ask if it were OK if Mel could come to stay with us for a short period of time. Only because, I love her and this is her friend of thirty years, I said yes. I prepared Trina's room for our guest and the following weekend she was here with plans for a new future. I helped her as much as I could. Working third shift, I could help her more than Yvette could, so we spent a considerable amount of time together. It was nice having her there, I seen a closeness between them that I myself had never had with another person. One morning, a month after she came to live with us, she needed a ride to check on a job that paid more money than the job that she currently had. I agreed to take her. I have something to tell you; she blurted out. I think that you are too nice to be kept in the dark any longer; she added. Since I've been here, all that I've seen, was the love that you've shown to both her and everyone around you, she paused. I watched as she seem to be in turmoil about whatever was on her mind. My curiosity had peaked, go ahead and tell me. It's OK, I added.

The day that you came to the job to take Yvette out to lunch? She said, peaking slowly. Yes, I remember, while smiling as I remembered locking myself out of my car. It took us a long time to get to you because we were out at the mall for a total of two hours or so, I believe; she added. Well that's not a problem, I mumbled. I know that she buys things without my knowledge; I added, smiling. We weren't there alone; she added, with another long pause. We were there with Grace; she said, while putting her head down. She wanted to see Trina and give Yvette money for the baby for her birthday; she added. What!!?? really? I was confused and I didn't want believe a word that she said. I pulled over into a parking lot and just sat there. I thought about all the hell that Grace put us or shall I say, me through. The fact that I was facing jail time because of her lying ass. Yvette watched me go through all that shit, this was just wrong, if this is true. Interrupting my thought, she continued; I watched a lot of touching and probing and playing around between the two of them; she added. The more she spoke, the more unbelievably disheartening it all was, to me. I drove her to her destination. While waiting for her, I wondered where was my woman's moral compass when she was out there gallivanting around. I wondered if any of our friends saw them together. I had a lot going through my mind, still in shock. I made a decision not to say anything to her about what I had just heard. I just wanted to see how much longer, it would take her to come clean about this.

When I made it home, I felt anger beyond belief. How could she do this to me, I thought. After all that I've done to make life comfortable for us. I told no one because, I was too embarrassed. I showed no difference in my mannerism. I laid beside her thinking day after day, how could she lay here as if nothing ever happened? I even watched her during the day move around as if...This made me angrier. Mel, got the job and moved into her new apartment all in the same week. She needed help moving in. Because of Yvette's new position she wasn't able to help so, of course, I helped her. I was fine with it because, she was someone that I could talk too about Yvette, it felt good to have someone that I could vent too. When she was all settled in. I shared, that I was going to let Yvette know that I knew what she had done this evening. But, I had no idea what I was going to do about it, as of yet. Mel, suggested that I wait until I had a solution to my problem. I did just that, in the meantime I watched as my girl went on being all that she could be. That evening, I sit watching her as she put on her night clothes, I think that you have something you need to tell me dear; I blurted out. What? She ask in surprise. Have you done anything that maybe you should admit too; I ask. No! She shouted, playfully.

Sit down; I instructed. As she sit on the bed, I saw the concern on her face that instantly turned stern. Remember, when I came to your job to take you to lunch and you weren't there? Yes; she answered. I was told, that you were out at the mall with Grace, {her face was instantly contorted}you were there with her for at least two hours, making me look like a dam fool; I added. I could see the wheels turning as I looked into her eyes. She opened her mouth, I stopped her by putting a hand up and calmly repeated what I've always said to my children. {You'll be in more trouble telling a lie, than you will telling the truth; I said, sternly.}I instantly saw change in her facial expression. I could only assume that her story would change as well. She, looked up to meet my eyes and held them captive. She had money that she wanted to give me for Trina; she said. Three hundred, as a matter a fact. I didn't mean for it to take so long and I didn't tell you because I didn't want you to be upset about it.

I took a moment to breath, my thoughts had ran off without me. I could picture me whoopin her ass all the way up the street and back. Instead, I sit in silence to think of my next words. What ever you do while we are together should represent us and our well being, not just you dear; I said harshly. You were there to witness the fear and anguish that I went through because of this woman and yet, for your own selfish gain you met with her, allowed her to touch you in places that only I should be allowed; I shouted. I don't want to hear any more, I want you to decide where you want to be from this point on. I will drop you off where ever you want to go. She looked at me with a surprised look on her face. She means nothing to me, it was all about the money and you know this; she insisted. I want to be here with you; she blurted out. I walked outside, and went into the garage. I ask myself, why did I let her off so easy? After a minute of honestly thinking. It was because I genuinely loved what we had, and I wasn't ready to loose it over something that I though was a miner hiccup. I was weak, even in my own thoughts, so I decided to punish her by cutting off communication, giving her the silent treatment. I walked back into the house still choosing to remain silent, she offered to fix me something to eat. I looked in her direction, shaking my head and continued walking past her. The silent treatment, went on well throughout the travel to her aunt's birthday bash in Illinois. Where I sit at a table with Mel and four other people that I didn't know. It was a nicely decorated event, I watched as Darion and her children continued to bond, which was very important to me. I also noticed that she was in the kitchen helping out most of the night. She also helped with the serving and cleaning. The more that I watched her in her element, the more prideful I became. She would come to the table to bring me a plate and converse with me to make sure that I was OK. Of course I would answer, I nodded. Only because I felt that it was nobodies business what was going on in our home. As the night came to an end, Mel and I walked the grounds waiting for Yvette to finish up. She and I talked about the events of the night and Yvette and her demeanor.

It wasn't until she exited the building that I realized that she had been drinking. I looked at her with anger in my heart. We weren't past the last shit that she did, I thought. Mel looked over at me to gauge my anger, I imagined. I had no words, I turned and started walking to my Jeep. I called my sons name and listened for his footsteps and when I heard him running behind me, I added speed to mine. At that moment, I was prepared to leave everyone behind. When I made it to my vehicle, her kids ran up to meet with my son to say their goodbyes. I slowly moved past them and got into the jeep and started it up. I looked out at the kids and said goodbye and instructed my son to get in. I watched as my son put his left leg in, I then heard her loud laughter; so you trying to leave me; she yelled. I said nothing and instructed my son to close his door, he acted as if he were confused about my instructions, once more I told him; close your door. I watched as he did what he was told, and then the door flung open. Looking at me with that look of anger, she instructed my son to get in the back. She got in the front, Mel, Trina and Justin got in the back with my son. Yvette looked over at me; so you really tried to leave me? She snarled. I said nothing and put the Jeep in drive. Mel, tell me how to get to Emmy's house, please, she agreed. Yvette, snapped at me the entire ride, it was so bad that Mel intervened and ask that she stop. Yvette told her to mind her business. Finally, pulling in front of the house, I waited for the kids to get out. Get out! I said in a low tone. Before she could utter another word. Get the fuck out, now! I yelled. I watched as she exited the Jeep, while still talking that drunk talk. I told my son to get in, I could here Mel whisper to me; can you take me home please, of course I can; I said, and pulled off. She and I talked about the events of the night until I dropped her off in Chicago. I made it back to the hotel, that I was staying in, to see Yvette standing and waiting outside without the baby, I could only imagine that she's come to her senses again.

Our lives from that point on were as any other relationship to those looking from the outside, in. We were very good at keeping our personal business out of the streets. We had gone through a lot together. I knew that there would be more because we were recovering addicts learning how to live without the use of drugs together, I told myself. I loved her and I wanted the world to know this as well. Months later, I got up the nerve to ask all of my friends to join me at the Sea Horse at eleven o'clock on that next Saturday. I then proposed to her on stage. Six months later on June 8th 2008 we had a ceremony, although it wasn't legal in the state of Indiana, it was very nice. There were four ladies that wore beautiful black firm fitting full length dresses and my guys wore traditional black tux. The church was filled with all of our friends and one member of my family. Her family from Illinois came as well, although her mom was against it, she showed up, mask on tight. It didn't matter to me because at the end of every day, I wanted her daughter to be in my life.

There were constant trips planned too Illinois, which was fine with me because I was finally feeling comfortable about being around her family after all that had happened. As time passed, I could feel in my spirit, there was something that my father wanted of me. We were so busy being the pillar of the Gay community that I didn't take heed and then without warning I was laid off work for six months, which in a short time depleted my savings. I worried. This put me into survival mode, the hustle became real. I had a gift for gab and I used it to get what I needed from people. Little did I know, things happen for a reason, what I needed was to slow down. And because I didn't, I had a mini stroke. On the left side of my lip I felt a tingling. A numbing feeling that cascade down the left side of arm, the left leg wasn't quite cooperating as well. I rushed to med point, they sent me to the emergency room. I drove, being as cautious as I could. I was admitted immediately. I stayed a week in the hospital, followed by eight weeks of therapy. I worked hard towards recovery. In time, I was almost 90 per cent back to normal. I even went to a Christmas party thrown by my job, with the help of a cane of course.

Fast forward, there was a feeling stirring inside, that there was something more that was needed of me. I've always been in tune with my spirituality. I ask God what more would you have me do. And on November 9, 2009 we received our first foster child by the name of Jeremiah. He was the most beautiful little boy that I had the pleasure of having in my care. He was three years old with fair skin and a head full beautiful curly hair. It was love at first sight for me. We were told by DCS{ Department Of Child Services} that his mother loved him enough to bring him in, so that he may have a chance at a better life. When I was told this, I knew in my heart that he was home. Trina instinctively took him under her wing, and the boys, well...they were boys. They attempted to talk hip to him but he wasn't feeling it.. As days past, we all noticed little things about him, he was very smart, his pronunciation of words were better that most adults. He was three years old and knew how to write small sentences. He seemed to be a little dyslexic but he knew his numbers up too one hundred and fifty.

He played by himself, even when other children were present. He organized every toy and put them in rows and if anyone would move or disrupt what he had accomplished, he would go into a rage, where he would shake as if convulsing, in total silence. It wasn't until we enrolled him into the daycare which was where Yvette worked, that they pointed out that he may have something called Asperger or Autism. I couldn't get upset about it because I had yet to look it up, to find out what it was. How could you come up with this assumption? He's just a baby, I ask. Once I made it home and looked up these things, I could see some of these traits in him. I also noticed he showed no affection, nor did he show any emotions, unless his play was disrupted. I called our case manager to ask if she could get him in to see a therapist. After explaining what was going on, she agreed. After a few sessions, they said the same as the ladies at the daycare. I was told that he is too young for testing but, they would continue with therapy. Yvette had began to complain that I seemed to spend more time with him than I did with Trina. I didn't see it that way, he just needed more of my attention than she did at the moment. Trina was in school now and Jeremiah had quite a bit of dental work that needed to be done as she did. So, with a few visits, he had shinny new caps on his teeth.

I was relieved that the weekend was approaching, I thought that I could possibly get some rest, when she yelled in and ask that I not make any plans. With Darion being the only one my boys living at home now. I went down stairs to chill with him in the sitting room. I heard a knock at the door but chose not to move. I heard a scream and my son and I ran upstairs to see what was happening. When I made it to the living room, it looked like a scene out of Coming to America.

They seemed larger than life to me, standing there in my little home with their jackets with fur around the neck. Large ear rings, hair cut close to their scalp looking like women of royalty. In shock, I walked over to say hello to her mother Carrie, brother Raymond, and his wife Theresa and their two small girls. Bringing in the rear was her aunt Jasmine with a smile as genuine as the day that I met her. I couldn't believe that after three year of us being together that they were finally here in our home. Seeing how happy she was, made me happy for her. I, at that moment felt less than and needed to excuse myself to put on more appropriate clothing. When I returned, I walked in on conversation about going to a restaurant to be more comfortable, which were words coming from her mother. Whew; I said to myself. Yvette, standing close enough to hear me, chuckled. I suggested that we can go to Ryan's restaurant to eat, they all agreed. Once seated and our food ordered, her aunt Jasmine spoke first.

Chapter 15

Trouble Don't last always

Tru, our family goes on vacation every year and we would like for you to join us this year; she ask. We understand, that you have never been on a cruise before but we will help you all, with whatever you may need. On a what? I ask. A cruise, she stated. We are also aware of your financial circumstance and are willing to help with that in any way possible. I looked over at Yvette, thinking; how could she, without discussing this with me first? I took a moment more before answering, battling with my pride, while thinking about the fact that we will be on all of that water. It sounds like an opportunity of a lifetime however, next year would be a better time for me; I insisted. The adults at the table sit in silence and almost simultaneously, all but her mother, began the talk of persuasion on Yvette's behalf. I listened to all that was said and with great hesitation, I agreed to go.

The preparation for this trip was overwhelming for me. I had to prove to myself that I could do this, by myself. I didn't want to borrow money and set up a payment plan with her aunt to pay it back. Yvette and I sit down to discuss how we were going to make this happen for us, for all of us? She explained, that there were rooms available on the ship that were paid for by people whom were no longer going, that would be free due to them dropping out for whatever reason. She mentioned that there would be sixty eight people going, I could not believe this number. I go on to mentioned, that I had to ask my older boys to see if they wanted to go. I know that I am taking Darion and Jeremiah, I mentioned. She turned, giving me a confused look, why would we take him? She said, sternly. He's a ward of the state, he can get respite care while we go away; she added. I chose not to answer right away for fear that I would say words that I didn't mean....In my heart; I started, he belongs to us and when we look back on pictures that I will take of this vacation, he will be in them; I promised. Well, I'm sure that you'll make it happen; she said, and walked off. As I said; I had to prove to myself that I could do this all by myself.

My older boys didn't want to go but promised that they would participate if I wanted to do this some other time and with a smile, I told them; you just want to see if I'll make it back alive; we all laughed. I ask her about her kids, she told me that their father was going to pay for them. Now, Jeremiah. I had four months to get things together for myself, Darion and Jeremiah. I first had to get permission from the state of Indiana to take this baby out of the country. I was told that this would require an appointment to stand in front of a judge. On the day of court, I was afraid and leery of the outcome. I explained to Her; I believed that he is already a part of my family and I didn't want to look back years from now at memories that he wasn't a part of because of a minor technicality, your Honor. I believe in my heart that this is in the best interest of the child and will be for his future; I pleaded. I then stood in silence waiting on instructions, while praying that she granted my wish. She took a moment, ask that the bailiff along with the case manager, to come and stand before her. She whispered something to them and when they all walked back to their places, she then spoke to me.

For as long as I've been on the bench here in Indiana. I have never had a case like this come across my desk. A foster family is requesting that a child in their care goes out of the country with them on their vacation. A truly amazing request I may add. However, my question to you Miss Benevolence. Will I see you back in my courtroom to adopt said child in the future? Yes, your Honor; I replied with a smile. Well, I'm going to grant your request, you may pick up the paperwork that you will need for his travel from your case manager. Good Luck Miss Benevolence and may God Bless you. This court will adjourn, while the gavel hit the block. When I received the paperwork, I requested his birth certificate and social security card as well. After receiving those items, I went to Meier to get pictures taken so that I could send them off, for him, my son and my passport. However, Jamie gave me the blues, he argued that he didn't want his son going out of the country, the crazy thing about all of this, is that he could not go without the signature of his father. I was angry, that once again, I had to put power in his hands to abused as he had in every other aspect of my young life. He rambled on for three days on this subject and only God knows why but he finally decided to sign. When I received everything, I went to the post office and quickly sent the paperwork and pictures in and then started on the financial part of this trip. I went to Gordons food service and purchased five boxes of candy bars to sell. I also ask a co-worker who collects cans at the job. If she would donate a couple of bags for two weeks to help pay for Jeremiah's flight, she not only said yes but allowed four bags for two weeks also. My co-workers raised money without my knowledge to help out as well. Finally, I filed my taxes that next week and this got me over the hump, so when her family called to notify us that the flights were low, I was proudly ready to purchase three of them for us. From that point on things were better, we followed the guidance of the family as to what was needed for the kids.

Flying into fort Fort Lauder dale was quite an experience for me. There were fifteen of us on this flight, I watched as everyone gathered their things and moved towards the exit. There was a man standing beside a van holding a sign that had the families name on it. As we rode through the city, there was an excitement inside of me that was truly overwhelming. Upon making it to the hotel, I could see others whom I met at family functions, that shared welcoming smiles. As we made our way to the desk to check in, I could see that everyone was in good spirits and that put me in a good mood as well. Fifteen floors up, I visually prepared a large one bedroom, suite for seven children and two adults to occupy for this one night. Once this happened, we went down to survey the area. When the elevator doors opened to the lobby, we noticed more people that we knew, checking in. As we proceed past them, I looked out the door of the hotel and could see the water in the distance. I took Trina and Jeremiah's hands and walked crossed the street headed to the beach, where I felt that I could take the time to reflect on where I am, in my life today. Night life, was just a meet and greet in the beautiful lobby and restaurant and then off to bed for an early rise.

We had a wake up call at seven. Had a beautiful breakfast in the most amazing looking atrium that I had ever seen. The shuttle was due to leave at ten for an arrival at the port at eleven am. I worked hard at getting the babies ready, while she yelled at the teenagers. Finally able to make our way to the lobby, to finally step out the door too an enormous commercial tour bus just for us. To my surprise we filled it up. It was beautiful to see all of these people in their orange tee shirts with the ships logo on it, being happy and ready to have a wonderful time. In a short time we were at the port, where there was a large vessel waiting. Freedom Of The Seas, it was called. The closer we got to the ship the more that I was able to admire it. I was truly impressed, afraid and excited at the same time because of what I was about too experience. We were told by the handlers to leave our luggage right where it was in the parking lot, which had our room tags on them, we were assured that they were in good hands. We were told by the others in our group that the check in process is a long one. Looking ahead, I could see hundreds of people walking through a maze of sorts. Take out your passport and paperwork; a voice yelled into the crowd. It took a while but finally we made it up to the desk. We were all separated, going to the next available person. I could hear the gentleman yelling in the distance regarding passports again. I heard a voice say; next person in line. I stepped up with Jeremiah and Darion with paperwork in hand. I gave her all three passports along with signed documents for the kids. She checked them once and then checked them again. Although the documents were in her hand, she ask what relations are these children to me. When she was satisfied she told me to keep all documents out as she allowed me pass through, I thanked her and moved forward and waited on the rest of our party to come through. We all walked around a large hallway to see an escalator as tall as a two story building.

When making it to the top, I looked down to see how far I had traveled up, whew; I said. I turned to notice a sea of people waiting to go through, what I found to be customs. My heart thumped around a bit from the excitement of knowing that this was about to happen. I could see hundreds of people being separated and moved through lines to be checked. It was my time to approach the officer that appeared to be larger than he actually was due to the height of the booth that he sit in; passport and legal documents; he said with a stern voice. I calmly reached up to him, handing him what he ask for. And then, waited for him to let me know if everything was in order. He looked down at the documents and then down at us, enjoy your trip; he said, and the gate opened for us to pass through. Once through, I prepared to stand to the side however there were two huge officers that rushed me around the corner and away for the customs area.

When we were all united again, we pushed our carry on luggage around and through a long hallway that allowed us to walk along side of the ship. I was truly impressed at how big and beautiful it was up close. We finally made it to a large opening, where eight personnel were waiting there to greet everyone that stepped across the threshold. But what I saw, was not expected. I couldn't train my eyes to focus on just one thing, there was so much to see. As I proceed, I noticed that the space looked as if from a scene in a movie of a big and luxurious hotel, called; THE PROMENADE DECK. I laughed at my myself and continued on. It was beautiful, with all of the large pieces of art hanging and sculptures positioned through out. The stores and shops on either side with the elevators encased in glass to make it easy to see as you ride. I was in love at first sigh. I turned to Darion to get his response and he seemed to be as amazed as I was. Finally told that we could carry our bags to our state rooms, once we went to customer service to receive our sea pass. I learned that this was a type of prepaid card that we loaded ourselves and used like a credit card on the ship.

Once we made it on our floor, I ask that my son come with me to our room first and I will walk with you to your room to see where you will be staying. We all waited while Yvette used the sea pass card to open the door. We all stepped inside, to see a beautiful balcony suite. It was an open space, with a king sized bed a curtain that separated another space with a couch that let out into a bed and a spacious bathroom. I walked through to stand on the balcony that overlooked the town below and the vast body of water in the horizon. Truly an amazing sight of Forte Lauder dale. We left our bags in the suite and walked with all of the kids to find their rooms. Their rooms were nice, dorm sized rooms. I decided at that moment, that while they were on the ship and they kept themselves out of trouble, that I wouldn't police them as much. I wanted them to enjoys their experience as well but when we are off the ship, we all were going to stay together for safety.

I gave them their walkies talkies and left the teenagers to themselves, with the agreement that we would meet on deck in an hour for the set sail party. An hour later I heard a loud horn coming from the ship and the party began. Music blared from all directions as people stood by the rails waving goodbye to the crowd down below as the ship eased from port. This was an opportunity for me to overcome my fear of heights and large bodies of water. I eased to the rail afraid to look over however I needed this. I stood there until I was able to conquer my fears. Finally, I stepped away to notice orange shirts everywhere, I smiled because it was us.

The cruise went on and it was beautiful, there was nothing that I needed that wasn't provided. Every night was a party, although I wasn't always a part of it. She had hopped that her mom would keep the kids on a couple of nights but when she said, No.... There were times that I just chose to allow Yvette to go out with her family and I stayed with my babies. We didn't stay in the room though, we walked around the ship exploring and making it fun for them. There were two nights that we had the teens watching them for an hour or two but most of the time they were with me. There were things going on during the day while they were in day care, that the ship provided for free for most of the day with the exception of when we were at port. We had a fabulous time and I was very happy that I chose to go and I promised that I would go back again if God Blessed and said the same. After seven days of pleasure the journey had come to an end. We were told to put our luggage outside of our rooms the night before and when we got off the ship our luggage was already near the bus and ready to go. Our flight wasn't for two more hours. It was already planned that we tour the city which was a very good idea. It was nice seeing the big and luxurious home and yachts awaiting beside them but what amazed me most, was seeing coffins above the ground. It's said, that this was because of the storms that cause flooding. Finally making our way thought the airport to our destinations, there was lots of happy chatter about the trip. I thought to myself; it was a glorious time had but now back to reality.

It was good to be home after the long drive. The kids seemed well rested after sleeping the whole way home however it was the wee hours of the morning. I remembered that I had the next two days off work. I made a decision that when I go back, that I would work hard and save money to do things like this without going through what I had to go through for this trip. I couldn't wait to get back to work to share my experience and insist that they do the same.

Two days later, I received a call from DCS from my case manager, Mira. {It seemed that when we came back from our vacation, we received many calls for cases back to back although we had reached our limit of children at times but I didn't mind, if I could I would}. She ask if we could take two siblings who were boys, I agreed but only because they were a year younger than Jeremiah. I vowed never to receive a child older than him, I called Yvette at work to get the OK and Mira process their paperwork to bring them in an hour or so. I prepared the bunk and the single bed for her to see that we were ready for them. I started a conversation with Trina and Jeremiah about what was going to unfold but I'm not sure that I got through to him, so I continued to prep for them anyways. When they arrived, I could see sadness and confusion in their faces, I knew then that my work was cut out for me.

When she finally left our home, I ask the kids if they were hungry. Without their answer, I went in to fix snacks for all four kids. I watched as they ate, careful not to make any sudden moves to startle them because I've scanned over their paperwork which gave me some insight on their situation. When they were finished, do you guys want to go out to play; I ask. Neither one, was ready to talk however they would nod. I opened the back door and allowed them all to walk past me to go out. Ten minutes had passed and I heard a loud scream. I quickly ran to the door to find that it was Jeremiah, being frantic from what I could tell because the youngest child touched his hair. The boys reached over and touched it again and Jeremiah screamed and began to shake in what I believe to be anger. I went to them in attempt to defuse the situation by telling the young man, that he needs permission to touch another person's hair or any part of their body. He looked up at me; she didn't tell me no; he snarled. I smiled, well, for one thing, she is a he and yes you have to have permission to touch; I said. Why do you call she a he; he ask. Because, he is a boy; I added. With a confused look on his face, he looked up at me; NO SHE AIN'T; he shouted. And walked away. Jeremiah has a long beautiful ponytail, not to mention that he's a beautiful child, with a lighter complexion. This may have confused the little guy. However, it was an everyday conversation between him and Jeremiah which turned into a stalking situation. The young man had become so obsessed with my son that he began touching him even more on other parts of his body. He seemed to be grooming him. This was a bit disturbing to me and I felt that I needed to protect Jeremiah from not only this little guy but his brother's overly aggressive nature, as well. I called my case manager and ask if she could place them into another home and when I explained what was going on, she agreed. The process took about two days and I was ask to bring them to the parking lot on Western ave. to meet a foster mom that takes in special needs children.

Once this chapter in our lives was done, I thought that we could take a moment to breath however I received another call for two beautiful mixed babies that were only 3 and 18 months of age. I was told in the foster parenting classes, not to get emotionally attached but how could you not, when they are so young, precious and helpless and not to mention, beautiful. Soon after the babies were dropped off, I received a phone call from Yvette's mother. I quickly made her aware that her daughter wasn't available, no I need to talk to you, she muttered. I was quite surprise because I knew in my heart that she really didn't like me, so much to the point that she told her daughter last month that she was cutting her from her WILL, so that I didn't benefit from any of her money{ I wished that Yvette never had shared that information with me}.Yvette told me with tears in her eyes. I comforted her; while making her aware, you can't miss something that you've never had. Yvette entrusted this information to me not knowing that I have always retained what a person has said or done against me but this truly astounded me. How I had so much control over a persons thoughts, that I could control an outcome as well.

Good afternoon Miss McDeer, what can I help you with? I ask. I needed to speak to you about something; she admitted. Well, if I could call you back in about an hour, I'm in the middle of something, I added. She agreed. The entire time that I was getting the girls situated, she was all that I could think about{what could she possibly want with me, I wandered}. When the girls had eaten and were changed and sitting quietly near me playing, I called her back. Hi, Tru; she started. I just wanted you to know that I was happy to have gotten to know you better on the cruise; she said. You seem like a very nice person, especially how you take on all of those kids; she added. Thank you; I said. I need you to know this because I know your a good person through conversations had by my family. I understand your struggle to remain clean and sober and I wish this for my daughter as well, someday. I told her this on the ship. While she was indulging, I believed that she now has heard me; she said. Now, I have to go, I hope that you have a good day and I'll see you soon; she said. I could hear the dial tone as I held the receiver in my hand in silence. Confusion consumed me, as I tried to think back wondering how and when I could have missed it. I truly understood what she was telling me. When Yvette walked through the door, I made her aware that her mother called and what was said, I decided to leave it alone. She started to speak, I stopped her, to make her aware that, it's OK, as I closed the door. But it wasn't OK with her, her mother had committed a cardinal sin among family, she snitched on her daughter.

We were coming up on one year of having Jeremiah in our care, the state contacted the biological father to see if he wants custody of the child and if no response within six months, we could file for adoption. Finally, we were given the all clear. She and I talked extensively about it. I knew in my heart when we got him, that I didn't and wasn't going to throw him away. As I listened to her speak about what could happen, my mind was already made up as to what was going to happen. She and I agreed that we were going to bring this little guy with all of his differences into our family. We filled out the paperwork and left the lawyers office elated. However, the next week we received information that there was an issue, a rather large one that involved me.

The lawyers found that I was a felon after running a more extensive background check. I couldn't believe it, I was under the assumption that I had been cleared from my past, after all of these years. Sort of a good behavior deal. Reality of it all, was that I just didn't know how the judicial system worked. However, my attention turned towards the baby and what happens to him now. The findings were sent to DCS right away, they contacted me, they were back and forth but had to make a decision if they were going to remove Jeremiah or not. The process had already begun with the other children in our custody, this was a scary moment for me. I didn't want to loose him, especially knowing that he would go to people that he doesn't know. I stayed in constant contact with them, making them aware that I'm willing to do what ever it takes to rectify this problem. I'm also aware that this was a huge oversight where the agency was concerned and I made sure not to stir the pot in fear that I would loose him indefinitely. Here is where God stepped in, he was allowed to remain in our home until I was able to clear things up on my end. The following day, was very challenging. I was on the phone most of the day calling SanDiego California, in hopes of getting information as to how I could attain a lawyer there to fight my case from here in Indiana. I learned that, what I needed was for my cases to be expunged from my record, which from the sounds of it, would take time and money. Finally, I called Vista county jail to find that there was a woman that holds an office in San Diego that would take the case. I immediately called Mrs. Rodriguez, she did just that. The entire process was as it was explained to me, she called me every step of the way about every part of the process and if she needed more information, I had to get it. This entire process was expensive and took a year and a month of my life away. During this time, I felt that this was my problem alone. I could tell that because there wasn't anything that she could do about this, that she wasn't very supportive of it.

In the process, I strayed away from my duties at home. I don't know how it happened but before I knew it, there was someone standing before me by the name of Betsy Mae, who promised me the world and the world was what I needed at this moment, so I obliged. I was honest, I spoke to Yvette about it, I felt that honesty was always the best policy, she knew that this was a good thing for us at this moment. I assured her that it wouldn't last longer than needed. Surprisingly, she agreed, although there were demands, I agreed to them. I felt that it was only fair that everyone involved knew what was to be expected. In the meantime, I had to keep DCS informed the whole step of the way about what was going on in California. Having too attain letters from neighbors, family, friends and not to mention a few important people that I lucked up on knowing in the community that had a few kind words to say about me. I sent certificates that I had attained throughout the years from my job and various other achievements from foster parenting class, that had to be searched for and presented to help show that I'm a changed person. As of March 29th 2010 I received a letter stating that my Expungement had been granted. I could feel my heart beating once again.

Once the agency was satisfied with the documents that I presented to them, we were allowed to proceed with the adoption. As of October of 2010 we were officially the parents of Jeremiah. It was quite a happy occasion for us and everyone that went through the process with us as well. We celebrated by going to Illinois to Shed aquarium with seven car loads of family, friends and co-workers from my job, behind us. I'm not quite sure if he understood that this was all for him but I believe that he had a good time. And when we made it home later that evening, we adults went to Smokin Annies to celebrate as well. We were able to relax and get back to love. I showered her with affection, knowing that I was the reason that it was needed. I was aware of how tense things were in the house between us. I accepted responsibility, however it was now back to business.

Officially, being a changed woman, gave me a feeling of pride but when my survival mode kicked in, I wasn't very proud of the way I handled things sometimes but, in my mind it had to be done. I found that walking away from Betsy Mae wasn't as easy as I thought. She believed that because of all that she had witnessed of my relationship with Yvette, that I would be better off being with her. I could hear her talking in an attempt to persuade me but I could only hear bits and pieces of what she was saying. When she finished, she could see it in my face, she yelled; How Could you stay with her! Because…. I love her; I whispered. She stepped towards me; looking me in the eyes and pushed me into the closet doors, that came off the track causing me to land on top of them. I stood to my feet, attempting to regain my balance. When I did, I walked out of her room and out of the front door. When I made it to my car, I could here footsteps coming near, as I opened the door to get in and start it up, I pulled off and heard rocks hitting the rear window and the trunk of the car. But, I continued to drive. From that day forward, every day spent with my wife was cherished. We choose to leave our past behind us and look towards the future. Because of my seniority at work, I was finally able to move from third too first shift. It felt good coming home to her every evening, sometimes I would have to work over but it still put me home at 7pm.

It was a Friday night, all of the older kids, including my sons Jamie and Darion, were on their computers when I came in from work. Two of the boys had cell phones in their hands. What are you guys doing; I ask. Trying to get a job; Justin said. I continued walking to the kitchen and in walked Yvette. How would you like to move to Illinois? She ask, with a smile. My aunt Jasmine, told me that there were openings at her job and I applied for it; she added. I also told the kids to put in an applications as well, she added. You know how dangerous this is for you, right? Going back to your old stumping grounds, may bring back old feelings dear, I added. I'm OK, I want something out of my life now; she said with no hesitation, I think that you should fill out one for yourself, as well; she added. OK, I answered, cautiously. I sit beside Jamie, watching as he finished up, I proceed to fill out one for myself.

From that night on, every conversation that was had was about our going to Illinois. Our, life was in a state of purgatory. We were going out to the club more and if we weren't going out, we were meeting up at someones home to party. Saturday nights, were not ours anymore because there was always people in our lives now and if, I didn't want to participate she would head out to her friends home alone. One night, I decided to drive to the bar alone, walked in and sit at the bar and thought and thought about how much of a turn that our lives had made in such a short time. I sat feeling sorry for myself, thinking of what's to become of the only family that I've ever really loved being a part of. I ordered a rum and coke. I sit starring at it, knowing that I was giving up fifteen years of sobriety if I lifted it to my lips. It sit there so long that I could no longer see the ice in it. Before I changed my mind I took that first drink, followed by four more. The alcohol rushed through me like a freight train.

I don't know how I made it home. I heard someone shout; she got the Job! In the weeks to follow, there were trips that she made alone to Illinois for drug tests, orientation and classes for the job. I was proud of her, as I was for every other thing that she had accomplished for herself. However this was different. Every time that she came home it seemed as if she left a part of herself there. There was no more talk of home, no cleaning the home or anything that had to do with this home, very much. I watched her behavior and conversation change. Although she added me to the equation to somehow make it about us, she spoke of me as if an afterthought. We received a call from DCS, asking if I could take a preteen lesbian whom they thought would be a great fit in our home. I chose not to disclose any of our plans to the agency as of yet, only because I was in denial. Sandy, was her name, she is a sweet girl, that wanted to be liked by everyone, I noticed. She knew right a way that she didn't care for my wife however, I ask that she get to know her before she drew a conclusion; she agreed. Her and Yvette were getting along just fine after that. However, the distance between Yvette and I was happening at an alarming rate. I ask her out on a date as I always had but this had more urgency for me. I planned it well, it was a beautiful dinner for two on the deck overlooking the river. I couldn't help but ask; would you please consider staying? While listening to the sweet sounds of Freddie Jackson {you are my lady, that played on my zune player}. You could pursue the dreams that you originally had, that were the reasons for your Associates and Bachelor's degree that you attained. She never said, no. But the smile and the kiss, killed me inside.

Emotionally, I was in trouble but I dare not let it be known. My friends all knew about the break that we were taking and attempted to comfort me by saying; you guys will be together soon, she's going ahead to hook things up for y'all. But I felt something different and needed to voice my opinion about it. Your already gone; I said to her, with conviction. I can feel you slipping further and further away from me and this child, as days grow near; I added. My suggestion; is that you go on and move with your mom, too properly motivate you to start your new job; I said. Why are you saying this, Tru? she ask. Because I can't continue to watch all of this, knowing that there is absolutely nothing that I can do to stop it; I said. We can continue with our plans for me to come there however all that your doing is a distraction and if you were there with your mom, you can get and stay on track; I added. She, disagreed at first and then agreed that it was a good idea. You can Leave Trina in school if you like and we will all come out together; I suggested. No; she said. I'll take her and get her enrolled in school there; she admitted. Well, take him, so that I can get things wrapped up her? I ask. I think that you should keep him because he's so young and my mom…. She added. I listened but I couldn't believe what I was hearing but, I said nothing.

It was a Tuesday, when we talked about this, she said that she would take a few things and go to Illinois this Friday. I knew that I had to work but I explained that I would have Jamie Jr there to help her if she needed. All that I could think about was her while I worked. I wanted to call to talk to her but what would I say? I believed that I had said all that needed to be said and still, this is happening. However, by the afternoon I did call to talk to Jamie to see how things were going. You are being robbed, he said, in a joking manner. Boy; I said. Help her with what ever she needs, OK; I said. I hung up, feeling a surge run through my body as I returned back to work. Again, all that I could think about was, what was happening at my home. I clocked out, having a heavy heart and made the twenty minute long ride home. When I pulled up in front of the house, I sit for a moment attempting to push the feeling of dread aside. As I walked up the walk way, I notice my son standing in the doorway silently waiting for me. When I stepped passed him, I heard the echo throughout the room as my feet stepped over the threshold. My heart reacted before my eyes were able to see what had happened.

I looked up, waiting for my eyes to focus, just to see an empty room that was once full of furniture. I remembered the day, that she ask if she could bring her brothers furniture here after his death. I looked around to notice that the television was still there, trying to hold my head up and appear strong in front of my son, I continued walking into the bedrooms. All of Trina's things were gone as it should be; I thought to myself but when I walked into Jeremiah's room, the bunk bed that that he slept on, was gone as well, which caused me too cringed. I turned to walk towards the stairs that lead down into the basement, which is where we moved when the boys were old enough and move into their own. She took an over sized desk that belonged to her family and a computer with a modem that had a manuscript on it that belonged to me. I had no idea that she was even interested in knowing what was in the book because I've given it to her before to read and she didn't. I felt the need to breath, I sit on the bed to take a moment to reflect on the life that I felt that we had together. My thought were drifting back and forth, 9 ½ years of patience, tolerance and as much love as I could conjure up. It took me years too build up these walls to protect my heart. I thought that they were impenetrable, enough to create a barrier so strong that it would withstand any type of pain. I was wrong obviously. It hurt, more than any trauma that I had ever experience during my childhood or in my adult life. I finally opened up and actually loved someone with all of my heart and what was so crazy? I wanted to make her responsible for my feelings, as if she had control of the happiness that I felt in our relationship. As time pressed on, I stuffed my feelings into a bottle, exhibiting bad behaviors. There were tragedies of war going on inside of me, I wasn't responsible for my own feeling, never the less someone else. There were women, many women that when we came in contact, were told that I was broken and fresh out of a relationship but they felt that they could fix me and make me all better. But my heart was under construction, I had to build those walls back up. If not for the children, I would have probably fallen off of the deep end, I found it better to suffer in silence. I had no idea which way to turn, I had friends that I could party with but none that I could call on to help me manage my life as it was. My siblings were not ones that I could depend on, I had no idea what I would do with Jeremiah if something were to happen to me. In the past, we as a family took care of the little ones, never have we had to go outside of the home for help. Justin dated a slightly older woman named Carrie. She was nice but I really didn't get to know her very well when they were together, she seemed quiet to me or maybe she didn't care to get to know us, I'm not sure. But she came to my rescue when they left us, I couldn't believe it but she did. She made me aware of how nice she thought that I was, when she came to our home, way back then. I was too emotional, to the point of having no words. She told me her hours of work, I knew then that I would have to go back on third shift in order for this to work because her job was during the day. She was that friend that God sent.

Meanwhile……

I attempted to keep in contact with Yvette in the beginning. But after a year of trying I realized that it was one sided, we then made a decision to separate and agreed to remain friends for the sake of the kids. I then found that I was the only one of us, interested in keeping the kids in contact but I still kept traveling there, trying to stay in my daughters life, as well. The young lady that I was fostering was happy that Yvette was gone, she showed that she wasn't very fond of Jeremiah either. We knew this for sure, when she urinated in a bottle and poured it on his face as he slept. I couldn't believe that she would do something like this because she was such a sweet person to me but, she showed something different towards others if she didn't care for them. I was afraid for his safety after that, so I called the agency. Soon after, I began making plans to take my son to Disney World. Although he wasn't able to express his feelings about his mother leaving. I knew, that not only I were going through something behind all this but he had to be as well. So, for that whole year, I worked and saved for our trip and received a blessing on top of what I saved. I made a conscious decision, that because I was blessed that I would bless Carrie's son Cameron by taking him along with us, free of charge on the strength that I was truly grateful for what she was doing for me. Although, she wasn't having it, I continued trying to convince her to allow me too pay for it all. Finally she agreed to let him go only if she paid for his flight, I agreed. I wanted him to have an experience of a lifetime. There was a conversation had between my daughter and I about her going with us but I thought that it would be best that she stay home and prepare herself for the cruise that she and her family were all going on in a month after our trip. I was angry that our son wasn't invited to go with them and even angrier that she choose this time to share that she was getting married to a guy named Billy. I can't and won't explain what I felt behind this information but congratulations came across my lips.

==

It was nice watching the boys run through the park to get to the next ride or the next character walking around. They were able to swim in an over sized pool while watching a Disney movie on the large screen out doors. Although I was alone, I was having an amazing time. I made sure that the kids had great memories and gifts in hopes that they would remember this for a lifetime. I also had a lot of footage on the camcorder and pictures that I shared with his mother when we made it home. I walked into our house, it wasn't a home any more, it was a place to come after a long day at work but nothing more. I decided that I would start traveling, Jeremiah and I began hitting the highway pretty often. There were times that Carrie would keep him for the weekend or my son, Jamie and his new girlfriend Elise, would keep him as well, just to give me a break and allow me to be an adult. Elise was a nice girl, once I got her to talk to me. She was very quiet and reserved. She had three brown skinned beautiful girls that kept my son on his toes.

Going to Illinois was the main place at first because it kept me in close with my daughter. I met a woman on the internet by the name of Cassie, who I talked too for two months. She was from a place called Stony island which wasn't far from where my daughter moved with her mom and stepdad. Cassie had a mean streak in her but I figured that was due to her being sixty plus years of age. She was good to me, I came to visit her every other weekend, like clock work. She and I, established an understanding{as I called it}. I gave her what she needed and I got what I wanted. She and I planned a cruise at my request, soon after all the monies had been paid and we were no longer able to back out without being penalized. Soon after, she began to have small outbursts that were a bit disturbing to me. She, accused me often, of not being present and being emotionally unattainable. She also accused me of still being in love with Yvette. She was right about one thing, I was emotionally unattainable. Two and a half years of friendship, we decided that after the cruise, we would go our separate ways.

It seemed as if one door closed and another opened, it may have been wrong for me too think of it in that manner but it was true. It was as if I were sent another distraction that kept me alive longer. The alcohol seemed to become a special part of my life as well, it kept me from being in touch with me. Although my drinking wasn't an all day affair or even an everyday occurrence. The damage was done usually on a Friday nights. Now, there were a few Saturday nights thrown in on special occasions but not often. What bothered me the most about all that happened to us, I had no one that I felt comfortable enough to talk too about what I was going through. Carrie and I, we'd chat about it sometimes but I couldn't go deep with it, for fear that I would seem weak in front of her.

Chapter 16

Learning to love

  I hung out with friends that I couldn't tell what was on my mind, I was a firm believer, that if you give a person too much information they'll use it against you one day. Life was crazy that way for me, especially when dealing with my own people. Health issues arose, so I slightly pulled back from those friends and continued having conversation with a young lady that I met on line some time ago. There were things that I felt comfortable telling her only because she didn't live here and didn't know those people that I knew. In the meantime, I chose not to listen to my body until the pain became too great to ignore. My doctor, sent me for an ultrasound that revealed that there was a growth in my pelvic region that was benign but had to come out. The fact that I didn't understand the severity of this issue, didn't mean that I didn't care. I worried about my boy and how I was to care for him while I was down. He was still young and unable to do most things that boys his age could. She offered to literally come and help but I, with my severe trust issues declined. I thought of other options however, there were none. I called back days later and ask if the invitation was still open, Yes; she admitted. Surgery was scheduled on Thursday June of 2011. The doctors were describing a new contraption that they were going to use on me called; De Vinci Robotic system that would allow them to cut up the mass and bring it out without causing a lot of scarring, however once in, they found that it was much larger than they anticipated that caused them to make a larger incision that lead to a longer recovery time. I stayed in the hospital for two day for observation. When I was allowed to go, I drove home quickly and carefully to lay on the couch, there was no pain at first, I was just weak.

 An hour later I was on my way back out, heading to the Greyhound bus station. Within twenty minutes of my showing up, she walked out. Ajia Nyee, showed up, looking like a woman that was ready to go to work. I gestured to get out, she immediately instructed me to stay where I was, I watched as she tossed her bags in and walk to get in the truck. Hello, thank you for coming to help me; I said. Your welcome she said; sounding as if she was an island girl. Now, lets get you home too bed; she added. As she spoke to me informing me as to what her plans were to help me. I watched at how she used her hands to express what she was saying but I could feel the pain coming on and her words were slurred to me. When we pulled up at the house, I hurried to open the door and sit on the couch again, waiting for her to come in. After the polite introductions, she help me downstairs and into the bed. I took one of the pills that we picked up from the pharmacy, it wasn't long after, I was out. When I wake, a fear came over me that something wasn't right. I quietly and slowly while ignoring the pain surging through the lower region of my body, made my way upstairs. I sit on the chair closest to the kitchen to meet her coming out of my sons room. My heart jumped, what are you doing out of bed; she said. She looked surprised to see me. Everything's OK, up here; she admitted. Are you hungry? I can fix you something right away, she added. I couldn't shake the feeling that I had, so I rose up from the chair to walk past her. I gave her a smile and walked into my sons room to see that she had cleaned and organized it.

In disbelief, I turned to look into the other room and saw the same thing, I quickly looked into the closet that I stood next too, noticing that she re-organized every piece of linen in there, not to mention the bathroom next to it. Full of gratitude and humility, I turned, smiled and thanked her. Now, let's get you back to bed, OK; she said calmly. Without words, she and I walked back into the basement, where I returned to bed and back to sleep. Later in the evening, Jamie jr. called to tell me that they were bringing Jeremiah home in the morning which was fine. She catered to me all night, making sure that I was comfortable in every way. Although, in the back of my mind, I thought that she would take something or had an ulterior motive for coming here. I just couldn't get my trust issues under control. When my son came home, he was brought to the basement to greet me. I had to steal some kisses. I knew that he missed me but showing emotions wasn't his forte. I turned and introduced her to my son and his girlfriend, Elise too Ajia. I thanked them for keeping him. As she walked them upstairs and to the door, I pulled my son close, to have a conversation with him about what to do if he's uncomfortable about anything while being with her. She then came downstairs, walked over to my son and calmly ask if he wanted something to eat. I watched how she interacted with him, being cautious and calming. I believed, because of the information that I gave her pertaining to him. She was wonderful with him, he warmed up to her really quickly, which was a first. I stayed up to listen to their interaction. I could hear everything with my room being off of the kitchen. I stayed up as long as I could but the pain was getting the best of me, I grabbed a pill and fell off to sleep right away.

This brown skinned girl was an amazing person. To have my son feeling her so soon after meeting her, it must have been genuine. She made him a priority. She changed my bandages, helped me to the shower, got me dressed, had me to sit in the chair as she changed the bedding. The love that she showed was consistent, in my opinion, she was another Angel that God sent to help me, in my eyes. The healing process was moving along smoothly. I felt funny being dependent on her. I noticed that I would rebel at times because of it. Feeling much better now. The day approached for me to go back to work, she and I were getting close, real close. I was able to sit up and we played board games, laughed and became friends. I was afraid to call it anything else because I didn't quite know what I was going to do with her as of yet. Healing brought on feelings. I tried to focus on how to show her that I appreciated her. Selfishly, I tapped into her mind, doing things to her body that no one has ever done}I head her yell. I knew that this was the wrong way. My mind told me no but my body told me yes as R-Kelly, sings. I went back to work and while there I came up with an idea; I would take her out on the town, a little dinner and dancing, I thought. I called my sister in law and ask if my niece could come by to babysit for me this up coming Saturday. I also called my friends as well. She and I took a ride to Macy's on Thursday. She was so excited. While there, they catered too her. She loved that they showed her how to apply makeup. She seemed very happy. She choose a very pretty dress and shoe from there, I couldn't wait to see her in it. This was my way of giving back what she selflessly gave to me.

The night went like clockwork. We had a very good time, all night long. As we made the ride home, she made me aware that she loved me, through the slurred words. I smiled and thank her. We made it home safely, remembering that I had to take my niece home, I waited for her to get her things together and pulled away. When I made it to their house, I stood around shootin the shit for a minute with my sis-n-law, I turned said my goodbyes, and left. I felt a little nauseous but held it in until I made it to my truck. I knew it was the alcohol. When I made it up the street, I turned the corner, I had the urgency to hurl. I opened the door and let it all out.

When I woke the next morning, the sun shined so bright in my eyes that I couldn't make out my surroundings. Once my eyes adjusted, I could see that I was parked on Thomas street, right off of Chapin. I looked down and noticed that my truck door was wide open and my glasses were on the ground. I reached down to get them and noticed that the street was bare. No cars, nor where there people walking. There were only a few homes left of this street, there was an enormous amount of gratitude that came over me, when I thought of how the situation could have gone for me, had it been a few years earlier. I remembered; Chapin Street and this whole area was party central for blacks at night back then. There were no rules in these streets. I looked for my phone and found it on the floor dead, I searched my back pocket for my wallet and finally found it between the middle console of my seat. I sit in silence searching my thoughts, wondering how did I not realize that I was this inebriated. I just couldn't believe that I drove my niece home while in this state. I was immediately ashamed. I knew that I was tipsy but not to the point that I blacked out. I was truly grateful that nothing bad or worse happened. I lowered my head and said a prayer. When done, I grabbed the keys and turned the ignition to hear a click-click-click and then nothing. And realized that I ran the battery down, leaving the door open all night. With no cellular service, I had no choice but to leave my opened truck, to walk back to my families home to call AAA.

Fast forward….four Years. Ajia was still with us, however I thought that it would be better if we lived in separate home. I visited but mostly at night or when ever she needed to go somewhere or sometimes just to check up on her. I remember asking her; if she wanted to return home when the split happened. She loved me and her decision to stay was clearly based on that. She was intertwined with my family but it was always me and my son that was her focus. When the day came that it finally became apparent to her that I was truly broken and unable to love another, she made the decision to return home to A.T.L. She explained the obvious, that she tried. This move, had me torn but it crushed my son, to the point he cried profusely. This was something that he didn't do when Yvette left him. I felt like the villain, to the point that I attempted to mend what I had broken. But after four years of hoping for change, she couldn't take that chance with me. I, again was left with the deed of putting my sons heart back together again. I witnessed the ultimate of sadness and in my opinion, I caused it, yet again. He reacted in a way that I didn't think that he was capable of. On the ride to the bus station the kiss was long, loving and seductive. Why haven't you ever kissed me like this before; she ask. Because, I'm broken, baby. TO BE CONTINUED...

TURNING

THE

PAGE

~

~

~

CHAOS

Moist, can't feel that I've cried

Having memories of distant thoughts equivalent to better days derived

Pick up, gathering to salvage, what was back when

To be unsure if it was...wondering, why did it end

Cries traveling through the wind in the night

Questions the fight

Imagination, elevating to it's highest heights

Of what will be or what's in sight

Pure chaos brooding, manifests inside

To revisit what's mine, Oh, the level of pride I hide

Breaking peace I feel, hard to conceal the truth of what's false and what's real

Having dreams, dreamt that weren't mine to emulate trauma of being BLACK

In these times

Even when proclaimed to be healed, still I stand

AND

Wait to be lifted up into GOD'S hands.

Until then, the chaos inside still

a friend.

EPILOGUE

It's 2021, we're still in the middle of a pandemic. My mask on the table, ready to be applied to my face at a moments notice. Sitting outside in front of the cafe, sipping on a glass of wine, eating a light meal. I notice the pasta had a different taste than usual as did the wine with a different consistency as well. Watching as people walked hand in hand down the lane, with the look of love in their eyes. I couldn't help but remember when that look was mine. While enjoying the differences in the way they moved, strolling as appose too walking, yet noticing how the love felt free to express here, too me. Looking around, taking it all in, I felt blessed that I sit in the middle the Piazza Navona in Rome Italy, admiring the fountain of the Four Rivers, while looking down the lane to see the Fountain Del Moro. How could I be so blessed; I ask myself, again.

But then…... I must explain how I made it here.

The journey to healing, was a long and gruesome process for me. Pushing past my trauma, P.T.S.D and servere trust issues were harder than anything that I had ever gone through in my life. Addressing those underlined issues such as; drug addiction, alcoholism, abandonment and although I wasn't apart of his life, I dealt with issues resulting from our relationship. I learned that trauma bonding, was a thing that needed addressing. However it was very necessary to take those necessary measures to change my way of thinking and apply those ways in my everyday living in order for me to come close to functioning as a productive member of society.

I first had to admit that I was powerless over my addiction which made my life unmanageable. I continued working the steps as suggested. I felt it necessary too move on to step #8 and apologize to those that I had harmed. My son was the first on my list. Because in his young mind, Trina and Ajia, were the only two people that truly loved him other than I and I was the one that made them go away. So once Ajia was settled into her own home, in Atlanta Georgia. I brought two airline tickets and flew him and I to visit her. He was overjoyed and I was yet again the best mom ever. Trina, was always my focus, I put many miles on my truck trying to stay connected to her. I remember "Yvette and I, shopped around and found a 2008 Chrysler Aspen too transport our large family. It was very important to me that we not have to drive in two different vehicles. I had a thing about not being present to here what the little ones had on their minds when they were in the other car as we traveled. I was approved for a loan of $30,000 and some change and I signed on the dotted line however, I spent the next six years being reminded of how much of a fool in love I was. Had I known that there was a plan put in place for us to separate a month and a half later, I would have never done this. Separating, was a hard pill for me to swallow, it was heartbreaking and unforgivable but forgiving her for everything that she had done within our relationship was what I had to do to move on and attempt to heal. This didn't happen over night but it did happen. She, I and her husband have become cordial. I've been invited to events in their home and they have come to mine, once. Again, I am the only who cared enough to try. Therapy didn't come right away for those other behavior issues but it came. Not long after the first blackout on Scott street, I had another. I knew then, a change was coming. I envisioned, something horrible happening that would land me in jail and my child back into the system.

Therapy helped me to realize, that I was harboring resentments about things that transpired throughout the course of my life. I struggled, life itself seemed too great and yet I wanted more of it. I suffered in silence for many years. I've always felt; if I told people things that were on my mind and in my heart, that they would use it as a weapon towards me, to do with as they wish. And they did but my therapy sessions where essential and many for at least two years, until I felt that they weren't needed any longer. I attended many AA and NA meetings as well as talked to my sponsor about those things that I wouldn't share around the tables. Although, I've always felt the distance between she and I as well. I never felt as if I could honestly have an intimate conversation with her for fear of feeling as if I would say the wrong thing to offend her because of her Christianity. I fired her as my sponsor, not only because of this but I've felt for a long time that I wasn't receiving what I needed from this arrangement. I worked on my self every day taking inventory while wearing a smile that took a long time to feel genuine. I then forgave my Mother, the cliche, take it to your grave, was an understatement as far as my mother was concerned. She died taking secrets that no one else would or could not divulge. Throughout my life spent with her, everything seemed to be a secret held tight to her bosom. I knew nothing about my mother when she past, this was not what I wanted for my children, this is the reason for this book. I then forgave my Mother... again. For all of my childhood woes. While writing this book and being transparent with self, there were many things that I had to remember about my life once again that re-hatched feelings that I am now currently working my way through, yet again. I have also attempted to mend the relationship between my siblings. I knew that it would be an uphill battle but because we are family, it matters.

I've made many friends through out my life and have lost many more and for that, believe it or not, I am grateful. People are normally here for a season but all for a reason with lessons learned along the way. I have found a peace that I never would have know had some of them been in my life. Being the introvert/ extrovert as I am today, allows me to exercise the strength that I feel that I possess inside, which is quite amazing. Although, I've never thought of them as being bad people, I believe that some people value friendships differently. I've also had a few that may have wanted more of me than I was able to give and when this didn't happen for them, I found that they had no reason to remain. Being a lesbian, has been wonderful for me. I now know who I am as a woman. My life now consist of healing and building relationships that add substance to my life. The cliche, knowing better is doing better, holds precedence with me. I use this mindset in my daily method to a healthier me. I thank God, much more now because without all of the outside interference I am able to better stay in tune with him and hear with my spiritual ear, what it is that he wants from me.

I've earned my degree in the streets of hard knocks. I'm in the process of owning my second home. I've driven nice cars and still dress to my liking. I am an author of three books and working on my fourth. I have the respect of many as I have for them. My children are productive members of society, however, I miss them. Ajia and I, whom I am truly grateful for, are very good friends with boundaries put in place by her that are not to be broken by me. I respect this because, it was I who hurt a very good woman and for that I apologize.

Since that first cruise that was mentioned in this book, I've since been on seven others to places like; Jamaica, Haiti, Cozumel Mexico,

Bahamas, St. Martin, Rome and Barcelona Spain. I've traveled in the States as well to; San Francisco, Reno, San Diego, Oceanside, Texas, Nevada, Georgia and countless other places. My travels have opened my eyes to a many different cultures. I had the pleasure of watching the changing of the guards in London England. Eating Pizza in Italy, while walking the grounds of the Colosseum. I had the pleasure of watching a Marathon in Barcelona, which was truly amazing but most of all was the Louvre in Paris and seeing, Da Vinci's Mona Lisa and then walking into the Sixteenth chapel. I say to my self... I am truly blessed and highly favored by my father whom I give honor too.

Jamie died on February 4th 2020 and Larnice died June 8th 2020. I was torn. RIP

    God Bless you all on your own journey's in life.
        Break Barriers

LIVE LIFE TO THE FULLEST

Special thanks to

L. A. H.

My best friend from Michigan

IN LOVING MEMORY OF

J. OGLESBY

R. M. GUNN

W. BULLOCKS

L. TYLER

R. ANDERSON

L. B. B.

J. B.

MAY YOU ALL REST IN HEAVEN

PEACE BE UNTO YOU

MAMMA

www.ingramcontent.com/pod-product-compliance
Lightning Source LLC
LaVergne TN
LVHW010315070526
838199LV00065B/5573